Alain Resnais

Manchester University Press

FRENCH FILM DIRECTORS

DIANA HOLMES and ROBERT INGRAM *series editors*
DUDLEY ANDREW *series consultant*

Jean-Jacques Beineix   PHIL POWRIE

Luc Besson   SUSAN HAYWARD

Bertrand Blier   SUE HARRIS

Robert Bresson   KEITH READER

Leos Carax   GARIN DOWD AND FERGUS DALEY

Claude Chabrol   GUY AUSTIN

Jean Cocteau   JAMES WILLIAMS

Claire Denis   MARTINE BEUGNET

Marguerite Duras   RENATE GÜNTHER

Georges Franju   KATE INCE

Jean-Luc Godard   DOUGLAS MORREY

Diane Kurys   CARRIE TARR

Patrice Leconte   LISA DOWNING

Louis Malle   HUGO FREY

Georges Méliès   ELIZABETH EZRA

Jean Renoir   MARTIN O'SHAUGHNESSY

Coline Serreau   BRIGITTE ROLLET

François Truffaut   DIANA HOLMES AND ROBERT INGRAM

Agnès Varda   ALISON SMITH

Jean Vigo   MICHAEL TEMPLE

FRENCH FILM DIRECTORS

Alain Resnais

EMMA WILSON

Manchester University Press
MANCHESTER AND NEW YORK

distributed exclusively in the USA by Palgrave

Copyright © Emma Wilson 2006

The right of Emma Wilson to be identified as the author of this work has been asserted by her in accordance with the Copyright, Designs and Patents Act 1988.

Published by Manchester University Press
Oxford Road, Manchester M13 9NR, UK
and Room 400, 175 Fifth Avenue, New York, NY 10010, USA
www.manchesteruniversitypress.co.uk

Distributed exclusively in the USA by
Palgrave, 175 Fifth Avenue, New York NY 10010, USA

Distributed exclusively in Canada by
UBC Press, University of British Columbia, 2029 West Mall,
Vancouver, BC, Canada V6T 1Z2

British Library Cataloguing-in-Publication Data
A catalogue record for this book is available from the British Library

Library of Congress Cataloging-in-Publication Data
A catalog record for this book is available from the Library of Congress

ISBN 13: 978 0 7190 6407 4

First published 2006 by Manchester University Press

First paperback edition 2009

Printed by Lightning Source

Contents

LIST OF PLATES	*page* vi
SERIES EDITORS' FOREWORD	vii
ACKNOWLEDGEMENTS	ix
Introduction	1
1 **Documentaries 1948–58**	16
2 *Hiroshima mon amour* (1959)	46
3 *L'Année dernière à Marienbad* (1961)	69
4 *Muriel ou le temps d'un retour* (1963)	87
5 *La Guerre est finie* (1966), *Je t'aime je t'aime* (1968), *Stavisky* (1974)	108
6 *Providence* (1977)	131
7 *Mon oncle d'Amérique* (1980), *La vie est un roman* (1983), *L'Amour à mort* (1984), *Mélo* (1986), *I want to go home* (1989)	147
8 *Smoking/No Smoking* (1993), *On connaît la chanson* (1997), *Pas sur la bouche* (2003)	171
Conclusion	195
FILMOGRAPHY	199
SELECT BIBLIOGRAPHY	207
INDEX	210

List of plates

1	First impression, *Nuit et brouillard*, 1955	page 39
2	Memory in Japan, *Hiroshima mon amour*, 1959	39
3	Liminal image, *L'Année dernière à Marienbad*, 1961	40
4	Mirroring, *L'Année dernière à Marienbad*, 1961	40
5	The gardens at Marienbad, *L'Année dernière à Marienbad*, 1961	40
6	Fantasy and the tactile, *L'Année dernière à Marienbad*, 1961	41
7	In the night, *L'Année dernière à Marienbad*, 1961	41
8	Last image, *L'Année dernière à Marienbad*, 1961	41
9	Bernard, *Muriel*, 1963	42
10	Hélène, *Muriel*, 1963	42
11	Janine as a child, *Mon oncle d'Amérique*, 1980	43
12	Janine, *Mon oncle d'Amérique*, 1980	43
13	Laboratory rat, *Mon oncle d'Amérique*, 1980	44
14	Titles sequence, *Mélo*, 1986	44
15	Camille and Nicolas, *On connaît la chanson*, 1997	45
16	Arlette and Gilberte, *Pas sur la bouche*, 2003	45

Series editors' foreword

To an anglophone audience, the combination of the words 'French' and 'cinema' evokes a particular kind of film: elegant and wordy, sexy but serious – an image as dependent on national stereotypes as is that of the crudely commercial Hollywood blockbuster, which is not to say that either image is without foundation. Over the past two decades, this generalised sense of a significant relationship between French identity and film has been explored in scholarly books and articles, and has entered the curriculum at university level and, in Britain, at A-level. The study of film as an art-form and (to a lesser extent) as industry, has become a popular and widespread element of French Studies, and French cinema has acquired an important place within Film Studies. Meanwhile, the growth in multi-screen and 'art-house' cinemas, together with the development of the video industry, has led to the greater availability of foreign-language films to an English-speaking audience. Responding to these developments, this series is designed for students and teachers seeking information and accessible but rigorous critical study of French cinema, and for the enthusiastic filmgoer who wants to know more.

The adoption of a director-based approach raises questions about *auteurism*. A series that categorises films not according to period or to genre (for example), but to the person who directed them, runs the risk of espousing a romantic view of film as the product of solitary inspiration. On this model, the critic's role might seem to be that of discovering continuities, revealing a necessarily coherent set of themes and motifs which correspond to the particular genius of the individual. This is not our aim: the *auteur* perspective on film, itself most clearly articulated in France in the early 1950s, will be interrogated in certain volumes of the series, and, throughout, the director will be treated as one highly significant element in a complex process of film production and reception which includes socio-economic and political determinants, the work of a large and highly skilled team of artists and technicians, the mechanisms of production and distribution, and the complex and multiply determined responses of spectators.

The work of some of the directors in the series is already known outside France, that of others is less so – the aim is both to provide informative and original English-language studies of established figures, and to extend the range of French directors known to anglophone students of cinema. We intend the series to contribute to the promotion of the informal and formal study of French films, and to the pleasure of those who watch them.

DIANA HOLMES
ROBERT INGRAM

Acknowledgements

I am grateful to Diana Holmes and Robert Ingram: their interest in this project and their care and attention as editors have been invaluable. Matthew Frost and Kate Fox at Manchester University Press have been unfailingly helpful: I am grateful for their guidance and support. Sara Peacock has proved a meticulous and thoughtful copy-editor; any errors which remain are my own. Keith Reader first discussed the possibility of a Resnais project with me and has been the source of rich insight into Resnais's films. Edward Dimendberg has deepened my understanding of Resnais's documentaries. Both have also provided video copies of less accessible films. In Paris, I thank the staff of the Bibliothèque du film and of the bookshop Aux films des temps for their help in tracing critical and visual sources; staff at the Bibliothèque de France have offered help with audio-visual recordings. I thank Astrid Kurth warmly for her expert assistance collating critical material and Kristy Guneratne for her very assiduous checking and indexing in the final stages of the project. I also thank Wendy Bennett, Victoria Best, Nadine Boljkovac, Sarah Cooper, Martin Crowley, Colin Davis, Georgina Evans, Alison Finch, Alex Hughes, Bill Marshall, Tim Mathews, Judith Mayne, Isabelle McNeill, Edward Nye, Kathryn Robson, Mireille Rosello, Lynsey Russell-Watts, Libby Saxton, Michael Sheringham, Emily Tomlinson, Edward Baron Turk, Virginia Vacy-Ash, Rachel Volloch and, retrospectively, my college supervisor Ann Duncan. My mother, Jacqueline Wilson, encouraged me to watch *Hiroshima mon amour* while I was still at school and shared her interest in Duras. My partner, Josephine Lloyd, has offered patient help with images for the book. I add personal thanks to Laurence Pierre de Guyer for permission to reproduce the cover photograph, an image by Georges Pierre taken on the set of *L'Année dernière à Marienbad*. Material in this volume has formed the basis of papers given at the UCL/SOAS workshops on 'Tradition and Modernity', and in Cambridge, Nottingham and Tallahassee, Florida.

Introduction

In Resnais's film of 1980, *Mon oncle d'Amérique*, there are images of an island, one of the four hundred islands in the gulf of the Morbihan. The camera slowly approaches the island across the sea as dark trees become visible, their shapes reflected in the white waters of the bay. The image has reminded critics of Arnold Böcklin's painting *The Isle of the Dead*. In interview Resnais says that he would visit such an island in his childhood and the film conjures a sense of nostalgia for this haunting, water-locked place, outside time. Resnais's films deal very rarely with the director's personal memories, yet Resnais has been considered perhaps the most important French film director to treat questions of memory and forgetting. Looking beyond his personal history, his work explores cultural and popular memory, mass trauma and individual losses, pursuing such issues in both documentaries and feature films.

For Resnais, memory is part of a broader network of issues. Rather than speak of memory alone, he says: 'Je préfère parler de l'imaginaire, ou de la conscience. Ce qui m'intéresse dans le cerveau c'est cette faculté que nous avons d'imaginer dans notre tête ce qui va arriver, de se souvenir de ce qui s'est passé' (*Positif* 2002: 277).[1] Resnais is interested in memory, but in memory as one part of our broader mental or imaginative capacity. As Youssef Ishaghpour notes: 'Resnais conçoit le cinéma non comme un instrument de représentation de la réalité, mais comme le meilleur moyen pour approcher le fonctionne-

[1] 'I prefer to speak of the imaginary, or of consciousness. What interests me in the mind is that faculty we have to imagine what is going to happen in our heads, or to remember what has happened'. (Translations are my own.)

ment psychique' (Ishaghpour 1982: 182).[2] Resnais is fascinated by mental or subjective images, the virtual reality which makes up individual consciousness and is itself composed of both what we have known and what we have imagined. This interest in the finest workings of the mind – in the mind itself as an internal cinema where images both virtual and real coexist – calls for an extraordinary reshaping of cinema and rethinking of the capacity of film to show us reality as it is imagined, as well as lived.

Resnais's films are often perceived as demanding, cerebral or soporific. I do not want to underestimate their difficulty, and challenge to the viewer, but I draw attention in this book to some of the more tangible or moving pleasures of his filmmaking: in particular his address to the senses and his interest in the pathos and uncertainty of human interaction and exchange. Resnais's films are watchful and sensitive. His caution and reflection as filmmaker have resulted, in *Nuit et brouillard* and *Hiroshima mon amour*, in two of the most searching testimonies to the trauma and horror of the Second World War. His later filmmaking, turning in new directions, has continued to reflect on mortality, guilt, chance and human doubt, and on the capacity of cinema to reveal, and not betray, the subtlest mental process.

Chronology

Alain Resnais was born on 3 June 1922 at Vannes in Brittany. He is circumspect about his personal life, and is cited by many as modest and diffident (Monaco 1979: 2). A few elusive details surface in interviews. Like his heroine in *Hiroshima mon amour*, he had a father who was a pharmacist. He was an only child and sickly, with asthma, through his childhood. Gaston Bounoure, whose study is most imaginative in its description of Resnais's life, conjures an image of a child nurtured and spoilt by his parents. He dwells in particular on the influence of Resnais's mother, credited for introducing Resnais to writers such as Katherine Mansfield and Marcel Proust (Bounoure 1974: 9). (Elsewhere Resnais withdraws from this image, claiming to have read Proust later and with no particular affection (Goudet 2002:

2 'Resnais conceives of cinema not as an instrument for the representation of reality, but as the best means to approaching the workings of the mind'.

281).) While Resnais apparently attended school infrequently, due to illness, his passion for cinema developed early: when he was 13, his parents gave him a super-8 camera, bought, according to Bounoure, in one of the arcades in Nantes filmed by Jacques Demy. With his camera, Resnais made films of local children and also began a re-adaptation of *Fantômas*. Bounoure offers a rich image of life in the Resnais pharmacy, surmising that it might have held the Surrealist journal *Minotaure*, possible source of Resnais's interest in the art of Ernst, Magritte and others. Such fragments offer a possible collage of Resnais's childhood, a virtual image of his past.

In interview Resnais cites a trip to the theatre in 1937 as particularly significant in the development of his ambitions and career. He saw a production of Chekhov's *The Seagull* by the Pitoeff company at the Mathurins theatre in Paris and this ignited a passion for theatre and inspired him to become an actor. He enrolled in acting classes in Paris at the Cours René Simon and attended these for two years. He later decided to take the entrance exam for the Paris film school, IDHEC (Institut des Hautes Etudes Cinématographiques), in 1943 and he spent a year there (*Premier Plan* 1961: 39). From here, he began to gain experience as a film editor, assisting on Nicole Védrès's *Paris 1900* (1948) and other films. His interest in the visual composition of meaning is apparent from the start: he comments that working as an editor he was already keen to express himself and make his own films. Agnès Varda, director of *La Pointe courte* (1956), which Resnais edited, recalls that he first refused to take it on: 'Il m'expliquait que cela ne lui était pas possible: ce cinéma correspondait trop à ce que lui-même rêvait de faire' (Bounoure 1974: 140).[3]

Resnais's directorial ambitions were first realised in a series of documentaries and, from 1959 onwards, in feature films. As his career develops, his filmography replaces his biography in the spotlight of critical interest, and I follow this pattern allowing the films to take predecence (his open comments on those films, from various interviews, nevertheless interweave this discussion). The films are treated here in chronological order. This may seem ironic where one of the major traits and innovations of Resnais's filmmaking is his rethinking of time in the cinema. Resnais rejects the chronological

---

3 'He would explain to me that it was not possible for him: this cinema was too close to what he himself was dreaming of doing'.

representation of events in order to reflect on film form (the way cinema orders events) and to represent the complexity of the human process of imagination and recall (where events may be repressed, repeated, re-construed in the human mind). Treating such formally challenging and temporally fragmented films (watching a film by Resnais may sometimes feel like looking at changing images through a kaleidoscope), a linear order foregrounds the increments and transformations of his long career. Resnais claims that he does not review his films (Jousse 1993: 27), however; the repetitions and returns of his filmmaking may occasionally be involuntary, unbidden.

Introductions to individual films are offered in the eight chapters which follow. Depending on their level of familiarity with Resnais, readers may find it preferable to read chapters on the individual films before exploring the more theoretical and integrated discussion in the second half of this introduction.

Trauma and memory

Reflecting on the disruption of chronology in Resnais's films, and their focus on intense pain and rarefied mental activity, notions of trauma and post-traumatic stress disorder have been key to recent critical discussion. Post-traumatic stress disorder refers to a response to an event which is outside the range of usual human experience. Cathy Caruth suggests that trauma is defined not by the nature of the traumatic event itself, but by the form of the responses generated by that event; she writes: 'there is a response, sometimes delayed, to an overwhelming event or events, which takes the form of repeated, intrusive hallucinations, dreams, thoughts or behaviours stemming from the event, along with numbing that may have begun during or after the experience, and possibly also increased arousal to (and avoidance of) stimuli recalling the event' (Caruth 1995: 4). As this description indicates, traumatic responses are typified by their involuntary nature; for Caruth, 'to be traumatized is precisely to be possessed by an image or an event' (Caruth 1995: 4–5). She speaks of the 'radical disruption and gaps of traumatic experience' (Caruth 1995: 4); of the ways 'trauma unsettles and forces us to rethink our notions of experience' (Caruth 1995: 4) and brings about a new ignorance. Caruth claims that 'Psychoanalytic and medically oriented psychiatry, sociology, history, and even literature all seem to be called upon to explain, to cure, or to show why it is that we can no longer simply explain or simply cure' (Caruth 1995: 4). Trauma brings us to the limits of our understanding; it instructs us that knowledge may be delayed or belated, always partly fictional or partial; it shows us that some experiences may always resist representation or comprehension. Resnais's films, in their doubt and disruption, are entirely in line with this new traumatic knowledge.

Both literal questions of bearing witness to traumatic events and broader questions about trauma and the limits of understanding are crucial to Resnais's cinema (Caruth herself offers a fine discussion of *Hiroshima mon amour* (Caruth 1996)). Resnais explores major traumatic subjects of the twentieth century: the Holocaust and the dropping of the atomic bomb; he reflects on colonialism and on torture. Indeed, Serge Daney describes Resnais as a 'sismographe' who has made 'trois films géniaux, trois témoins irrécusables de notre modernité' (Daney 1998: 28) (he refers to *Nuit et brouillard*, *Hiroshima mon amour* and *Muriel ou le temps d'un retour*).[4] Naomi Greene, whose study *Landscapes of Loss: The National Past in Postwar French Cinema* offers one of the most distinctive recent readings of Resnais, reveals the influence of questions of testimony and trauma in her thinking about his films. For Greene, Resnais's films are 'peopled by men and women for whom time has stopped – numbed survivors chained to the past by remembered trauma' (Greene 1999: 32). Resnais explores the experience of physically and mentally marked victims and survivors of trauma, yet he also, more experimentally, moulds the form of his films to the structures and temporality of traumatic experience. For Greene, in Resnais's films, 'repressed and shifting memories seem to hold thought and action captive' (Greene 1999: 30). Resnais's films rarely show experience directly; instead they show protagonists attempting to piece together a narrative of their lives. In the form of his films, Resnais follows the hesitant time structures of remembering and forgetting, interlayering time-levels, allowing events to resurface in unexplained flashbacks. There is little sense of teleology or even, sometimes, of forward movement in his films. Equally, they often resist closure or any definitive meaning or outcome; as Leo Bersani and Ulysse Dutoit write: 'Resnais ...

4 'seismographer'; 'three films of genius, irrefutable witnesses to our modernity'.

discourages the authoritative and knowledge-hungry ego of his viewers' (Bersani and Dutoit 1993: 7). Like trauma theory, Resnais teaches us a new ignorance, a refusal of resolution or meaning. Jean-Luc Godard, commenting on Resnais's cinematic experimentation, states: 'Alain Resnais, plus qu'aucun autre, donne l'impression qu'il est parti complètement de zéro' (*L'Avant-scène* 1966: 40).[5]

Trauma theory is one of several models for understanding the circularities and repetitions of Resnais's filmmaking; various readings will be kept in play through this book. A further strand in discussion derives from the work of Gilles Deleuze, one of the most brilliant readers of Resnais's films (discussed extensively in *Cinéma 2: L'Image-temps*). Deleuze sets Resnais in a broader historical and philosophical argument about the development of cinema. Where, for Deleuze, cinema up until the post-war period depends primarily on the action-image – on editing motivated by action, reaction and forward movement – from the post-war period onwards (in an immobile, arguably post-traumatic, ruined Europe) the action-image gives way to the time-image where film is less teleological and transparent, where different layers of past events, subjective and virtual layerings of reality, take precedence. Deleuze comments on *L'Année dernière à Marienbad*, in words which are resonant for many of Resnais's films: 'les immobilisations, les pétrifications, les répétitions témoigneront constamment pour une dissolution de l'image-action' (Deleuze 1985: 136).[6] The stasis and immobility of Resnais's cinema provoke a rewriting and reimagining of cinema and its formal invention. Deleuze allows us to move away from the numbness, the stasis of the trauma victim, to focus more specifically on a new visual aesthetics. Resnais's cinema is concerned, precisely, with cinematic reinvention in the face of excessive (often traumatic) experience.

His work is not merely art for art's sake. His films attempt to give a closer, more detailed imprint of traumatic and other excessive mental and bodily experience. Politically Resnais is engaged in making us imagine this experience, bringing it close before our eyes, in order to prevent its recurrence or reinvention. He is quoted (in English) as saying, in 1962: 'My intention ... is to provoke in the

---

5 'Alain Resnais, more than anyone else, gives the impression that he started completely from zero'.

6 'the immobilisation, the petrification, the repetitions will constantly bear witness to the dissolution of the action image'.

spectator a change, no matter how small or remote' (Hughes 1962: 60). His work is about compassion and proximity; it is in this context that his interest in states of pain and disrepair returns. Resnais is particular too in evoking aleatory and creative means of escape from traumatic experience, revealing a fascination with forgetting, displacement and denial. Often these means of forgetting are bound up with the sensory, with everyday sensate experience and sometimes with eroticism. Whilst his filmmaking is most widely celebrated for its attention to the mind, Resnais has always displayed an interest in the material world, in the senses and the ways in which they reflect, enhance or deny the subjective and the imaginary.

Resnais's art and the senses

In her study *The Skin of the Film: Intercultural Cinema, Embodiment and the Senses*, Laura Marks argues that many works of intercultural cinema 'evoke memories both individual and cultural, through an appeal to nonvisual knowledge, embodied knowledge, and experiences of the senses, such as touch, smell, taste' (Marks 2000: 2). In particular she is concerned with the ways certain images appeal to a 'haptic, or tactile, visuality' (Marks 2000: 2) Such images invite the viewer to respond in an embodied way. Key to Marks's thinking is her intimation that 'many works of intercultural cinema begin from the inability to speak, to represent objectively one's own culture, history, and memory; they are marked by silence, absence and hesitation. All these works are marked by a suspicion of visuality, a lack of faith in the visual archive's ability to represent cultural memory' (Marks 2000: 21). Appeal to the haptic, to the senses and embodied knowledge, originates for Marks in this hesitation, this suspicion of visuality. She is clear in her study that her argument is specific to intercultural cinema; nevertheless the effect of her disclosure of the sensory textures of cinema as medium, and the appeal of her linking of such material filmmaking with hidden, unseen, denied histories, may tempt us to transfer her findings to other contexts. Resnais is even briefly mentioned by Marks where she speaks about the critique of ethnographic visuality, arguing:

> Trinh's films *Re:Assemblage* (1982) and *Surname Viet Given Name Nam* (1989), like Chris Marker's *Sans Soleil* (1982), Claude Lanzmann's

Shoah (1985), Alain Resnais's *Hiroshima mon amour* (1959), and Peter Kubelka's *Unsere Afrikareise* (1961–66), use both poetic and aggressive strategies to compel the viewer to consider the destructive effects of believing that one can know another culture or another time through visual information alone. (Marks 2000: 134)

Through his early filmmaking, Resnais appears indeed to register the limits of visual information alone and seek instead, in line with the intercultural cinema Marks analyses, to open up possibilities of a tactile visuality in a bid to change our relation to the image viewed and to find a more prescient, sensitive, even prehensile mode of representation.

Resnais's interest in touch and the image of hands and tactile contact has already drawn comment from critics, in particular in discussion of *Hiroshima mon amour*. Following Marks, we may also want to stretch a reading beyond such literal images of contact. Marks writes: 'Looking at hands would seem to evoke the sense of touch through identification, either with the person whose hands they are or with the hands themselves. The haptic bypasses such identification and the distance from the image it requires' (Marks 2000: 171). For Marks, prohaptic properties in video and film might be seen to be changes in focus, graininess, and effects of under- and overexposure. She sees these techniques discouraging the viewer from distinguishing objects and encouraging a relation to the screen as a whole. She speaks more generally of sensuous effects achieved through haptic imagery in combination with sound, camera movement and montage; she speaks more specifically of the use of tactile close-ups. Marks is concerned with film (and video) as material, both in terms of what they represent and as media in themselves. She observes that film and video become more haptic as they die, as we witness their gradual decay. Optical printing, solarisation, and scratching the emulsion are all seen to work with the very physical surface of the medium. In words which seem to resonate with Resnais's editing practice, she adds, 'film can be actually worked with the hands' (Marks 2000: 173).

Resnais is particularly distinguished as a filmmaker, in his early years, for his use of editing and creative editing effects (as Ishaghpour writes: 'Pour Alain Resnais, le cinéma c'est d'abord le montage' (Ishaghpour 1982: 181)).[7] He has been aligned with the Soviet

---

7 'For Alain Resnais, cinema is first and foremost editing'.

filmmaker and theorist of montage Sergei Eisenstein. Godard calls him second only to Eisenstein (*L'Avant-scène* 1966: 40). Resnais himself comments on his proximity to Eisenstein (*Premier Plan* 1961: 89) as do his critics (see Benayoun 1980: 67). Eisenstein is associated with editing which depends on collision, rupture, and a play of similarity and dissimilarity. Editing works here to create signification and meaning through association, juxtaposition and disjunctive effects (rather than through continuity and the illusion of a photographic transcription of the real). Ishaghpour draws attention to the ways in which Resnais collages together his films with images of very different visual specificity and effect, using

> le montage métrique, rythmique, harmonique, contrapuntique, intellectuel, en jouant des luminosités, des tonalités, des infimes nuances du gris pour les paysages, de la netteté, de l'intensité, des grosseurs des plans, des durées, des volumes, du graphisme, des directions, des motifs musicaux multiples et du non-synchronisme du son et de l'image.[8] (Ishaghpour 1982: 191)

Ishaghpour's attention to these infinite variations in Resnais's cinema draws us back to Laura Marks's evocation of the various ways in which some filmmakers emphasise film as a tactile, material as well as visual medium. Thinking about Resnais's cinema as collage – as massed inventory of images of different substance, texture and effect – allows us to perceive the way that Resnais is self-consciously concerned with cinema as creative medium, and more broadly absorbed with ways of creating sensation and awakening the senses and memory with that medium.

Such honed editing effects allow Resnais to focus in particular on fine detail and on difference in scale and perspective: Mettey remarks on 'le souci de détailler certaines actions avec précision, par des gros plans très explicites' (Mettey 1970: 68).[9] For Prédal, Resnais 'cultive aussi l'art du détail infime qui précipite toute l'émotion d'une scène' (Prédal 1996: 67).[10] These close-ups and details are also used to draw

---

8 'metric, rhythmic, harmonic, contrapuntal, intellectual editing, playing on degrees of light, tonalities, infinitely small nuances of grey for landscapes, precision, intensity, the scale of shots, duration, volume, graphic effects, directions, multiple musical effects and effects of non-synchronicity between sound and image'.
9 'the concern to detail certain actions precisely, with very clear close-ups'.
10 'also cultivates the art of the tiny detail which releases all the emotion in a scene'.

attention to scales and modes of viewing, to the image as at once so close and proximate it seems tangible and, at times, as so different in scale and so disorienting as to seem unassimilable, abstract, strange. Sometimes, indeed, Resnais's camera literally moves us between these two viewing positions, making the position and distance from which we view his images integral to our perception and appreciation of them (Prédal comments: 'Resnais sait rendre étrange et dense tout ce qu'enregistre sa caméra parce qu'il a un sens extraordinaire de l'endroit où se placer pour voir' (Prédal 1996: 32)).[11]

Resnais is not interested merely in viewpoint, or in distance, but in a moving, unfixed mode of perception. Ishaghpour comments that in addition to his disjunctive editing techniques, Resnais also uses a resource Eisenstein himself used very little: 'le mouvement, qui transforme le cadre, l'expose au hors-champ' (Ishaghpour 1982: 191).[12] Speaking about his use of tracking shots (shots where the camera moves horizontally or more rarely vertically through space), Resnais emphasises his urban sensibility and his love of motion: 'Mais j'aime beaucoup les rues. J'aime beaucoup me promener dans les rues. Cela aussi c'est du travelling et je me promène souvent dans les rues à bicyclette' (*Premier Plan* 1961: 80).[13] Resnais's alignment of the tracking shot with a sensory experience of space draws attention to the very sensation created in movement. In particular this may be linked with Resnais's exploration of the transport of the emotions, their ebb and flow, states of moving forwards and moving on. In *Atlas of Emotion*, Giuliana Bruno, looking at Madeleine de Scudéry's map of the emotions writes that '[e]motion materialises as a moving topography' (Bruno 2002: 2). This materialisation of the affective as a topography draws attention to the movement, the motion, that already inheres in the word *emotion* (as Bruno reminds us 'the meaning of emotion ... is historically associated with "a moving out, migration, transference from one place to another"' (Bruno 2002: 6)). In conjoining movement through space with affective movement, the transports of the emotions, Bruno draws out in particular the notion

---

11 'Resnais knows how to render what his camera records rich and strange since he has an extraordinary sense of the vantage point he needs'.
12 'movement, which transforms the frame, and opens it up to what is outside the field of vision'.
13 'But I like streets a lot. I like walking in the street. That is a type of tracking shot too and I often cycle through the streets'.

of the haptic and contact (taking Marks's thoughts in a new direction), writing: 'haptic means "able to come into contact with"'. She continues: 'As a function of the skin, then, the haptic – the sense of touch – constitutes the reciprocal *contact* between us and the environment, both housing and extending communicative interface. The haptic is also related to kinesthesis, the ability of our bodies to sense their own movement in space' (Bruno 2002: 6). Resnais's films with their moving camerawork, their trajectories through space, remind us of our bodily journeys and bodily contact. In this sense the haptic and tactile in Resnais's work relate to literal touch, human contact and the handling of tangible objects, yet also to passage, to navigation, to movement through a three-dimensional space. As we see spaces and landscapes open before us on screen, Resnais reminds us that spectatorship may be upset from a fixed viewing position, that film viewing may be more bodily, more visceral, that the film may be a journey, a space of contact and encounter, playing on the senses and emotions conjured.

Crystals and virtuality

Writing about Resnais's early documentaries, Cyril Neyrat identifies the ways in which they reveal Resnais's development of editing effects and the tracking shot: 'La série de courts métrages de Resnais montre l'invention, le déploiement et l'aboutissement d'un système formel dont l'élément principal est le travelling et le principe dynamique le montage' (Goudet 2002: 51).[14] He draws attention, implicitly, too, to another feature of Resnais's filmmaking: the notion of the series. Resnais is interested in repetition and degrees of difference, both between particular films as he returns to and refines techniques and thematic clusters, and also within a particular film. This aspect of his filmmaking comes to the fore from *L'Année dernière à Marienbad* onwards (indeed the film is pivotal in this study). Susan Sontag comments on the film: 'The burden of [the] double intention – to be both concrete and abstract – doubles the technical virtuosity and complexity of the film' (Sontag 1963–64: 24). *L'Année dernière à*

14 'Resnais's series of short films show the discovery, the development and the completion of a formal system whose principle element is the tracking shot and whose dynamic principle is editing'.

Marienbad is a film which apparently draws attention to the tactile: in the grand hotel setting and filming of his heroine, Resnais closes in on a material world of stucco work and sumptuous fabric, gilded, diaphanous, moulded against skin. He uses leisurely tracking shots which move the spectator through space, mapping the labyrinth of his film, making of viewing a haptic, emotive encounter. Despite this materiality and tactility in the mode of representation, however, *L'Année dernière à Marienbad* is primarily a film of the mind, of mental images and formal experimentation. Commenting on both the film's structure and its material setting, Sarah Leperchey writes: '*Marienbad* donne l'impression de répétitions foisonnantes. Tout est clos, tout est reflet, répétition, retour; c'est le cristal décrit par Deleuze: le film cristalise, en formant des circuits de plus en plus vastes, autour d'un germe, d'un petit circuit originel, qui met en relation une image et son image virtuelle (son double ou son reflet)' (Leperchey 2003: 20).[15] Deleuze himself writes: 'c'est tout l'hôtel de Marienbad qui est un cristal pur, avec sa face transparente, sa face opaque et leur échange' (Deleuze 1985: 102).[16] For Deleuze, the crystal image is a film image which encompasses a real image and its mirrored reflection, in such a way that the relation between the two, actual and virtual, is drawn into question. Such an approach to cinema draws attention to the ways in which cinema is not merely a reflection of reality, but a self-conscious construction which has the capacity to reflect the world as it is imagined and fantasised, as well as viewed. To find the crystal image in *L'Année dernière à Marienbad* seems particularly apt since the mansion Resnais creates is itself encrusted with many mirrors in whose crystalline, reflective surfaces we see much of the action of the film take place. The film disrupts our knowledge of actual and virtual in its filming of mirrors, in its creation of *mise en abyme* and *trompe-l'oeil* effects. This visual effect is reflected too, however, in the status of the events in *Marienbad* where the viewer remains uncertain whether images we see represent actual

---

15 '*Marienbad* gives the impression of proliferating repetitions. Everything is closed, everything is a reflection, a repetition, a return; it is the crystal described by Deleuze: the film crystallises, forming ever vaster circuits, around a central idea, a little original circuit, which sets up a relation between an image and its virtual image (its double or reflection)'.
16 'the entire mansion at Marienbad is a pure crystal, with its transparent surface, its opaque surface and the exchange between them'.

events, remembered events or indeed fantasised events. Despite his attention to materiality here, Resnais shows materiality as a product of the desiring or remembering mind; he offers us mental images of a sensory world, the world of the senses as it is imagined. In an interview at the time of the making of *L'Année dernière à Marienbad*, he comments on the sensory precision of imaginary images, saying: 'Par exemple, je discutais l'autre jour avec une fille qui revenait de l'Inde, et je l'ai vue tout à coup devant le temple d'Angkor avec une robe bleue, alors qu'elle n'était jamais allée à Angkor et que la robe bleue était simplement ce que je lui voyais porter' (*Premier Plan* 1961: 84).[17] As he shows reality doubled in the imagination, projected and reconstructed by the desiring mind, Resnais already approaches in *Marienbad* a theme, and formal concern, which will dominate in his filmmaking in its latter decades: fate, chance and plural destinies. Resnais, like Kieślowski and others, moves in the latter part of his career from thinking cinema as a medium in which to represent subjective perception to thinking cinema as reflection of plural, virtual realities, lives which might be led. *Marienbad* already prefigures this turn as we see a hint of so many possible, proliferating encounters which might, or might not, have taken place. Cinema becomes a means of witnessing, vicariously, alternative destinies. In this way whole strands of Resnais's films, and arcs of his plots, can be seen to be virtual, as an experiment, not only in how a particular destiny might be lived, but how it might be filmed. This is witnessed in its ultimate form in his late pair of films, *Smoking* and *No Smoking*.

This introspective, and potentially prospective, concern emerges inevitably and eventually as a part of a broader thematics of destiny in the face of death. Proliferating destinies are imagined as an exit from the inevitability of death, as delay, or diversion. Resnais's films may be perceived at times as dreams of the dying, as a retrospective glance. Films as diverse as *Je t'aime je t'aime*, *Stavisky* and *Providence* each offer discomposed fragments of a remembered, or imagined individual life. Playing on hesitations between life and death, between animate and inanimate, Resnais's films largely offer protagonists who are increasingly insubstantial, phantom and death-defined. As

17 'For example, I was talking the other day with a young girl who had come back from India, and instantly I saw her in front of the temple at Angkor in a blue dress, while she never went to Angkor and the blue dress was simply what I could see her wearing in front of me'.

Deleuze writes, indeed: 'Le personnage dans le cinéma de Resnais est précisément lazaréen parce qu'il revient de la mort, du pays des morts; il est passé par la mort et il naît de la mort, dont il garde les troubles sensori-moteurs' (Deleuze 1985: 270).[18] In this respect, indeed, Resnais's films might be seen to move in repeating circles. Where the traumatic encounter with the visceral death of the other – a race, a population, an unknown woman, a lover – impacts on Resnais's early filmmaking, his late works trace life as it is imagined (and re-thought) from the perspective of death. Resnais's filmmaking finds material and mental forms for such extreme death encounters, even as he appears to treat the lightest subjects, the most transient forms of representation. For Serge Daney, 'le monde de Resnais est, aujourd'hui encore, un monde *convalescent*, fragile et compliqué' (Daney 1998: 29).[19] Fragile, certainly, his films are yet ever sentient, ever prescient in their attention to fear and desire. As Resnais enters his eighties, at the beginning of the twenty-first century, his filmmaking is enjoying renewed critical attention in France and beyond. There has been a flurry of critical writing (as cited variously in this volume) and international retrospectives of his work. It is in this context that his films re-enter the viewer's arena, arriving where they started, and knowing the place for the first time.

References

L'Avant-scène du cinéma: Hiroshima mon amour, 61–2 (July–September 1966).
Benayoun, Robert (1980) *Alain Resnais: arpenteur de l'imaginaire* (Paris: Stock/ Cinéma).
Bersani, Leo and Ulysse Dutoit (1993) *Arts of Impoverishment: Beckett, Rothko, Resnais* (Cambridge MA: Harvard University Press).
Bounoure, Gaston (1974) *Alain Resnais* (Cinéma d'aujourd'hui 5) (Paris: Seghers).
Bruno, Giuliana (2002) *Atlas of Emotion: Journeys in Art, Architecture, and Film* (New York: Verso).
Caruth, Cathy (1995) *Trauma: Explorations in Memory* (Baltimore MD: The Johns Hopkins University Press).

---

18 'The protagonist in Resnais's cinema is Lazarean precisely because he comes back from the dead, from the land of the dead; he has passed through death and he is born out of death, keeping death's sensory-motor disturbance'.
19 'Resnais's world is, still today, a *convalescent* world, fragile and complicated'.

Caruth, Cathy (1996) *Unclaimed Experience: Trauma, Narrative, and History* (Baltimore MD: The Johns Hopkins University Press).
Daney, Serge (1998) *Ciné Journal. Volume II 1983–1986* (Paris: Petite bibliothèque des Cahiers du Cinéma).
Deleuze, Gilles (1985) *Cinéma 2: L'Image-temps* (Paris: Minuit).
Goudet, Stéphane (ed.) (2002) Positif, *revue de cinéma: Alain Resnais* (Paris: Gallimard [Folio]).
Greene, Naomi (1999) *Landscapes of Loss: The National Past in Postwar French Cinema* (Princeton NJ: Princeton University Press).
Hughes, Robert (ed.) (1962) *Film: Book 2. Films of Peace and War* (New York: Grove Press).
Ishaghpour, Youssef (1982) *D'une image à l'autre: La représentation dans le cinéma d'aujourd'hui* (Paris: Editions Denoël/Gonthier).
Jousse, Thierry and Camille Nevers (1993) 'Entretien avec Alain Resnais', *Cahiers du Cinéma*, 474 (December), pp. 22–9.
Leperchey, Sarah (2000) *Alain Resnais: Une lecture topologique* (Paris: L'Harmattan).
Marks, Laura (2000) *The Skin of the Film: Intercultural Cinema, Embodiment, and the Senses* (Durham NC: Duke University Press).
Marks, Laura (2002) *Touch: Sensuous Theory and Multisensory Media* (Minneapolis: University of Minnesota Press).
Mettey, Marcel (1970) *'La Guerre est fini'*, *Image et son: la revue du cinéma*, 244, pp. 49–72.
Monaco, James (1979) *Alain Resnais* (New York: Oxford University Press).
Prédal, René (1996) *L'Itinéraire d'Alain Resnais* (Paris: Lettres Modernes [Etudes Cinématographiques]).
Premier Plan: Alain Resnais (1961), 18 (October).
Sontag, Susan (1963–64) '*Muriel ou le temps d'un retour*', *Film Quarterly*, 17: 2 (winter 1963–64), pp. 23–7.

1

Documentaries 1948–58

Resnais's early documentaries are meticulous, exquisitely edited works, encompassing both his interest in art – the visual arts and his own art as filmmaker – and his constant attempt to create a visual testimony to traumatic history. These documentaries offer models (sometimes in miniature) of the spectral and architectural worlds found in his feature films. Bounoure argues that the themes explored in the documentaries all return in Resnais's work, and he pairs the significant documentaries with later feature developments (Bounoure 1974). Resnais himself in an early interview takes a typically sceptical approach, however, shying away from any auteurist projection. He comments: 'Les films documentaires sont toujours commandés. Si je pouvais choisir je ne ferais pas des films d'art. Je voudrais faire un long métrage, mais j'ai la sensation de ne pas connaître encore le métier. J'aimerais faire les films musicaux' (*Premier Plan* 1961: 37).[1] He realised this ambition to make musicals in the latter part of his career. Despite this, for many Resnais will remain a filmmaker of the mourning heritage of the mass horrors of the twentieth century: Guernica, the Holocaust, Hiroshima.

As he reminds us, his first films were commissioned. His work in piecing together these films, however, honing the skills as editor he learned at IDHEC, led to Resnais's development as a director and his opportunity to make his first feature film, *Hiroshima mon amour*. Viewing the documentaries through the optic of Resnais's later

1 'Documentary films are always commissioned. If I could choose I would not make films about art. I would like to make a feature film, but I have the sense that I do not yet have the right skills. I would like to make musicals'.

features makes us attuned to the development of a sensibility, the director's analytical and sensuous manipulation of images, his ordering of the world.

Van Gogh (1948), *Paul Gauguin* (1950)

Critics often evoke the visual arts in describing Resnais's images, imagining his films echoing the figures of Piero della Francesca paintings, or the nocturnal scenes of Surrealist art. Resnais's early career as documentarist was devoted to making images of artists and their paintings, his works belonging to the genre of the 'film sur l'art' ('film about art') which developed in France in the period 1945–60. Such films sought to explore works of art filmically, creating pictorial narrative about the artist, the artwork and the process of production. In 1947, Resnais made a series of ten 16mm films about contemporary artists – Henri Goetz, Hans Hartung, Christine Boomeester and others – taking the camera into their studios and also creating a montage of their images (see Thomas 2002: 37–41). He chooses to leave these films in obscurity, however, and they are little seen; his first widely recognised work is *Van Gogh* (1948).

Resnais was encouraged to take advantage of a Van Gogh exhibition at the Orangerie in Paris to make a film about the artist (Benayoun 1980: 42). He made a 16mm film which was then blown up to 35mm for release. It won a double prize at the 1948 Venice Biennale and in 1950 was awarded an Oscar (Monaco 1979: 18). François Thomas comments on the similarities in technique used in the earlier 'visites d'atelier' and in the more successful *Van Gogh* finding 'un voyage à l'intérieur des oeuvres' (Thomas 2002: 38).[2] In *Van Gogh*, already, Resnais develops the two signature devices which return throughout his filmmaking: the expressive use of editing, cutting and pasting reality into a new collaged form, and the use of tracking shots where the camera moves around a painting, towards it and, more frequently here, away from it, creating an exhilarating mobility, yet also, insistently, guiding our vision.

Van Gogh forms its visual narrative of the artist's life entirely out of images by the artist: it uses the work to generate the life of the painter.

2 'studio visits'; 'a journey inside the paintings'.

Resnais wrote in a piece for *Ciné-Club* in 1948: 'Il s'agissait de savoir si des arbres peints, des maisons peintes, des personnages peints pouvaient grâce au montage remplir dans un récit le rôle d'objets réels et si, dans ce cas, il était possible de substituer pour le spectateur le monde intérieur d'un artiste au monde tel que le révèle la photographie' (cited in Bounoure 1974: 29).[3] Resnais's work exists like an animated film, using an evolving series of Van Gogh paintings and drawings to evoke the Dutch village of Van Gogh's youth, the rooftops and panoramas of Paris where he pursued his art, and the disturbing corridors of the *hospice de Saint Rémy* where he lived his last days. Resnais's aim is not merely to use Van Gogh's art as material evidence, substituting paintings for snapshots of the artist's life; more subtly, as he suggests above, he uses the paintings to show us the world apparently as Van Gogh saw it, to show us not merely the object world of nineteenth-century Holland and France, but to conjure the subjective images of that world perceived by the artist and captured by him on canvas. Resnais's investigation in the film is not merely art historical therefore: he seeks already, as he will in his later films, to reveal the work and process of the imagination, the shots of reality that we view, distorted, in our mind's eye. As Resnais said in interview with Truffaut in 1956: 'Pour moi, *Van Gogh* est moins un film sur Van Gogh qu'une tentative de raconter la vie imaginaire d'un peintre à travers sa peinture' (cited in Bounoure 1974: 100).[4]

For the contemporary viewer, Van Gogh's images are some of the most recognisable in modern art (though as Resnais points out the artist was little known when he undertook the film) (Resnais 1972: 34). Filming them in black and white Resnais strips them of their strident blue, yellow, black and emerald. There is still sensory pleasure in *Van Gogh*, evoked, for example, in the backwards tracking shot away from the images of trees in blossom, in the subtle fades as one painting gives way to another, and another. Yet Resnais's *Van Gogh* – with its monochrome images, its form dissolves, where editing is dictated by shape – also looks forward to Resnais's own

---

3 'It was a matter of finding out whether painted trees, painted houses, painted people could, through editing, play the part of real objects in a narrative and if so, whether it was possible to replace the world as revealed by photography, for the spectator, by the interior world of the artist'.

4 'For me, *Van Gogh* is less a film about Van Gogh than an attempt to narrate the imaginary life of a painter through his painting'.

later, bleaker black-and-white documentary and feature images. The viewer may find resemblances between the early, borrowed Van Gogh images and the skeletal figures of *Nuit et brouillard* or the contorted trees in the Nevers of *Hiroshima mon amour*. Seeing the artist's work, his imagining of the world, in black and white, focuses our attention on the form and shapes in his paintings, aligning his art with that of Resnais himself.

Resnais followed *Van Gogh* with a further short documentary, *Paul Gauguin* (1950), which he acknowledges as less innovative. It is a companion piece to *Van Gogh*, beginning with a self-portrait by Gauguin and following his flight from Paris to an island in Oceania (Tahiti). The film adopts the tranquillity and composure of Gauguin's images of Tahitian women. But this evocation of paradise on earth is shifted as Resnais also evokes Gauguin's images of dream and nightmare. In his later documentary, *Les Statues meurent aussi* (1953), Resnais will be more self-conscious about self/other relations, colonial and post-colonial tensions (the commentary suggests 'le Blanc projetait sur le Noir ses propres démons, pour se purifier' Cornand 1969: 196).[5] *Paul Gauguin* is a largely pictorial film by contrast; it is in his next documentary, *Guernica* (1950), that Resnais develops his politicised, mourning sensibility.

Guernica (1950)

In *Guernica*, Resnais extends his work outwards to encompass not only personal tragedy but a broad traumatic history. In its editing, the film recalls *Van Gogh*; as Alain Fleischer writes: 'le célèbre tableau de Picasso est utilisé comme un scénario à découper, à mettre en scène' (Fleischer 1998: 25).[6] While the painting *Guernica*, which hangs in the Reina Sofía art gallery in Barcelona, is central to the images of Resnais's *Guernica*, his film moves beyond this painting, and its shattered, exploded composition, finding its visual echoes throughout Picasso's painted *oeuvre*. As with *Van Gogh*, this is not a film about a painting, or paintings, it is an attempt to convey an artist's vision of the world, and in the case of *Guernica* to use that vision in order to

5 'whites projected their own demons onto blacks to purify themselves'.
6 'Picasso's famous painting is used like a script to be cut up, to be dramatised'.

animate and respond to an event of enormity and horror: the bombing of civilians at Guernica during the Spanish Civil War. There were 2,000 deaths, all civilian, at Guernica in the bombing on 26 April 1937. Resnais says of Guernica in interview: 'Guernica nous paraissait la première manifestation de la volonté de destruction pour le plaisir de la destruction: faire une expérience sur du matériel humain, pour voir' (*Premier Plan* 1961: 36).[7]

In his words about Guernica, Resnais signals the bombing campaign as destruction for pleasure. In making a film about Guernica, Resnais experiments with the documentary form, moulding and manipulating his film art in such a way as to attempt to make us feel the horror of experiments with human flesh, with human lives, material creation, artistic and urban fabric. Georges Sadoul writes in *Les Lettres françaises*: '*Guernica* se situe dans le domaine de la poésie lyrique et ne pretend jamais être didactique' (cited in Bounoure 1974: 147).[8] Lyrical the film certainly is, and uncertain about the possibility of didacticism; yet such readings neglect the passion and engagement of Resnais's filmmaking, his incitement to think critically about trauma and his search for an apt mourning aesthetic.

Guernica is a source for the experimentation of *Nuit et brouillard*, *Hiroshima mon amour* and later films. It foreshadows them materially and formally. Like them, it draws on a creative relation between soundtrack and image track. A text by poet Paul Eluard is read by Maria Casarès (an actress who starred in films by Bresson and Cocteau). *Guernica* opens with a shot of the city in ruins; this still image remains as we hear the voice-over. The film starts and ends with the name of the city, Guernica. Resnais uses the name of a place which became a topos in the twentieth-century imagination, a place synonymous with destruction and horror. In Cayrol's commentary to *Nuit et brouillard*, he writes: 'Le Struthof, Oranienbourg, Auschwitz, Neuengamme, Belsen, Ravensbruck, Dachau, Mauthausen, furent des noms comme des autres sur les cartes et les guides' (Cayrol 1997:

---

7 'Guernica seemed to us the first manifestation of the will to destroy for the pleasure of destruction: experimenting on human matter, to see what would happen'.

8 '*Guernica* is situated in the domain of lyric poetry and never claims to be didactic'.

9 'Le Struthof, Oranienbourg, Auschwitz, Neuengamme, Belsen, Ravensbruck, Dachau, Mauthausen, were names like any others on maps and in guidebooks'.

18).[9] Guernica too was another such anodyne site. Resnais begins with this place once ruined and then leads the viewer backwards to imagine the inhabitants of the city. Here he uses figures from paintings of Picasso's blue period (before Guernica historically). There is a strange pathos in seeing the composure of these figures, and seeing how their dimensions and features will erupt in Picasso's art. *Guernica* draws much, visually, from this mapping of pictures from different periods of Picasso's work. Yet it draws emotive effect too from Resnais's own filmic fragmentation of Picasso's human forms. Resnais brings us close to the images, lighting discreet sections of paintings, making the painted figures appear to emerge from their dark backgrounds, making their presence more tactile, yet momentary, illusory. The attempt to animate still images, to make film out of painted art, is most experimental here in the scenes which evoke the bombing itself. Extremely rapid editing of images is coupled with discordant music, assaulting the viewer's senses. In the horror of the bombing we see Picasso's frantic animal images – bulls, horses – as well as contorted human figures. Drawing attention to the imprint of this atrocity on animal and human flesh, Resnais shows a series of close-ups of body parts, of mouths, of tongues. Like Picasso, Resnais does not shy away from horror, showing us emblematic images of anguish and despair, pausing in close-up, for example, on an image of a mother and her dead child.

Guernica is an emotive, if small, film in comparison to Picasso's painting. Its greatest effect comes not merely from its sensitive cutting and pasting of Picasso's images, but from the reflections it offers in retrospect in the context of Resnais's career. Resnais's images are moving, they have an impact on the viewer. Yet these are only shadows of the real events. These morbid, mobile images hide the reality of Guernica as they also point to its horror. In close-ups, in images of hands and tongues, Resnais recalls sentient flesh, but all he shows us is its fine, aesthetic after-image. His films, after *Guernica*, continue to grapple with the divide between inanimate matter and sentient flesh, with matter changing state, with horror being felt in art.

Les Statues meurent aussi (1953)

Les Statues meurent aussi has been little seen in France. The controversy surrounding the film anticipates the censorship and reticence around the release of the later *Nuit et brouillard*. *Les Statues meurent aussi* was commissioned by Présence Africaine in 1950, though not completed for another three years. It was a co-authored project between Resnais and his contemporary and friend, documentary maker Chris Marker. Like *Nuit et brouillard*, which followed it, the film won the Prix Jean Vigo. As James Monaco writes, *Les Statues meurent aussi* 'describes the disintegration of African art as a result of the cultural imperialism of French colonial powers' (Monaco 1979: 20). The film was banned in France for fifteen years after it was completed (full details of the film's censorship, including a copy of the letter banning it can be found in Cornand 1969). A complete print was first seen by the French public in November 1968 in a programme of short films grouped under the theme 'Cinéma d'inquiétude'. Until its release on DVD in 2004 it was difficult to access, though a print is occasionally shown in the *cinémas d'art et d'essai* in Paris.

Resnais says in interview, with nice ambiguity, 'nous n'avions pas, au départ, l'idée de faire un film anticolonialiste et antiraciste' (*Premier Plan* 1961: 54).[10] Resnais and Marker intended instead to make a film about African art, which was little seen or appreciated in France in the 1950s. As he researched the film, Resnais wondered why African art was placed in the Musée de l'homme (an ethnographic museum) while Assyrian, or Greek art, by contrast, was on show in the Louvre. He was overwhelmed by the beauty of the African art objects he viewed in special collections. Resnais says that before working on the film 'la notion même de colonialisme [lui] était pratiquement inconnue' (Resnais 1972: 34).[11] Colonialism and its impact become apparent as Resnais traces the history and trajectory of African art objects and their relation to their culture. In studying African art, making it visible, Resnais and Marker ironically trace its erosion and loss. Marker writes in the film's commentary: 'puisque le Blanc est acheteur, puisque la demande excède l'offre, puisqu'il faut

---

10 'at the start, we did not have the idea of making a film that was anti-colonialist and anti-racist'.
11 the very notion of colonialism was practically unknown [to him]'.

aller vite, l'art nègre devient l'artisanat indigène' (Cornand 1969: 197).[12]

Les Statues meurent aussi denigrates the commercialisation of African art and its western appropriation, by extension indicting the force of colonialism. The very title of the film speaks of entropy, loss of meaning. It puts forward ideas, too, about art, death and commemoration which return in Resnais's later works. Marker's commentary specifies that the African statues we see are images of ancestors, establishing a link between life and death: 'Gardiens de tombeaux, sentinelles des morts, chiens de garde de l'invisible, ces statues d'ancêtres ne forment pas un cimetière. Nous mettons des pierres sur nos morts pour les empêcher de sortir, le nègre les conserve près de lui, pour les honorer et profiter de leur puissance, dans un panier rempli de leurs ossements' (Cornand 1969: 196).[13] In this simplified image of African culture, statues, images of the dead, are seen to live until they are buried in the museum: 'Et puis ils meurent à leur tour. Classés, étiquetés, conservés dans la glace des vitrines et des collections, ils entrent dans l'histoire de l'art' (Cornand 1969: 197).[14] The death of statues is illustrated also in the opening images of the film where we see statues from western art, fragmented, the title seeming to refer to a Proustian sense of the friability of even hard matter, through time. In both motifs in the film, statues are rendered peculiarly animate (in particular in Resnais's moving shots which circle the material objects). Resnais introduces this uncanny theme of hesitation between life and death, flesh and stone, which will recur in his films as he shows ash-covered figures in Hiroshima, statues and shadows at Marienbad. In *Les Statues meurent aussi*, this material concern shadows the more trenchant awareness of the loss and embalming of a living civilisation. In the images of broken marble, in the images of African statues, objects in western glass cases, Resnais counterpoints two narratives of loss, of the erosion of art through time and the acts of the (colonial) other. It is an irony that

12 'because whites are keen to purchase, because demand exceeds supply, because speed is a necessity, African art is becoming indigenous craft'.

13 'Guardians of graves, sentries of the dead, guard dogs of the invisible, these statues of ancestors do not form a cemetery. We put stones on our dead to stop them coming out, the African keeps his close to him in a basket filled with their bones, to honour them and profit from their power'.

14 'And then they die in turn. Classified, labelled, preserved behind glass in museums and collections, they enter into the history of art'.

the film itself was lost for viewers, through censorship, for many years.

Nuit et brouillard (1955)

In *Landscapes of Loss*, Naomi Greene explores the effect of censorship on representations of nation, history and memory in post-war French films. She writes: 'Censorship restrictions in force throughout the 1950s and 1960s ensured that these works could only hint at some of the darkest zones of the French past' (Greene 1999: 9). Greene refers to restrictions on representations of the Occupation and France's relation to the Holocaust, an issue which Resnais tackles, although in part indirectly, in his documentary *Nuit et brouillard*. The film was commissioned by the 'Comité d'Histoire de la Seconde Guerre Mondiale' to mark the tenth anniversary of the liberation of the German concentration camps by the Allied forces. It has been one of Resnais's most widely viewed films, both in the decade in which it was made and subsequently (shown on television and in *lycées* in France as part of a campaign to encourage people to remember the Holocaust and to resist anti-semitism, and racism more broadly). In 1994, France Culture devoted a four-hour radio programme to the film's fortieth anniversary.

Resnais first declined to make the film since he had no direct experience of the Holocaust. He reconsidered the commission when writer Jean Cayrol, who had been a political prisoner in Mauthausen, was willing to work on the project. Cayrol provided a measured commentary (read in the film by actor Michel Bouquet). Hanns Eisler, a contemporary German composer who flew to Paris to work with Resnais, composed music for the film. Allowing the project to be layered by Cayrol's commentary and Eisler's music, Resnais opened it up to different voices and effects. The film would work as a composite, intersubjective piece. In interview Resnais says: 'Les courts métrages qui ont été faits sur les camps en 45 et 46 n'ont atteint aucun public. Avec *Nuit et brouillard*, j'ai eu la volonté de faire un film susceptible d'atteindre un grand public' (*Premier Plan* 1961: 37).[15] With historical

15 'The short films which were made about the camps in 45 and 46 did not reach their audience. With *Nuit et brouillard*, I wanted to make a film which was likely to reach a wide public'.

assistance from Olga Wormser and Henri Michel – who had previously organised an exhibition and written a book, *Tragédie de la déportation 1940–1945* – with the support of producer Anatole Dauman, with help editing words and images together from Chris Marker, Resnais achieved this aim. Work on the project was painful. Resnais had nightmares throughout his research on the film and recalls that he would wake screaming in the night (though the dreams passed when he was shooting at Auschwitz). Cayrol became seriously ill during the writing of the commentary. Bounoure quotes him saying: 'Quand je me suis retrouvé chez moi avec le tas de photos sur les camps, j'ai vraiment cru devenir fou' (Bounoure 1974, 133).[16]

The commission came in May 1955 and the film was completed by December 1955 and sent to the board of censors. In a telephone call to Resnais a request came for a shot to be cut 'since it might be offensive in the eyes of the present-day military' (Raskin 1987: 30). It is a shot of the camp at Pithiviers, one of the two main camps for foreign-born Jews arrested in France (Raskin 1987: 31). In the lefthand corner of the frame, an officer can be seen surveying the camp from a watchtower. His *képi* signals his French nationality. The still photograph, acquired from the Centre de documentation juive contemporaine, squarely offers an image of French collaboration and responsibility. Resnais resisted censorship, requesting that the demands of the censors be placed in writing and refusing to remove the image. He stresses in interview: 'c'était quand même important de montrer que la France avait organisé des points de départ pour les camps' (Raskin 1987: 56).[17] Indeed, as well as Pithiviers, he shows shots of the Vél-d'hiv, the cycling stadium where Jews were forced to assemble before deportation to the camps. *Nuit et brouillard*, anticipating Marcel Ophuls's far more specific project *Le Chagrin et la pitié* (1970), is a film which questions French collaboration with the Nazis. With respect to the image of the French officer, a compromise was found after negotiations between the censors and the film's producers: the image remained in the film but a beam was superimposed, supposedly obscuring the officer's nationality. (Resnais points out the irony that if anything this act of censorship drew attention to the image of the

16 'When I found myself at home with the pile of photographs of the camps, I really thought I was going mad'.

17 'it was still important to show that France had organised points of departure for the camps'.

officer).The 'visa de contrôle' was granted and Resnais was allowed to leave in images of bodies in the last sequences which had initially been deemed too violent.

The film met further censorship at the Cannes film festival of 1956. It was unanimously selected to compete in the *court métrage* category, but then withdrawn from competition at the request of the West German Embassy. As Raskin reminds us: 'Article 5 in the festival regulations stipulates that if a film is deemed offensive to the national sensibilities of a participating country, that country's representatives may request that the film be withdrawn from competition' (Raskin 1987: 35). The film was still shown in Cannes, but out of competition. This wary reception, by the censors and at Cannes, was swept aside by critics. In *Cahiers du cinéma*, Truffaut writes: '*Nuit et brouillard*, le "film" le plus noble et le plus nécessaire jamais tourné, nous plonge dans une perplexité honteuse et provoque de nos idées et de nos sentiments la déroute' (cited in Raskin 1987: 138).[18]

Criticism has come latterly, however, and rightly, over the film's inadequate treatment of the Holocaust as Jewish experience. *Nuit et brouillard* makes only glancing reference to Jewish specificity. The term 'juif' appears only once, in the evocation of 'Stern, étudiant juif d'Amsterdam';[19] there are also a few images of deportees bearing the yellow star sewn on their clothes. Charles Krantz writes: 'a close analysis of the film reveals not a single statement of the fact that the Holocaust was a particularly Jewish experience' (Krantz 1985: 5). Robert Michael continues: 'No one can doubt the humanistic intent of Resnais and Cayrol. But their silence unintentionally mirrors Himmler's imperative that "in public we will never speak ... of the evacuation of the Jews, the annihilation of the Jewish people"' (Raskin 1987: 159). Krantz takes up the issue with Resnais: 'Alain Resnais recently suggested to this author that to have dealt with the fate of the Jews would have been inappropriate in that it might have diverted attention away from the universal message of vigilance that he wanted to convey, though he conceded the possibility of an error of judgment' (Krantz 1985: 6). For Serge Klarsfeld, cited on France Culture, the failure to show the Jewish experience of the Holocaust was the major fault of *Nuit et brouillard*. Claude Lanzmann, in the same programme,

---

18 '*Nuit et brouillard*, the most noble and necessary "film" ever made, throws us into shameful confusion and redirects our thoughts and feelings'.

19 'Stern, a Jewish student from Amsterdam'.

corroborates this view, also offering a series of strong reflections on the differences between his own approach in *Shoah* (1985) and Resnais's in *Nuit et brouillard*. In particular, against Resnais, *Shoah* refuses the use of archive shots, demanding instead, in Lanzmann's words 'tout un travail de réflexion intérieure'. (Adolphe Nysenholc argues, however, that without the work of *Nuit et brouillard* in disseminating images of the Holocaust, *Shoah* would not have been able to depend only on spoken testimony; see Nysenholc 2003).

Not Jewish himself, Cayrol was a prisoner captured under the 'Night and Fog Decree' signed on 7 December 1941, which set up new guidelines for the treatment of civilians arrested in occupied countries for offences against the Reich. The chalked capitals 'NN' (for 'Nacht und Nebel') are seen on a prison uniform within the film. For Krantz: 'Naming the film after them [NN prisoners] was an act of French patriotism' (Krantz 1985: 9). Raskin, also referring to comments by Olga Wormser, reminds us, though, that 'in the aftermath of the war, "nuit et brouillard" came to stand for the nightmare suffered by everyone who had been deported by the Nazis, whether on the basis of ethnic background, political conviction or resistance activities' (Raskin 1987: 22). In naming the film *Nuit et brouillard*, Resnais also chooses a title with sensory impact. Resnais uses the senses, and in particular images of the bodily, the animate and the inanimate, to provoke the viewer's response. Lanzmann has spoken disparagingly of the catharsis of *Nuit et brouillard*; Bazin writes: '*Nuit et brouillard* est avant tout un regard d'amour et de confiance en l'homme' (cited in Raskin 1987: 139).[20] Raskin himself writes: '"Douceur" and "tendresse" are among the terms most often used to characterize the tone of *Nuit et brouillard*' (Raskin 1987: 134). Such readings overlook how unsettling to the senses the film may be. Leo Bersani and Ulysse Dutoit remark: 'for all the smoothness of its visual presentation, [the film] is constantly setting up obstacles to undisturbed vision' (Bersani and Dutoit 1993: 183). *Nuit et brouillard*, like much of Resnais's cinema, attempts to grapple with the filmic representation of human matter and sensation, fantasised, sensed and felt. Resnais risks lyricism and aestheticism, qualities which make his film memorable, in representing a real excess of horror, mortification and desecration of the flesh. Hesitation and unclear values, sickly uncertainty, are key.

20 '*Nuit et brouillard* is above all an expression of love and confidence in mankind'.

The film opens with a colour image of an open landscape shot in the present; against this we hear the words: 'Même un paysage tranquille, même une prairie avec des vols de corbeaux, des moissons et des feux d'herbe, même une route où passent des voitures, des paysans, des couples, même un village pour vacances, avec une foire et un clocher, peuvent conduire tout simplement à un camp de concentration' (Cayrol 1997: 17).[21] Resnais's camera travels backwards so that barbed wire becomes visible at the edges of this image of a 'paysage tranquille', the camera illustrating what can be cropped from the shot. Resnais's colour images, shot on location at Auschwitz, offer a visual testimony to the remains of the camp in the present (1955), a phantom, forgotten city only visited by the camera. The film plays on the contrast between these vivid shots of the Polish landscape and the historical documents, photographs and archive film, all in black and white, which make up its memorial and emotive substance.

The shooting script transcribed by Raskin gives the provenance of these documents (Raskin 1987: 65–131). The opposition of colour images with black-and-white photography appears to create contrast between past and present (Lanzmann, for example, shoots in colour). Images in black and white appear as documents of the past; images in colour are part of Resnais's engagement with what remains in the present. Yet, as Vincent Pinel notes, it seems that Resnais himself shot some of the black-and-white footage. Pinel cites by way of example the shots of the night-time arrival at the camps (these are in fact shots from another feature film), the shots of objects made by the camp prisoners, the shots of the Kapo's bedroom (cited in Raskin 1987: 145). If Pinel is right, *Nuit et brouillard* may tacitly blur the distinction between colour and black-and-white shots, moving not specifically between past and present, but between two modes of representation, two approaches to the experience of the camps.

In the colour sequences Resnais develops his use of tracking shots. These moving camera shots are used primarily to map the spaces of the camps which Resnais and his film production team visit. Critics have interpreted these tracking shots variously. Robert Benayoun writes: 'Le lent travelling avant de Resnais (il l'appellera "ma figure de

21 'Even a tranquil landscape, even a field with crows, a harvest and grass fires, even a road with passing cars, peasants, couples, even a holiday village, with a fair and a belltower, can quite simply lead to a concentration camp'.

style") ailleurs solennel ou exalté, se veut ici inquisiteur, culpabilise l'image dans la fausse innocuité' (Benayoun 1980: 54).[22] For Vincent Pinel, the tracking shot has a power of animation in this dead landscape: 'Resnais tire un parti étonnant des lents glissements de la caméra dans un décor immobile qui semble alors s'animer' (cited in Raskin 1987: 145).[23] Annette Insdorf offers a more melancholy reading, countering that 'while confronting and investigating, this fluid camera suggests transience, or the license of smooth mobility that can exist only after the fact' (cited in Raskin 1987: 157). Following this line, the moving camera might suggest not merely transience, but movement onwards into the future. The tracking shots coerce the viewer into following the eye of the camera; this camera movement speaks of inexorability, of the sweep onwards of time and motion as we lose the time to pause and contemplate. Resnais shows us the process of the past being forgotten, this deathly sweep of time and oblivion indicated both in the abandonned sites we see and in the movement of the camera.

In the face of forgetting, Resnais seeks material traces of presence in the camps and finds these most memorably in shots of the gas chamber ceilings at Maïdenek. This human trace in concrete can be likened too to the images of human shadows imprinted on stone in *Hiroshima mon amour*. The concrete of the gas chamber bears human traces and imprints, all but illegible signs of the suffering which took place and which Resnais's camera attempts to make visible, even palpable. Yet, as the camera moves over this scarred concrete, in a single tracking shot, the relation between the human markings and the atrocity to which they bear witness and of which they offer material proof challenges rationality and sense-making. In his move between animate and inert matter, Resnais offers evidence in the form of grotesquely malleable concrete. The gouging of this matter, the oxymoron it embodies, challenges and nauseates the viewer. Resnais brings us up close to these images; they fill the screen of his film. We have no purchase on these images, images which are abusively tactile, a record of the deathly, devastating imprint of dying

---

22 'Resnais's slow forwards tracking shot (he will call it his personal trait), elsewhere solemn or exalted, seeks to be an inquisitor here, showing up the blame in the falsely innocuous image'.

23 'Resnais takes astonishing advantage of the slow glide of the camera in a still setting which seems to come to life'.

hands on concrete. Expressly tactile, these images are yet obtrusive and resistant as we fail to apprehend their content.

Where Resnais shows concrete as vulnerable to human fear and pressure, so he shows the sheer horror of human bodies which have become invulnerable, immobile, petrified in death. Indeed one particular horror of *Nuit et brouillard* is felt in its protracted hesitation between life and death, between animation and lifelessness, a privilege cinema as medium can offer and a reflection Resnais presents on the mortal terror of the death camps. In his 1962 film *La Jetée*, Resnais's sometime collaborator Chris Marker presents a series of still frames which compose the visual narrative. At only one point does the film offer a moment of animation as the phantom woman whose image haunts the time-travelling protagonist almost imperceptibly opens her eyes. In *Nuit et brouillard*, Resnais moves more extensively between still frames and animated footage. The editing of still images creates a jolt of movement, action or shock effect. *Nuit et brouillard* has been read as a human or humanist film, and such it may seem through Cayrol's commentary, through its emphasis on named individuals ('Schmulzki, marchand de Cracovie, Annette, lycéenne de Bordeaux'[24]) and on details of human experience: hunger, sleep, emotion, bodily functions. Resnais's images are more fearful and more doubting, however. *Nuit et brouillard* is concerned time and again with indiscriminate mass images: the crowd scenes from the Nazi rallies Resnais borrows from *Triumph of the Will* (1934) and German news footage, overhead shots of the deportees, shots of massed piles of spectacles, of human hair. To these mass images, the film adds a further proliferating set of images of the body distorted by fear, hunger, disease, labour, humiliation, torture and death. A terrifying and perverse new human anatomy is glimpsed in the film, in its collage of bodies barely surviving, near death, dying or dead. Many of these shots are glimpsed in still photos, as images from which we may know some distance. Yet some are film, not photographs.

Shots 169–174, images of deportees in the camp hospital, are unexpectedly live. We see the deportees in the hospital beds, their bodies almost reminiscent of the corpses the film shows elsewhere. Yet, with more shock than in *La Jetée*, we find that these bodies are moving in the film. The shots are described in the shooting script: a

24 'Schmulzki, a shopkeeper in Krakow, Annette, a schoolgirl in Bordeaux'.

deportee trembling beneath a blanket, a deportee gasping beneath a blanket. As we see these moribund figures still moving, caught on film, Resnais disturbs our sense of the division between living and dead, between animate and inanimate. The shots are closed by a still image, entirely reminiscent of the previous shots in form and content but showing a man in bed, still living but very near death. In *Remnants of Auschwitz*, Agamben, in part following Primo Levi, argues that 'the complete witness ... is the one we cannot see: the *Muselmann*' (this was the name given to deportees who had reached the worst deprivation, the limits of their lives) (Agamben 1999: 162). Drawing on texts by Jean Améry, Primo Levi and others, Agamben writes that the death of the *Muselmann* had begun before that of his body. The *Muselmann* is described as a staggering corpse, as a mummy-man, as the living dead. Agamben notes: '"Finally, you confuse the living and the dead," writes a witness of Bergen-Belsen. "Basically, the difference is minimal anyhow. We're skeletons that are still moving; and they're skeletons that are already immobile. But there's even a third category: the ones who lie stretched out, unable to move, but still breathing slightly"' (Agamben 1999: 54). Resnais shows the remaining documentary images of the *Muselmann*; further, he makes the hesitation between life and death which the *Muselmann* embodies part of the visceral effect of the film on its viewers as he unsettles our sense of the difference between stillness and movement, death and life.

The hesitation between life and death imaged in the hospital scene, played out in the unexpected live images, is repeated all the more horrifically in shots of the liberation of the camps by the allies where bodies are moved in the mud by a bulldozer (Resnais uses British news footage from Belsen, also used by Godard in *Notre Musique* (2004)). The inanimate bodies are made to move through the mechanical action of the bulldozer, their flesh and limbs horrifically vulnerable again in this illusion of animation. The images seem unthinkable as we attempt to link prior human emotion and sentience to the desecrated mass of human bodies. Lanzmann states on France Culture that he would not have used such images; he says that if film had been available of the last moments inside a gas chamber, he would not have used it. Resnais makes a riskier decision, running risks of exposure and spectacularisation, of lack of respect for the dying, the dead and their relatives. In his text 'De la mort à la vie', which accompanies the commentary of *Nuit et brouillard* in the 1997

Fayard volume, Jean Cayrol envisages the possibility of art in response to the Holocaust. He names this art 'lazaréen', describing it as 'un art né directement d'une telle convulsion humaine' (Cayrol 1997: 51–2).[25] In creating such 'art lazaréen' in *Nuit et brouillard*, Resnais focuses materially on the trope of the living dead, on the body alive but near death, on the body dead but still moving, allowing his images to oscillate between petrification and the illusion of filmic reanimation. The viewer is confronted with visceral images bearing the imprint, the marks and scars of this 'convulsion', of this traumatic, infinitely damaging and irredeemable history. In response to these body images, permanently marked, signalling endless brutality there is no catharsis, no relief.

Nuit et brouillard details the uses made of bodies and body parts in the infernal productivity of the concentration camps: hair made into fabric, bones into fertiliser. (As Krantz writes: 'Bones, human hair, body fat, nothing is to be "wasted"' (Krantz 1985: 3)). This is one of the few moments where the commentary peters out several times, replaced by silence in which we are left to contemplate the transformation of these once sentient bodies into useful material. In this moment of sickness in the film, Resnais might be seen to reflect implicitly on the horror of his own filmmaking, itself (though very differently) recycling bodies as art. This caveat does not break the cycle of collaged images that make up *Nuit et brouillard*, but it offers some reflection on the horror of this material process, which sickened Resnais and Cayrol in the making of the film. In 1956, Jacques Doniol-Valcroze writes in response to the visceral images of *Nuit et brouillard*: 'Tous ces corps confondus aimons-les comme s'ils étaient vivants, car ils nous quitteront jamais' (Doniol-Valcroze 1956: 38).[26] For Žižek, those murdered in the Holocaust continue to haunt us, the living dead, until (unless) we can give them a proper burial (Žižek 1991: 23). Resnais in *Nuit et brouillard* chooses to show the murdered, their flesh once living, now dead, now eerily animate as we watch. He is disturbingly true to the aesthetic and material interest in objects, fabric and human matter he displays in his other films. He is peculiarly indiscriminate in his testimony to fleshly, emotional suffering in *Nuit et brouillard*. This is a very different film from *Shoah*

25 'Lazarean'; 'an art rising directly from such a human convulsion'.
26 'Let us love all these mingled bodies as if they were alive, for they will never leave us'.

but one which still effectively registers something of the impact, the imprint of the Holocaust in the collective imagination and in individual lives.

The film also functions not only as commemoration, but as warning. Emily Tomlinson refers to the work of Dominick LaCapra, arguing that commentators on history 'display a tendency to overlook or underrate the impact of traumatic scenes until more recent horror comes to light'; she continues: 'Auschwitz, thus, was not a pressing issue for French authors before the atrocities of the Algerian war began their course' (LaCapra 1998, cited in Tomlinson 2002: 44). This perspective allows *Nuit et brouillard* to be seen as a response to the present as much as the past; Raskin quotes Resnais saying: 'Et surtout, on était en France en pleine guerre d'Algérie, la guerre d'Algérie commençait en France, et il y avait déjà des zones dans le centre de la France où il y avait des camps de regroupement' (Raskin 1987: 51).[27] In this sense, too, *Nuit et brouillard* was a film about France, France under the Occupation *and* France in its colonial wars.

Toute la mémoire du monde (1956), *Le Chant du styrène* (1958)

Resnais followed *Nuit et brouillard* with a further documentary, about the Bibliothèque Nationale, the vaulted building in the rue de Richelieu in Paris which has since been supplanted, or supplemented, by the Bibliothèque François Mitterand at Bercy. The film was made for one of the cultural divisions of the French Foreign Ministry. As James Monaco notes, it had no censorship problems (Monaco 1979: 24). Jacques Doniol-Lacroze quotes Resnais writing in *Les Lettres françaises*: 'Client fidèle de la Nationale depuis des années, j'avais envie de découvrir ce qui peut bien se passer entre le moment où l'on remplit sa fiche et celui où l'on reçoit un livre' (Doniol-Lacroze 1957: 59).[28] The film reveals this investigative curiosity, analysing the system of the library and the process through which it functions.

---

27 'And above all France was in the midst of the Algerian war, the Algerian war was beginning in France, and there were already zones in the centre of France where there were internment camps'.

28 'A regular reader at the national library for years, I wanted to discover what can happen from the moment when one fills in one's form until the moment one receives a book'.

Critics have associated Resnais's filming of the function of the library with his filming of the diabolical system of concentration camps (see for example Doniol-Lacroze 1957: 59). Certainly the vocabulary of the commentary – where the library is described as a fortress and each book as a prisoner – and the very geography of the library, reminiscent of images by Piranesi, seem to uphold the analogy. For Christine Richardson, however, the relation is more contrastive: 'The anthropomorphic status of books and treasures in *All the Memory of the World* is reversed in *Night and Fog*, where humans are collected and systematically reduced to objects – corpses, things not worth mummification. When a book leaves its space in the stacks, a card takes its place as a "ghost". When an inmate finally deserts the cramped space of the barrack, the only evidence of his former existence is a line drawn through a name in the camp register' (Richardson 1979: 74). As it exists with and against *Nuit et brouillard*, *Toute la mémoire du monde*, retains not so much a 'concentrationnaire' view of the world, as an aesthetic vision which Resnais has developed in his early treatment of mass trauma but which, ethically or not, he will continue to rarefy and deploy in films treating a wider variety of subjects.

Forgetting, in particular, is given broader attention in *Toute la mémoire du monde*. Resnais does not give his investigation a specific post-war context, but the documentary gains resonance when viewed from this perspective. The commentary opens with a vision of the Bibliothèque Nationale as mechanism devised to counter forgetting: 'Parce que leur mémoire est courte, les hommes accumulent d'innombrables pense-bêtes'.[29] In its last shots, as it shows readers in the library, the film asks us to imagine these readers 'devant leurs morceaux de mémoire universelle'.[30] The books and documents are seen as part of an organic construction of cultural and collective memory. Historian Pierre Nora has explored changes in society and its relation to memory in the modern era; as memory is no longer retained through social and family groups, so its loss and failure are feared. He writes: 'moins la mémoire est vécue de l'intérieur, plus elle a besoin de supports extérieurs et de repères tangibles d'une existence qui ne vit plus qu'à travers eux. D'où l'obsession de l'archive qui

---

29 'Because they have short memories, people accumulate numerous aide-mémoires'.

30 'in front of their morsels of universal memory'.

marque le contemporain, et qui affecte à la fois la conservation intégrale de tout le présent et la préservation intégrale de tout le passé' (Nora 1997: 30).[31] In *Toute la mémoire du monde*, Resnais offers a tangible image of the archiving of memory. Nora looks at the construction or recognition of 'lieux de mémoire', places, monuments, rituals which defend against forgetting. He writes: 'la raison d'être fondamentale d'un lieu de mémoire est d'arrêter le temps, de bloquer le travail de l'oubli, de fixer un état des choses, d'immortaliser la mort, de matérialiser l'immatériel' (Nora 1997: 38).[32] Where Resnais, sweeping us through the camp, is cautious of seeing Auschwitz as a 'lieu de mémoire' – its horrors cannot be encompassed in this memorial process – the Bibliothèque Nationale, on the other hand is a 'lieu de mémoire' par excellence. Its building, its collections, its place within French cultural consciousness, history and knowledge mark it amply as such. Further, the 'lieu de mémoire' as defined by Nora, and constructed by Resnais in his filming of the library in *Toute la mémoire du monde*, preserves and commemorates the very obsessions of Resnais's cinema, his interest in the move between life and death, the material and the immaterial.

For Naomi Greene, who refers to Nora, 'designed as a "place of memory" to keep the past alive, the funereal library seems, instead, to have assumed the form of its tomb' (Greene 1999: 42). Christine Richardson, in evoking the film, comments too on 'the propensity for civilization to construct areas of death to preserve memory' (Richardson 1979: 62). A sarcophagus the library may seem, yet the work of the librarians is seen expressly as a 'lente bataille contre la mort'.[33] More lively still is the visual presentation of the library with its reading room like a cathedral shown through omniscient overhead shots. Resnais describes a changing spectacle in the library as he records the mass of readers absorbed in their work. We see how they change the patterns of Resnais's formal compositions, where, for

31 'the less memory is lived from the inside, the more it needs exterior supports and tangible marks of an existence which now only lives through them. This explains the archive obsession which marks the contemporary era, and which affects both the complete conservation of all the present and the complete preservation of all the past'.
32 'the fundamental reason for a place of memory is to stop time, to block the work of forgetting, to fix things as they are, to immortalise death, to materialise the immaterial'.
33 'slow battle against death'.

example, a young woman is glimpsed for an instance running back to her seat. In his interest in readers, Resnais animates the library, conjures the spectre of their infinitely diverse sampling from this repository of memory. Yet Resnais also moves to make the library his own 'domain of phantasms' (Foucault cited by Richardson 1979: 63). Amongst the chosen volumes and papers we see are comics featuring Harry Dickson, comics Resnais himself collects, and has variously tried to film through his career. Further we glimpse battle-scenes by Dürer, images by Odilon Redon – disembodied floating faces, reminiscent of the severed heads seen close to the end of *Nuit et brouillard*.

In *Toute la mémoire du monde*, Resnais propagates a notion of collective memory, of a 'mémoire universelle'. He shows, obliquely, how the shots of his own films are always already familiar, part of this cultural melting-pot or memory bank. His films will recall torture scenes in Goya, the bodily horror of passages in Kafka. His will be a collaged art, glimpsed first by a wider public as he edits together images by Van Gogh, pursued in the editing of *Guernica* and *Nuit et brouillard*. Resnais's response to the traumas of twentieth-century history is particular: he recognises the fear of forgetting, the blow dealt to memory, yet retains and refuses to relinquish the resonances of art, literature and popular culture, the fabric from which cultural memory is continually re-shaped.

The last non-fiction work of this early period in Resnais's filmmaking, *Le Chant du styrène*, described by Peter Cowie as the most abstract of Resnais's documentaries (Cowie 1963: 135), was a commissioned piece shot in the Pechiney polystyrene factories. For Edward Dimendberg, in a ground-breaking political reading of the film, 'it provides a revealing window onto the French political and global economy of the late 1950s and the obstinate materiality of capitalism and rewards close reading with a veritable return of repressed geopolitical relations' (Dimendberg 2005: 65). With a verse commentary by Raymond Queneau, and experimentation with time and process – the manufacture of the fabric is shown working backwards from product to raw material – the film also perpetuates certain traits of Resnais's filmmaking. The film's fascination with forms and patterns, with plasticity itself (and sensual, close-up, haptic images of stretched and moulded plastic), again links it to his earlier work. Yet his foray into colour, his references to abstract art, the apparent objectivity of his filming of the material world, already anticipates his work of the future, his testimony to the modern, the new, the unsettling of the senses, in *Muriel* and beyond.

References

Agamben, Giorgio (1999) *Remnants of Auschwitz: The Witness and the Archive*, translated by Daniel Heller-Roazen (New York: Zone Books).
Benayoun, Robert (1980) *Alain Resnais: arpenteur de l'imaginaire* (Paris: Stock/Cinéma).
Bersani, Leo and Ulysse Dutoit (1993) *Arts of Impoverishment: Beckett, Rothko, Resnais* (Cambridge, MA: Harvard University Press).
Bounoure, Gaston (1974) *Alain Resnais* (Cinéma d'aujourd'hui 5) (Paris: Seghers).
Cayrol, Jean (1997) *Nuit et brouillard* (Paris: Fayard).
Cornand, André (1969) 'Les Statues meurent aussi', *Image et Son*, 233 (December), pp. 193–201 [including a complete text of the commentary to the film].
Cowie, Peter (1963) *Antonioni, Bergman, Resnais* (London: The Tantivy Press).
Dimendberg, Edward (2005), '"These are not Exercises in Style": *Le Chant du Styrène*', *October*, 112 (spring,), pp. 63–88.
Doniol-Valcroze, Jacques (1956) 'Le Massacre des innocents', *Cahiers du cinéma*, 59 (May), pp. 37–8.
Doniol-Lacroze, Jacques (1957) 'La prisonnière Lucia', *Cahiers du cinéma*, 77 (December), pp. 59–60.
Fleischer, Alain (1998) *L'Art d'Alain Resnais* (Paris: Editions du Centre Georges Pompidou).
Greene, Naomi (1999) *Landscapes of Loss: The National Past in Postwar French Cinema* (Princeton NJ: Princeton University Press).
Krantz, Charles (1985) 'Teaching *Night and Fog*: History and Historiography', *Film and History*, 15:1, pp. 2–15.
LaCapra, Dominick (1998) *History and Memory after Auschwitz* (London: Cornell University Press).
Monaco, James (1979) *Alain Resnais* (New York: Oxford University Press).
Nora, Pierre (1997) *Les Lieux de mémoire* (Paris: Gallimard [Quarto]).
Nysenholc, Adolphe (2003) '*Nuit et brouillard*: Défense et illustration', *Contre Bande* 'Alain Resnais', 9, pp. 11–21.
Premier Plan: Alain Resnais (1961), 18 (October).
Raskin, Richard (1987) *Nuit et Brouillard* by *Alain Resnais* (Aarhus: Aarhus University Press). (This contains a full, reconstructed shooting script and many critical sources).
Resnais, Alain (1972) '*Les Statues meurent aussi* et les ciseaux d'Anastasie', *Téléciné*, 175 (January), pp. 32–6.
Richardson, Christine (1979) '*All the Memory of the World*: in retrospect', *Enclitic*, 3:1 (Spring), pp. 62–81.

Thomas, François (2002) 'Sur trois films inconnus d'Alain Resnais', in Stéphane Goudet (ed.), Positif, *revue du cinéma: Alain Resnais* (Paris: Gallimard [Folio]), pp. 37–41.

Tomlinson, Emily (2002) *Torture, Fiction, and the Repetition of Horror: Ghostwriting the Past in Algeria and Argentina* (PhD dissertation, University of Cambridge).

Žižek, Slavoj (1991) *Looking Awry: An Introduction to Jacques Lacan through Popular Culture* (Cambridge MA: MIT Press).

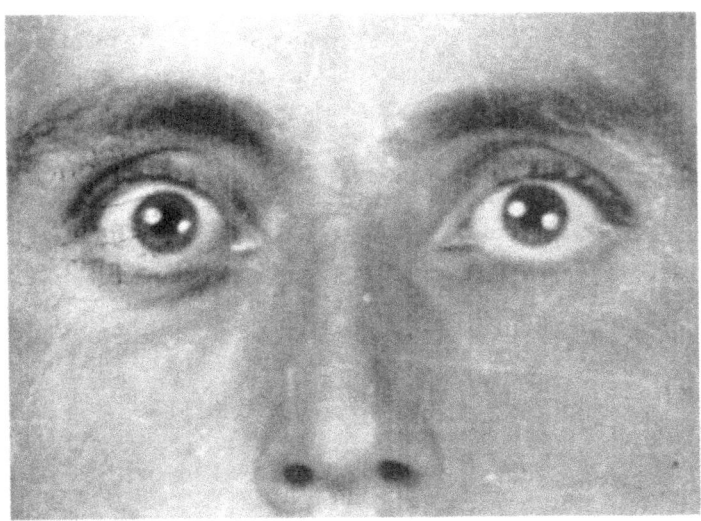

1 First impression, *Nuit et brouillard*, 1955

2 Memory in Japan, *Hiroshima mon amour*, 1959

3 Liminal image, *L'Année dernière à Marienbad*, 1961

4 Mirroring, *L'Année dernière à Marienbad*, 1961

5 The gardens at Marienbad, *L'Année dernière à Marienbad*, 1961

6 Fantasy and the tactile, *L'Année dernière à Marienbad*, 1961

7 In the night, *L'Année dernière à Marienbad*, 1961

8 Last image, *L'Année dernière à Marienbad*, 1961

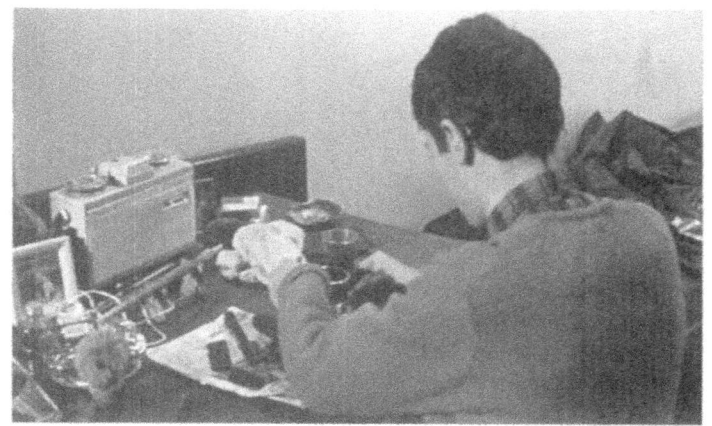

9 Bernard, *Muriel*, 1963

10 Hélène, *Muriel*, 1963

11 Janine as a child, *Mon oncle d' Amérique*, 1980

12 Janine, *Mon oncle d' Amérique*, 1980

13 Laboratory rat, *Mon oncle d' Amérique*, 1980

14 Titles sequence, *Mélo*, 1986

15 Camille and Nicholas, *On connaît la chanson*, 1997

16 Arlette and Gilberte, *Pas sur la bouche*, 2003

2

Hiroshima mon amour (1959)

At the start of Resnais's first feature, *Hiroshima mon amour*, two bodies are intertwined, clasping one another, skin against skin. Close-up and disorienting – expressive tactile shots emerging out of darkness – the body images are not attached to two individuals. Resnais cuts the distance between viewer and screen as we are enwrapped in this embrace, as the images summon our embodied knowledge and somatic memories, our sense of touch and physical sensation. The body images are moving, metamorphosing before our eyes, through a series of dissolves, as their material texture changes. Duras, screenwriter of the film, describes these 'deux épaules' visible on screen as 'trempées de *cendres*, de *pluie*, de *rosée* ou de *sueur*' (Duras 1960: 21).[1] The ashes which first cover the embracing forms, glowing in the monochrome shots, recall the atomic ashes of Hiroshima, calling us to imagine this deadly, corrosive fallout coating these still-moving, sentient bodies. The substance covering skin and flesh petrifies these limbs, offering them a new inanimate surface, recalling the frangible statues of *Les Statues meurent aussi*, and the contorted body images of *Nuit et brouillard*. Holocaust images, images reminiscent of the bodies held in lava at Pompeii, this opening speaks of the mortification of the flesh. Yet the dissolves, where one shot lingers on the screen as another, inexorably, moves into view, draw the viewer onwards as horror morphs into eroticism, as the bodies reappear now glazed in sweat, not ashes, moving with tenderness and pleasure. Through these dissolves, Resnais illustrates in smoothly contracted form the distance his film will stretch from Hiroshima to

[1] 'two shoulders'; 'covered in *ashes, rain, dew* or *sweat*'.

love, from trauma to the attempt to remember, and forget, in fleeting physical pleasures.

This opening proved immediately notorious. The sensuality of the film per se, rather than its dissolving between sex and death, provoked censure, a reviewer in *Films in Review*, for example, speaking disparagingly of the film as sexually titillating. As Jean-Louis Leutrat explains: 'Le film était précédé de la réputation d'être une oeuvre scandaleuse. La publicité a évidemment insisté sur l'image du couple, sur la relation entre un homme de couleur jaune et une femme blanche' (Leutrat 1994: 37).[2] On the response in Japan, Robert Jay Lifton reports: 'The film inevitably aroused opposition in Hiroshima, even while being made, because some *hibakusha* [Hiroshima survivors] felt that its sensuality was an insult to the A-bomb dead' (Lifton 1967: 468). Herein lies the moral puzzle of *Hiroshima mon amour*. For Duras, the screenwriter, this move between sex and death is not a sacrilege (indeed its dynamic will be repeated in much of her later fiction); she writes: 'Ce qui est vraiment sacrilège, si sacrilège il y a, c'est HIROSHIMA même' (Duras 1960: 10).[3] Lynn Higgins also, in a different way, champions the film's aesthetic wager. She writes of Resnais and Duras's work 'the desire to represent horror through a love story must be counterbalanced by an awareness of the danger of forgetting the horror entirely' (Higgins 1996: 22). A love story becomes one means of representation and commemoration, an inadequate means, but, as writers on mass trauma remind us, there are perhaps no adequate means to represent an event which annihilates its own witness.

In *Hiroshima mon amour*, the history of Hiroshima is embedded within the first traumatic and erotic images of the film. At this juncture Resnais's concern is to move beyond realist representation and to find a more condensed, poetic means of expression: 'le début n'est pas seulement une représentation du couple, c'est une image poétique. Et la cendre sur les corps, ça ne se réfère à aucune réalité anecdotique, c'est une pensée' (*Premier Plan* 1961: 58).[4] *Hiroshima*

2 'The film had the advance reputation of being a scandalous work. The advertising emphasised the image of the couple and the relation between a man of colour and a white woman'.

3 'What is really a sacrilege, if there is a sacrilege, is HIROSHIMA itself'.

4 'the start is not only a representation of the couple, it is a poetic image. And the ash on the bodies does not refer to any actual reality, it is a thought'.

mon amour elaborates its first meanings on the very skin of its protagonists, in the impressions of love and death. For Resnais: 'par associations d'idées, nous sommes passés de la peau source d'extrême plaisir à la peau source d'extrême douleur' (*Premier Plan* 1961: 69–70).[5] Leutrat notes that one of the main themes of the film, and its visual expression, is '[le thème] de la peau, des mains et des impressions tactiles'. He adds: 'Tout le début du film expose ce thème avec application' (Leutrat 1994: 66).[6] This theme is key to the material reading of *Hiroshima mon amour* I offer here.

Hiroshima mon amour, Resnais's first feature film, originated in a commission to the director from the producers of *Nuit et brouillard*. He was asked to make a documentary film on the atomic bomb. He considered the commission but decided that the cinematic result would be too similar in aesthetic and effect to his earlier film on the Holocaust; there were also already around fifteen Japanese documentaries on Hiroshima. He was persuaded to reconsider the project, however, in collaboration with a screenwriter. Françoise Sagan was approached but she turned the project down. Resnais had just read *Moderato Cantabile*, a new novel by Marguerite Duras, which had made a strong impression on him. Resnais went to tea with Duras in Paris and spent all afternoon talking about why he could not make a film about Hiroshima. This conversation initiated their collaboration, and, further, defined the film's aesthetic. In the synopsis she would later publish as preface to her script of *Hiroshima mon amour*, Duras writes: 'Impossible de parler de HIROSHIMA. Tout ce qu'on peut faire c'est de parler de l'impossibilité de parler de HIROSHIMA' (Duras 1960: 10).[7]

Hiroshima mon amour was a co-funded French and Japanese production, filmed on location in Hiroshima and Nevers, and in studios in Tokyo and Paris between September and December 1958. The film's première was at the Cannes festival in May 1959. The film has become so indelible in the public imagination that, as Lifton says: 'its international success has rendered it the source of many people's

5 'by association we moved from the skin as source of extreme pleasure to the skin as source of extreme pain'.
6 '[the theme] of the skin, hands and tactile impressions'; 'the start of the film carefully reveals this theme'.
7 'Impossible to talk about HIROSHIMA. All one can do is talk about the impossibility of talking about HIROSHIMA'.

imagery about the city and the bomb' (Lifton 1967: 467). Critical discussion of the film has been voluminous, with many coruscating accounts of the film's qualities and meanings. Critics are divided on the value of the film within Resnais's work as a whole, however. For Marie-Claire Ropars-Wuilleumier, one of the finest critics of Resnais, '*Hiroshima* precipitates a rupture of codes, through a forceful cinematographic *écriture* it dismantles the conventional order of cinema – hence the shock it felt in 1959' (Ropars-Wuilleumier 1990: 173). For James Monaco, writing in 1979: 'it remains by far Resnais's most complicated, difficult, confusing, and treacherous essay in the social, political, and linguistic/semiological ramifications of film' (Monaco 1979: 34). For Bersani and Dutoit, by contrast, 'thanks to Duras (especially to her commercially appealing fascination with the luxurious masochism of bourgeois love, a fascination weakly disguised by a great deal of pseudo-political intensity about the horrors of Hiroshima and the Nazi occupation of France), *Hiroshima* is Resnais's weakest film' (Bersani and Dutoit 1993: 189).

Hiroshima mon amour is a film which depends on division and merger. It begins as a co-authored project, dependent on the collision and *rapprochement* of Duras's words and Resnais's images. These images are themselves always already double. Resnais had two different cameramen: Takashi Michio in Japan and Sacha Vierny in France. Vierny agreed to shoot the Nevers scenes without seeing or knowing about the Hiroshima sequence (Hughes 1962: 54). Yet in late scenes in the film, shots from Hiroshima and Nevers are intercut as if the film showed one continuous imaginary city. Through editing the differences between the shots are gradually rendered indistinct.

Hiroshima mon amour shows two time sequences and interweaves two histories. The first and initially prominent history is that of Hiroshima, the city on which an atomic bomb was dropped at 8.15am on 6 August 1945. As one *hibakusha* writes: 'The thermal rays and blast force from the atomic bomb took the lives of hundreds of thousands of people, destroyed all the buildings in central Hiroshima in an instant, and turned most of them into ashes' (*Atomic Bomb Photo Testament* 1996: 1). The account continues: 'The damage caused by the A-bomb in Hiroshima city, an area of 72.7 square kilometers at the time, was 55,000 buildings totally burned, 2,290 partially burned, 6,820 totally destroyed, and 3,750 partially destroyed'. (*Atomic Bomb Photo Testament* 1996: 20). These events are recalled in the film from present-day (1958) Hiroshima, where a French actress is playing a part in a film about peace. On her last but one night before leaving Japan, she has a brief encounter with a Japanese man, an architect or engineer. In their embrace she speaks of her attempts to know and understand Hiroshima; her words draw commemorative images of the city and its tragedy onto the screen. The Japanese man's responses, returning, incantatory, are, however, negative as he says repeatedly: 'Tu n'as *rien* vu à Hiroshima' ('You saw *nothing* at Hiroshima'). (One critic suggests that he may be voicing the woman's qualms, her conscience, her fear that as untouched witness she has seen nothing (Callev 1997: 111)).

Resnais appears to commemorate the documentary he might have made about Hiroshima in the first fifteen minutes of *Hiroshima mon amour*. The film even sounds in places like his earlier film *Nuit et brouillard*. The editor, Henri Colpi, in a piece on music in the film, writes that a motif can be heard in the music which exactly recalls a theme from *Nuit et brouillard*, while Italian composer Giovanni Fusco had not seen the film or heard Eisler's score (Colpi 1960: 2). Constructing a self-conscious documentary on Hiroshima, Resnais offers a collage of images of the city and its survivors, yet this is always framed by return to the lovers in bed and to the doubting words of their dialogue. Our view of Hiroshima, recalled, is impeded like this, made self-conscious, dubious and interrogative. Resnais's images of Hiroshima are heterogenous, some taken, as in *Nuit et brouillard*, from news footage, some filmed in the museum at Hiroshima, some taken from both documentary and feature films about the tragedy. (Pauline Kael (1961–62) registers shock at seeing images of Hiroshima with which she was already familiar from Japanese films.) Yet Resnais says, quoted in English here: 'I used Japanese films that dealt with the explosion. I have always wanted to quote films within film as you find in literature' (Hughes 1962: 55). Through the Japanese man's words, through the self-consciously composite, 'false' documentary images, Resnais signals the inadequacy of images of this event, this city and its suffering. He opens out our perception of the voyeurism, and the failure, which inhere in his enterprise.

If the opening of the film casts doubt on approaches to remembering the A-bomb tragedy, Resnais and Duras appear, next, to distract us from Hiroshima altogether, telling instead the story of a Frenchwoman's love affair in Nevers in Occupied France. In the dialogue between the lovers, which continues in bed and in the bars and tearooms of the night city, a story the woman tells, coaxed by her Japanese lover, begins to take shape. As Resnais says, in interview: 'Pendant le tournage, nous racontions le soir toutes sortes d'histoires à son sujet, par example: elle est mythomane et cette histoire de Nevers qu'elle raconte à son Japonais n'a jamais eu lieu, ou bien: elle n'est pas à Hiroshima mais dans un asile, toute cette aventure c'est elle qui l'invente' (*Premier Plan* 1961: 57).[8] The story of Nevers is seen as one possible fiction; any verification, as seems to be offered in the film in the summoned flashback images, is registered as only illusory. Within the film even the French woman herself insists that the telling of the story of Nevers is only one possible narrative of many she might have shared with her Japanese lover; she insists that the telling of Nevers is his choice. She asks him why he has chosen Nevers and Duras's screenplay offers two different options for his response: 'C'est là, il me semble l'avoir compris, que j'ai failli... te perdre... et que j'ai risqué ne jamais te connaître' or 'C'est là, il me semble l'avoir compris, que tu as dû commencer à être comme aujourd'hui tu es encore' (Duras 1960: 81).[9] The film does not choose between the two responses, but offers both on its soundtrack, opening up layers and alternatives in our understanding of the man's motivation and the couple's interaction.

There is some sense that the woman's refusal herself to choose Nevers is disingenuous. Earlier in their dialogue she has said, indeed: 'Nevers, tu vois, c'est la ville du monde, et même c'est la chose du monde à laquelle, la nuit, je rêve le plus. En même temps que c'est la chose du monde à laquelle je pense le moins' (Duras 1960: 58).[10] Nevers returns insistently in her dreams, but not in her waking reality. (Like Antonioni's *L'Eclisse* (1962), like film noir, Resnais's film is substantially a night-time film, its action drawn out

8 'During the shoot, each evening we told all sorts of stories about her, for example: she is a compulsive liar and this story of Nevers which she is telling her Japanese man never took place, or perhaps: she is not in Hiroshima but in an asylum and is making up this whole adventure'.

9 'That's when, I seem to have understood, that I nearly... lost you... and that I risked never knowing you'; 'That's when, I seem to have understood, that you must have started being as you are today'.

10 'Nevers, you see, is the town I dream about most in all the world, is the very thing I dream about most. At the same time it is the thing I think about least in all the world'.

through a long waking night as the woman waits to return to France.) Nevers is a memory (or nightmare) by which the woman is possessed, but one which she does not consciously recall, or so we are led to believe, until this encounter in Hiroshima. Nevers is shown as an intrusive, unlocatable memory, at first for both the woman and the spectator.

The first inkling we have of Nevers in the film, though on a first viewing we barely recognise it as such, comes in a seemingly serene dawn scene. The Frenchwoman is awake in the early morning after a night with her Japanese lover. Dressed in a kimono, she stands on the terrace of her hotel looking out over awakening New Hiroshima. She moves inside and sees her lover's body dormant in the bed. In a point-of-view shot we see the man's hand as he sleeps. The image in Hiroshima is supplanted for a mere four seconds by a glimpse of another man lying in pain or dying, blood-stained, a tremor running through his body. The flashback is lost almost as soon as it is seen; it is not inserted into the narrative here, where the Japanese man wakes up and the woman pursues her dialogue with him in the present. Yet the force of this disruption, this sudden temporal convulsion, unsettles our viewing. The film here merges two senses of the term flashback. Flashback is used in film critcism to denote a sequence in a previous time or era; flashbacks are often understood to have an explanatory function in narrative cinema, offering us some key pre-history. In psychoanalytic discourse, by contrast, a flashback is an unwilled returning hallucination or memory which takes possession of the victim of trauma. As Caruth writes: 'the flashback ... provides a form of recall that survives at the cost of willed memory or of the very continuity of conscious thought' (Caruth 1995: 152). Resnais's cine-matic flashback takes on the properties and affect of the traumatic hallucination. It serves no explanatory function in the narrative, certainly not at this point, and works instead to disrupt our viewing of the film. The spectator's experience is aligned with that of the French woman involuntarily remembering. We sense some of her disorienta-tion, the way she may be the unwilling victim of these returning thoughts. Recalling Deleuze on the time-image, we see that the images we view are subjective, that the film records the woman's perceptions, not any supposed external or objective reality. The film will be inhabited by, and fall victim to, the intermittencies of her consciousness, her recall or her forgetting. In this sense Resnais seeks to offer a trace or imprint of the mind, here a traumatised mind, in process and action.

However even here, in identifying images as subjective, there are uncertainties. One of the risks of the film is the way it appears to allow the trauma of Nevers to take precedence over the mass horror of Hiroshima. This appears confirmed specifically in the way in which the film pays little or no attention to the Japanese man's recollection of Hiroshima, to his perspective. Yet the film may lead us to wonder, in this respect, about the man's investment in the story of Nevers. Nevers may indeed be his choice of narrative, as well as the space and time of the woman's involuntary memories. The images of Nevers may be his fantasies. When the couple are again in bed, in the afternoon, in moments after they have made love again the woman begins to summon a conscious narrative of Nevers which is accompanied by lyrical shots of herself as a girl cycling through the French countryside, watched by a German soldier and then meeting him in barns and in empty ruins. These shots may function as cinematic flashbacks – a previous layer of time, the images which accompany the woman's memories. Yet there is no sure indication that the implied subject conjuring these images is the woman and not the Japanese man. The images of Nevers, its river and forest, the Frenchwoman as a girl, may be imagined by the man, not recalled by the woman. Deleuze explains the man's interest in Nevers (and reciprocally the woman's fascination with Hiroshima) as follows: 'N'est-ce pas pour chacun une manière d'oublier sa propre mémoire, et de se faire une mémoire à deux, comme si la mémoire maintenant devenait monde et se détachait de leurs personnes' (Deleuze 1985: 154).[11] Immersion in the history of the other allows some reprieve, some forgetting (and this is a theme I pursue).

But first to address a risk implied by the dual structure of the film's plotting of Nevers and Hiroshima entwined: namely that the two events or experiences come to seem equal or equivalent to one another. Resnais has expressed surprise and dismay that some viewers of his film saw the two events, traumatic experiences, in any way as equivalent; he writes: 'on *oppose* le côté immense, énorme, fantastique de Hiroshima et la minuscule petite histoire de Nevers'

11 'Is it not for each of them a way of forgetting their own memory, of making a memory for two, as if memory were now becoming world and detaching itself from the individuals'.

(*L'Avant-scène* 1966: 41).¹² Deleuze specifies effectively: 'Il y a deux personnages, mais chacun a sa propre mémoire étrangère à l'autre. Il n'y a plus rien de commun. C'est comme deux régions de passé incommensurables, Hiroshima, Nevers' (Deleuze 1985: 154).¹³ The bombing of Hiroshima and the loss, for the Frenchwoman, of her lover at Nevers (and her subsequent treatment) are events of incomparable proportion and importance, globally or historically. *Hiroshima mon amour* shows them both, nevertheless, as events which bring about suffering, both mental and physical, which resist representation, and which open up questions about memory and forgetting. (As Resnais says elsewhere: 'Toute douleur est incommensurable. Nous avons rapproché ces deux drames, ces deux douleurs, pour mieux les appréhender' (*Premier Plan* 1961: 47)).¹⁴

The film shows the two events, and places, shadowing each other; parallels and echoes proliferate, not in an attempt to stress equivalence, but to show how subjective perception influences views of both personal and public histories. The woman arguably finds her own history in Hiroshima; the relevance of Hiroshima to her love story is a delusion, but one portrayed in the film with sensitivity. As Marie-Claire Ropars-Wuilleumier writes brilliantly: 'A deformed hand, a destroyed eye, hair torn out, a distraught woman breaking out of a cavernous dwelling, a twisted bicycle, legs of passers-by, river, anger, stone – long is the list of materials which the narrative of Nevers drags out of Hiroshima's museum and reconstructs into appeased, if not acceptable, forms' (Ropars-Wuilleumier 1990: 180). Nevers as history is constructed out of the same forms and material as Hiroshima (in Resnais's construction of images). Nevers inflects the woman's perception of Hiroshima; yet Hiroshima also shapes her narrative of Nevers. The narrative of Nevers and the narrative of Hiroshima work as two parallel, differently scaled histories which make us focus on ways of remembering, and forgetting, in particular through the flesh and materiality. Indeed two different means of

---

12 'we are *opposing* the immensity, vastness and unreality of Hiroshima and the trivial little story of Nevers'.
13 'There are two characters, but each has his or her memory which is foreign to the other. There is nothing in common any longer. Hiroshima and Nevers are like two immeasurable regions of the past'.
14 'Any suffering is beyond measure. We have brought together these two dramas, these two traumas, to apprehend them better'.

sensate remembering, and forgetting, can be found in the film: the first is eroticism, the second is in a sensory encounter with the city (both summoned in the film's title).

In her volume, *The Body in Pain*, Elaine Scarry writes:

> A deeply tactful, compassionate, and careful account of the alterations that occur in human tissue such as the Stockholm International Peace Research Institute's verbal and visual account of the effects of incendiary weapons in Vietnam, Dresden, Hiroshima, or Nagasaki may place the injured body several inches in front of our eyes, hold the light up to the injured flesh, and keep steady the reader's head so that he cannot turn away. (Scarry 1985: 65)

Scarry suggests that the injured body is an index of suffering and it if it is to act most volubly it needs to be seen individually: 'injury must at some point be understood individually because pain, like all forms of sentience, is experienced within, "happens" within, the body of the individual' (Scarry 1985: 65). In *Hiroshima mon amour*, in the woman's physical encounters with love and death – in her repetition of these, with her Japanese lover, at Hiroshima – she attempts to know her pain and the pain of the other, individually, in close-up. Her love in Nevers has dissolved boundaries between pain and pleasure, between life and death. Julia Kristeva opens questions about this love: 'Amour grevé de mort ou amour de la mort? Amour rendu impossible ou passion nécrophile pour la mort?' (Kristeva 1987: 240).[15] The woman's last encounter with the German soldier occurs as he lies dying on the banks of the Loire – the scene which we glimpse in flashback early in the film. Fragments of this scene return in the film until they are pieced into a narrative. The woman was due to meet her lover at midday but, as she tells the Japanese man: 'Quand je suis arrivée à midi sur le quai de la Loire il n'était pas tout à fait mort' (Duras 1960: 99).[16] The woman lies with him all day and all through the night (a time not dissimilar in length to the time she spends with her Japanese lover in Hiroshima). She lies on his body, protecting him and merging with him. She says to the Japanese man in Hiroshima: 'le moment de sa mort m'a échappé vraiment puisque... puisque même à ce moment-là, et même après, oui, même après, je

---

15 'Love weighed down by death or love of death? Love rendered impossible or necrophile passion for death?'.
16 'When I arrived at midday on the quai de la Loire he was not quite dead'.

peux dire que je n'arrivais pas à trouver la moindre différence entre ce corps mort et le mien...' (Duras 1960: 100).[17] Caruth, making a psychoanalytic reading, suggests that 'in missing the moment of his death, the woman is also unable to recognise the continuation of her life' (Caruth 1996: 39). Through melancholic identification, she attempts to absorb her lover's death, to take it into herself. Caruth speaks of the woman's 'attempt, in her entrance into madness, to maintain the event of death against the understanding of liberation' (Caruth 1996: 30). The woman is locked in a cellar at Nevers, entombed, both physically and in her psyche. After months have passed and her hair, shorn by the people of Nevers as she shares the common fate of women collaborators at the time of the Liberation, has grown, she escapes Nevers, cycling through the night to Paris. When she arrives at dawn, 'le nom de Hiroshima est sur tous les journaux' (Duras 1960: 101–2).[18]

As Sarah Leperchey writes: 'On part de Hiroshima et on y revient, ayant décrit le cercle de Nevers' (Leperchey 2003: 86).[19] The woman holds the memory and life of the dead lover inside herself until she reaches Hiroshima some fourteen years later. Her Japanese lover discovers that she has spoken to no one of Nevers until their encounter. Hiroshima is the place where she can tell this story; what is disturbing, for the woman, for the viewer, is that Hiroshima by this token becomes a place, not of remembering, but of forgetting. After she has told the story of Hiroshima we see her in a scene alone in her neutral, geometric hotel bedroom. She speaks to her reflection in a mirror (the image itself reflecting an image we have seen in the first part of the film of a young girl looking at the reflection of her burned face). The woman addresses her absent lover:

> Tu n'étais pas tout à fait mort.
> J'ai raconté notre histoire.
> Je t'ai trompé ce soir avec cet inconnu.
> J'ai raconté notre histoire.
> Elle était, vois-tu, racontable.

17 'I missed the moment of his death because... because even at that moment, and even afterwards, yes, even afterwards, I can say that I could not find the least difference between this dead body and my own...'.
18 'the name Hiroshima was in all the papers'.
19 'One leaves Hiroshima and returns, having followed the circle of Nevers'.

Quatorze ans que je n'avais pas retrouvé... le goût d'un
   amour impossible.
Depuis Nevers.
Regarde comme je t'oublie...
– Regarde comme je t'ai oublié.
Regarde-moi. (Duras 1960: 110)[20]

Caruth speaks of 'the very movement of the woman's own consciousness that acts as the betrayal of love, as the forgetting of her own lover's death' (Caruth 1996: 32). Emphasis has been placed by critics on the narrative act, on the expiation and betrayal found in offering an (analysand's) account of the past. Yet just as prominent in the woman's speech here is the sense of physical betrayal, being more literally unfaithful to her lover and, treacherously, rediscovering her taste for impossible passion.

This erotic betrayal, forgetting through desire, is also what Hiroshima, the city and the man, offers the Frenchwoman from Nevers. Her love at Hiroshima will be an 'amour nécrophile', in Kristeva's terms – the body of her lover reminds her in its form and shape of the dead man at Nevers. It will be an irradiated, painful love, and draw sick pleasure from its flowering in Hiroshima. To quote Kristeva again: 'l'explosion nucléaire infiltre donc l'amour même, et sa violence dévastatrice le rend à la fois impossible et superbement érotique, condamné et magiquement attirant' (Kristeva 1987: 239).[21] Linda Williams argues that the film tests a relation between Hiroshima and love: 'these violently disparate moments do have something in common, ... the horror of the atomic bomb has something to do with the ecstasy of lovers, ... a cold and dead German lover has something to do with a live and warm Japanese lover, ... destruction has something to do with creation, and ... memory has something to do with forgetting' (Williams 1976: 35). As we have seen from the outset, Resnais and Duras risk merging eroticism and traumatic response. Resnais has said in interview about Hiroshima: 'Partout on

---

20 'You were not quite dead. I have told our story. I have betrayed you this evening with this stranger. I have told our story. You see, it could be told. For fourteen years I have not refound... desire for an impossible love. Since Nevers. Look how I'm forgetting you... Look how I've forgotten you. Look at me'.

21 'so the nuclear explosion infiltrates the love itself, and its destructive violence renders it at once impossible and beautifully erotic, condemned and magically attractive'.

sent la présence de la mort. Par réaction, on ressent un violent appétit de vivre, une volonté de sensations immédiates' (*Premier Plan* 1961: 52).[22] To echo Caruth, we can say that it is this emergence of the life drive which the woman finds in Hiroshima. I suggest that she finds this in eroticism, in her physical encounter with the body of the Japanese man, privileged from the opening shots of the film, as much as, or more than, in language and narrative. The horror of this physical rebirth, however, for both the woman and the city of Hiroshima, as we shall go on to see, is that it entails survival through forgetting, through the anihilation of memory and the past.

As well as functioning as one of the most resonant films about traumatic experience – Ropars-Wuilleumier describes it as 'unmakable and never remade' (Ropars-Wuilleumier 1990: 173) – *Hiroshima mon amour* is also, as critics have begun to acknowledge, an extraordinary urban film. Giuliana Bruno in her very rich volume, *Atlas of Emotion*, writes: '*Hiroshima mon amour* – Hiroshima my love – is a title that speaks of two passions, superimposed: the difficult love for a city, and a city as the site of difficult love' (Bruno 2002: 39). She stresses: 'the city itself is imagined as a corporeal affair' (Bruno 2002: 242). As we have seen already in *Nuit et brouillard*, Resnais as filmmaker is fascinated by the possibility of mapping spaces, of tracing and transforming our experience of place with a moving camera. This is all the more evident, exultantly so, in his filming of the city of New Hiroshima. He speaks of his pleasure in cities at night: 'Comme ça me plaît... les villes où toujours il y a des gens qui sont réveillés, la nuit, le jour' (*Premier Plan* 1961: 79);[23] he tells us of his first experiences of Hiroshima as city: 'Quand je suis arrivé à Hiroshima pour la première fois, j'ai quitté l'hôtel à trois heures du matin et je suis parti au hasard à travers la ville. J'essayais de m'identifier à l'héroïne du film. J'ai erré, comme elle, dans les rues, en me laissant guider par les lumières, et comme elle j'ai abouti à la gare' (Resnais cited in Leutrat 1994: 34).[24] This exploration of Hiroshima, this pleasure in the night

22 'Everywhere one senses the presence of death. As a reaction, one feels a violent appetite for life, desire for immediate sensations'.
23 'I really enjoy that... cities where there are always people awake, in the night, in the day'.
24 'When I got to Hiroshima for the first time, I left the hotel at three in the morning and went wandering through the city. I tried to identify myself with the heroine of the film. I wandered, like her, through the streets, letting myself be guided by the lights, and like her I ended up at the station'.

city, is absorbed in the film which, despite its melancholy, is peculiarly beautiful in its images of the city.

Lynn Higgins comments: 'Most critics have considered Hiroshima to be merely the setting for a personal crisis' (Higgins 1996: 32). Seeing Hiroshima as more than stage or backdrop for the film, she argues: 'The film expands the notions of place from their initial meaning as literal geographical locale to a wider metaphorical conception of *topos*, at once spatial, rhetorical and political' (Higgins 1996: 35). Caruth, extending this point, suggests that the film asks 'what might become possible within a discourse that is not simply *about* Hiroshima (or Nevers), but within an encounter that takes place *at* Hiroshima, a discourse spoken, as it were, *on the site of a catastrophe*' (Caruth 1996: 34). Caruth's ultimately redemptive reading of the film ends by suggesting: 'a new mode of seeing and of listening – a seeing and a listening *from the site of trauma* – is opened up to us as spectators of the film' (Caruth 1996: 56). Caruth names Hiroshima a site of catastrophe, a site of trauma. I see the city represented by Resnais more as a fissured city, a city of peace, monuments and museums on the one hand, a rebuilt modern urban location on the other. In each the question of memory and forgetting is worked through.

Consider Hiroshima as museal (museum) city. In *Twilight Memories*, Andreas Huyssen writes (recalling in part Nora's ideas on the archive): 'A traditional society without a secular teleological concept of history does not need a museum, but modernity is unthinkable without its museal project' (Huyssen 1995: 15). Against the ideological critique of the museum, he asserts that the museum 'enables the moderns to negotiate and articulate a relationship to the past that is always a relationship to the transitory and to death' (Huyssen 1995: 16). Yet, as Caruth and others have suggested, massive trauma unsettles that articulation of a relationship to the past, to past catastrophe. The museum of mass trauma will never be secure or aptly commemorative. In *Hiroshima mon amour*, the first image we see of Hiroshima as a city is a model in the museum. We see a miniature representation of the destroyed city with the remaining dome of the Palace of Industry and surrounding devastation. With this dwarfed, impoverished representation as point of departure, Resnais moves to contemporary news footage and shots from other films: we see images of the burning city, survivors in the river, temporary camps. We see a photograph of Hiroshima after the bomb, a new desert, an image of catastrophe or oblivion (reminiscent of *Guernica*). The French woman says to her lover: 'Comme toi j'ai oublié. Comme toi, j'ai désiré avoir une inconsolable mémoire, une mémoire d'ombres et de pierre' (Duras 1960: 32).[25] Yet the memory images which remain of Hiroshima are seen in shots of souvenir shops where hundreds of models of the Palace of Industry are on sale; one such model, studded with pearls, is shown in close-up. Resnais shows a tour bus with the words Atomic Tour on its side. He shows tourists on the Place de la Paix, he shows the memorial built to a child survivor who subsequently died, he shows the remaining, commemorative structures of the A-Bomb dome. Such images in the film seem always framed by the words with which it opens about seeing nothing at Hiroshima. The woman wants to know the city, to have a material apprehension of its forms, she wants to hold its stones and shadows in her memory, but she remains a tourist. She is a museum visitor, she is an actress in a film in Hiroshima, she is a guest at the Hotel New Hiroshima, she passes through the city.

As Adrian Forty writes, with reference not to Hiroshima but to the Holocaust: 'against the inevitability of the Holocaust being forgotten, attempts to preserve its memory look futile, and if they take the form of artefact making, probably counter-productive' (Forty and Küchler 1999: 6). Forty explores the genre of anti-memorials which respond to the Holocaust, more ephemeral monuments which move outside and beyond the museum as site and testing ground. Resnais too, in *Hiroshima mon amour*, moves outside the museum; on her four visits the French woman can still see nothing of Hiroshima. The film follows her into the streets of the city to see whether in perambulation she may come to a different relation to trauma and the history of Hiroshima. Forty quotes Christian Boltanski, who, asked if he would make a Holocaust memorial, replied: 'If one were to make such a memorial, one would have to remake it every day' (Forty and Küchler 1999: 6). In walking through the city, in the traces of her footsteps, the French woman arguably seeks this creation and undoing of memory. Michel de Certeau, as Forty reminds us, writes that memory is an anti-museum, it is not localisable (Certeau 1980: 162). For Certeau, walking through the city articulates a relation between

---

25 'Like you I have forgotten. Like you, I have desired an inconsolable memory, a memory of shadows and stone'.

memory and forgetting. The meandering routes of the city walker, aleatory, lost in his passage through the city, install forgetting as process. To walk is to miss or lack a place (Certeau 1980: 155).

Pierre-Louis Spadone specifically connects Certeau's image of walking through the city with Resnais's tracking shots (Spadone 1996: 90). Particularly relevant to *Hiroshima mon amour* are possible links between the affect and sensation of the urban encounter for Certeau and for Resnais. For Certeau, the walker has a knowledge of the city that is as blind as in an erotic encounter. The words are resonant for Resnais: his night walker through the city is a woman, her adoption of the role of *flâneur* (stroller) is transgressive, her encounter with the city glancingly erotic as she recalls the image of the streetwalker. Yet more insistently her encounter is, like that of Certeau's walker, bodily, sensory, blindly corporeal.

Thinking Hiroshima as the city the woman attempts to embrace in her night wanderings brings Hiroshima, and love, disturbingly close. As she says: 'Comment me serais-je doutée que cette ville était faite à la taille de l'amour?' (Duras 1960: 35) and later repeats: 'Cette ville était faite à la taille de l'amour' (Duras 1960: 115).[26] This morphing of love and city into impressions of each other – this appropriative, cathartic embrace of Hiroshima – is reflected in Resnais's lyrical filming of the city as object of beauty: the shimmering water of the river Ota reflected through night-time café windows, the intermittent illuminations of the city's neon signs, cinema façades and amusement arcades. We come to question the relation between memorials and the museum aesthetic of Hiroshima as city of peace and the seeming art of forgetting celebrated in its shiny, rebuilt urban spaces. So much treacherous beauty, like the cornflowers and gladioli, the morning glories, which rose out of the ashes of the burnt city.

Two particular scenes are integral to this representation of a movement from memorial to amnesiac Hiroshima. The first marks the point of transition into the fictional narrative which makes up the main part of the film. In a division of soundtrack and image-track we hear the woman's solipsistic voice-over against tracking shots of the city. The camera glides on a moving vehicle across a bridge, through shopping arcades, past a cinema and down along the banks of the

26 'How would I have suspected that this city was made in the shape of love?'; 'This city was made in the shape of love'.

river, to see the A-bomb dome and to open onto the broad streets and rails running into the distance. With these tracking shots Resnais calls us to witness the rebuilt city; in a loving montage of these moving shots he runs through the links and lines of connection in the city, its routes, its rhythms of urban living, its ruins, its acts of remembering and oblivion. The film seems here to be fitted to the city, to bear the impression of the city's spaces and topography, its layers of past and present. Against this opening, this expansiveness, the woman's words, her inner monologue, addressed to an absent 'tu' who never responds, speak of how her love shapes her perceptions of the city. She seeks pleasure in annihilation in Hiroshima. She speaks of the 'lenteur', the 'douceur' of their love, their love-making, her pleasure in pace with the rhythm of the moving camera. But the urgency of her need to be formed, deformed and destroyed resurfaces. As the camera moves through the rebuilt, the restored city, the woman desperately tries to recall the city obliviated, the bodies destroyed and deformed by the atomic blast, by fire, by radiation sickness. Her sick wish to find annihilation in love, to find herself deformed, contorted in love, vulnerable, frangible like the victims of the bombing, is bound up with her wish to embrace the city, to find in it a fleshed image of her own fantasies of suffering and oblivion. Yet no such images are summoned on the image-track as the film moves with consummate lyricism through the urban spaces.

Later scenes in the film repeat and echo this transitional movement through the precincts of Hiroshima away from the past of this site of trauma. In the later parts of the film, however, the precincts are shot at night. The Frenchwoman walks through the streets of Hiroshima. She has argued with the Japanese man about whether she will stay with him in Hiroshima; we hear her interior monologue, voice-off, saying that she will remain in Hiroshima, with him every night in Hiroshima. Hiroshima will be her night city (as previously Nevers was her nightmare city). Hiroshima and Nevers, night cities, dream cities become interchangeable at this stage of the film.

The urban space to which she has tried to open herself in her erotic and mnemonic encounters, is now summoned as a reflection of her psyche, as screen for her subjective spatial connections. The film cuts from the covered arcades and signs of Hiroshima to the place de la République in Nevers. The rhythm of cross-cutting picks up as the film confronts us with emerging images of houses, trees, roads, a tower in Nevers, only to cut back to cinemas and shops in Hiroshima. While the architectural forms and linguistic signs of the two spaces remain entirely distinct, while the two urban spaces represent two distinct sheets of time (and time of day), the cross-cutting serves to represent their near fusion or merger into one moving, evolving city of the mind, night city, memory city. This effect is reinforced by the use of tracking shots through the streets of both Hiroshima and Nevers, the camera imitating the woman's blind, mnemonic pacing through these disparate urban spaces. The force of the connections in the woman's psyche, as (in Deleuze's terms) the film overlays virtual and actual images, forms one continuous, fused geography, a continuum of east and west, a no-man's land reminiscent of still further filmic spaces. Indeed, the style of filming of New Hiroshima by Resnais and his Japanese crew heightens the effect of this merger. The streets of night-time Hiroshima, inexplicably empty, are shot with low-key illumination. There are two series of expressive low-angle tracking shots where we see the woman's figure looming against the façades of the city, shop fronts and then an anonymous tower block. Hiroshima becomes not merely night city but *noir* city, the material surfaces and structures of the modern urban space viewed with reference to the idiom, the sense impressions, of the American crime film. Frank Krutnick speaks of the *noir* city as a space 'where sensation overwhelms sense' (Clarke 1997: 99); he continues: 'Dark with something more than night, the *noir* city is a realm in which all that seemed solid melts into the shadows' (Clarke 1997: 99).

The merger of Nevers and Hiroshima comes in the realisation that both are condemned to forgetting, forgetting in betrayal of the past and in the hope of survival in the future. Pingaud suggests that Resnais shows Hiroshima as 'une ville qui a oublié et qui vit à l'aise dans cet oubli' (*Premier Plan* 1961: 21).[27] For Leutrat, in the film, 'l'oubli est toujours le plus fort, elle a oublié son premier amour, les habitants de Hiroshima ont oublié la bombe' (Leutrat 1994: 63).[28] As Henri Colpi argues, considering the return of the musical theme 'Oubli' at the film's close: 'La distribution de la musique dans *Hiroshima* démontre tout d'abord que le film est circonscrit par le

---

27 'a city which has forgotten and lives at peace in this forgetting'.
28 'forgetting is always the strongest, she has forgotten her first love, the inhabitants of Hiroshima have forgotten the bomb'.

thème de l'Oubli' (Colpi 1960: 11).[29] At the end of the film, the woman also must come to acknowledge that she will forget her Japanese lover. She repeats the words spoken earlier into the mirror, now uttered to a different addressee: 'Je t'oublierai! Je t'oublie déjà! Regarde, comme je t'oublie! Regarde-moi!' (Duras 1960: 124).[30] As Pingaud writes, 'cela même que l'on avait cru unique, irrémédiable, peut se répéter' (Pingaud 2002: 67).[31] *Hiroshima mon amour* takes full account of the pain of suffering, recognising, in Proustian fashion, that, as Pierre Nora writes: 'la vraie tristesse est de ne plus souffrir de ce dont on a tant souffert' (Nora 1997: 43).[32]

In *Hiroshima mon amour* forgetting is visceral. The French woman, registering forgetting in her body, says: 'Je tremble d'avoir oublié tant d'amour' (Duras 1960: 99).[33] She seeks memory through bodily feeling and reaction, seeking to graze and mark her body, to deform it, to imprint it with love. Yet in the ecstasy and reminiscence she seems to find with the Japanese lover – his very body recalling that of the German soldier – she finds herself encountering again the forgetting of love, the inexorability of time and movement into the future. This she laments, yet enacts, as she wanders through the gleaming night streets of Hiroshima, this destroyed burnt city which, only fourteen years after the bomb, is rebuilt and appears, at least through her distorting eyes, and through the lens of the camera, a city reminiscent of any metropolis, or any urban film set. The woman is still untouched by Hiroshima as she sits alone at the station in the middle of the night, hearing the name of the city intoned, as she moves from tea room to nightclub, restlessly displacing herself yet failing to find any destination.

Ropars-Wuilleumier writes: 'To film Hiroshima ... means to show in what way the event exceeds the possibility of fixing it within filmic representations' (Ropars-Wuilleumier 1990: 179). Resnais does this in part through letting his film, and film viewer, fall victim to the discontinuities of traumatised perceptions. *Hiroshima mon amour*

29 'The arrangement of the music in *Hiroshima* shows straightaway that the film is circumscribed by the theme of Forgetting'.
30 'I will forget you! I am forgetting you already! Look how I'm forgetting you! Look at me!'.
31 'the very thing one had believed unique, irreparable, can be repeated'.
32 'true sadness is to no longer suffer from something that has caused one so much suffering'.
33 'I tremble from having forgotten so much love'.

does not let us organise its information easily: we are assaulted by images, both painful and pleasurable. We navigate without a map or structure, wandering like the female protagonist, open to each encounter with the film, to its visceral effects. In seeing the film as hallucinatory, as unwilled, we see the proximity between Resnais's approach to representing trauma and the analyses offered within trauma theory. Yet *Hiroshima mon amour* does not head towards testimony, expiation and commemoration. Speaking of Nevers, making her story 'racontable', reminds the woman of the fear of forgetting and betraying the past. The moments when she, and the film itself, might be seen to know some freedom from the clutches of the past are in the moments of sheer sensation, physical pleasure, the conjuring of visual beauty. These are troubling pleasures here; Resnais and Duras by no means condone or champion such sensory oblivion. Yet they show this indulgence, this emergence of the life drive, this search for exhilaration, as inevitable once more in the face of the impossibility of commemorating (or representing) the past, of keeping its emotion, its sense, intact.

References

Atomic Bomb Photo Testament (1996) [English Edition] (Hiroshima: Sasaki).

L'Avant-scène du cinéma: Hiroshima mon amour, 61–62 (July–September 1966).

Bersani, Leo and Ulysse Dutoit (1993) *Arts of Impoverishment: Beckett, Rothko, Resnais* (Cambridge, MA: Harvard University Press).

Bruno, Giuliana (2002) *Atlas of Emotion: Journeys in Art, Architecture, and Film* (New York: Verso).

Callev, Haim (1997) *The Stream of Consciousness in the Films of Alain Resnais* (New York: McGruer Publishing).

Caruth, Cathy (1995) *Trauma: Explorations in Memory* (Baltimore, MD: The Johns Hopkins University Press).

Caruth, Cathy (1996) *Unclaimed Experience: Trauma, Narrative, and History* (Baltimore, MD and London: The Johns Hopkins University Press).

Certeau, Michel de (1980) *L'Invention du quotidien. 1 Arts de faire* (Paris: Gallimard [Folio]).

Clarke, David B. (1997) *The Cinematic City* (New York and London: Routledge).

Colpi, Henri (1960) 'Musique d'Hiroshima', *Cahiers du cinéma*, 18: 103 (January), pp. 1–14.

Deleuze, Gilles (1985) *Cinéma 2: L'Image-temps* (Paris: Minuit).

Duras, Marguerite (1960) *Hiroshima mon amour* (Paris: Gallimard [Folio]).

Forty, Adrian and Susanne Küchler (1999) *The Art of Forgetting* (Oxford and New York: Berg).
Higgins, Lynn A. (1996) *New Novel, New Wave, New Politics: Fiction and the Representation of History in Postwar France* (Lincoln and London: University of Nebraska Press).
Hughes, Robert (ed.) (1962) *Film: Book 2 Films of Peace and War* (New York: Grove Press).
Huyssen, Andreas (1995) *Twilight Memories* (New York and London: Routledge).
Kael, Pauline (1961–62) 'Fantasies of the Art-house Audience', *Sight and Sound*, 31:1 (Winter), pp. 5–9.
Kristeva, Julia (1987) 'La maladie de la douleur: Duras', *Soleil noir: dépression et mélancolie* (Paris: Gallimard [Folio]), pp. 227–65.
Leperchey, Sarah (2000) *Alain Resnais: Une lecture topologique* (Paris: L'Harmattan).
Leutrat, Jean-Louis (1994) *Hiroshima mon amour* (Paris: Nathan).
Lifton, Robert Jay (1967) *Death in Life: The Survivors of Hiroshima* (London: Weidenfeld and Nicolson).
Monaco, James (1979) *Alain Resnais* (New York: Oxford University Press).
Nora, Pierre (1997) *Les Lieux de mémoire* (Paris: Gallimard [Quarto]).
Pingaud, Bernard (2002) 'A propos de *Hiroshima mon amour*', in Stéphane Goudet (ed.), *Positif, revue de cinéma: Alain Resnais* (Paris: Gallimartd [Folio]), pp. 66–86.
Premier Plan: Alain Resnais (1961), 10.
Ropars-Wuilleumier, Marie-Claire (1990) 'How History Begets Meaning: Alain Resnais's *Hiroshima mon amour*', in Susan Hayward and Ginette Vincendeau (eds), *French Film: Texts and Contexts* (London and New York: Routledge), pp. 173–85.
Scarry, Elaine (1985) *The Body in Pain: The Making and Unmaking of the World* (Oxford and New York: Oxford University Press).
Spadone, Pierre-Louis (1996) 'Les repérages urbains d'Alain Resnais: des espaces "empreints de temps"', *Espaces et sociétés*, 86, *Ville et cinéma* (Paris: Editions L'Harmattan).
Williams, Linda (1976) 'Hiroshima and Marienbad: Metaphor and Metonymy', *Screen*, 17: 1 (spring), pp. 34–9.

3

L'Année dernière à Marienbad (1961)

Resnais cites a trip to the theatre, to see Chekhov's *The Seagull*, as significant in the development of his career and ambitions. Reading the play, it seems in certain ways to prefigure Resnais's second feature film, *L'Année dernière à Marienbad*. Arkádina, an actress, remembers: 'Ten or fifteen years ago, there was music and singing here by the lake almost every night. There were six big country houses by the lake then. I remember the laughter, the parties – people were always shooting off guns, all night long – and the love affairs, oh, the endless love affairs!' (Chekhov 1997: 121). Her lover, Trigórin, intent on seducing a younger woman, says: 'I'll think of you the way you were that day last week... remember? The sun was shining, you were wearing a white dress, and we talked...' (Chekhov 1997: 137). *L'Année dernière à Marienbad* is a film composed of echoes of Chekhov, of French films – *La Règle du jeu* (1939) *Les Visiteurs du soir* (1942), *Orphée* (1949), *La Belle et la bête* (1946) and numerous others – of shadows of Hitchcock, *Vertigo* (1958) and, visually, *To Catch a Thief* (1955). It also depends on internal echoes as the film is woven out of a series of repetitions, of returning words and images. Critics have compared the film to Bergman's *The Silence* (1963), another sepulchral film set in a grand hotel, to Fellini's *8½* (1963) and more broadly to Antonioni's investigations of space and desire. It has been seen to have its own film progeny, inspiring such works as Chris Marker's *La Jetée* (1962), Duras's *India Song* (1975) and Peter Greenaway's *The Draughtsman's Contract* (1982). *L'Année dernière à Marienbad* can be located in this cultural context yet also exists entirely in its own terms as one of the most difficult, hypnotic and original works of cinema. Inevitably it is a film which has divided critics – adored by some, it also appears as metonym for all self-regarding, resistant art cinema of its period.

L'Année dernière à Marienbad was made in the autumn of 1960. It premiered at the Venice Film Festival in 1961 and won the top prize, the Golden Lion. Like *Hiroshima mon amour*, it was the product of a collaboration, this time between Resnais and another experimental modern novelist, *nouveau romancier* Alain Robbe-Grillet. Producers Pierre Courau and Raymond Froment asked Robbe-Grillet if he would be interested in working with Resnais. Agreement was reached and, as with Duras, Robbe-Grillet worked independently on the screenplay, which he subsequently published with an introduction. In this, Robbe-Grillet specifies: 'L'accord n'a pu se faire, entre Alain Resnais et moi, que parce que nous avons dès le début *vu* le film de la même manière' (Robbe-Grillet 1961: 9).[1] The film is faithful to Robbe-Grillet's script, bar a significant difference and divergence between writer and director which will be discussed below. Once the script was written, Resnais travelled to Germany to look for locations, taking a series of location shots. He settled on a number of baroque palaces in and outside Munich: Nymphenburg, Amalienburg, Schleissheim, the Munich Antiquarium (interiors were shot in the Photosonor studios in Paris).

The series of locations, collaged together, which make up the film, are not insignificant. Robbe-Grillet writes in his introduction: 'Il n'y a pas d'année dernière, et Marienbad ne se trouve plus sur aucune carte' (Robbe-Grillet 1961: 15)[2] (though T. Jefferson Kline discovers happily that Jacques Lacan, the psychoanalyst who theorised the 'mirror stage' in human development, once gave a paper at Marienbad before the Second World War). The imagined location of the film – a baroque palace overlooking expansive, ornate and frozen gardens – is itself not properly Marienbad. As a man tries to persuade a woman that he knew her and loved her, last year at Marienbad, he recalls: 'La première fois que je vous ai vue, c'était dans les jardins de Frederiksbad' (Robbe-Grillet 1961: 57).[3] As she demurs and denies this, he continues: 'Eh bien, c'était ailleurs peut-être ... à Karlstadt, à Marienbad, ou à Baden-Salsa – ou même ici, dans ce salon' (Robbe-

---

[1] 'Agreement could only be reached, between Alain Resnais and myself, because from the beginning we *saw* the film in the same way'.

[2] 'There is no last year, and Marienbad is no longer on any map'.

[3] 'The first time I saw you was in the gardens at Frederiksbad'.

Grillet 1961: 74).[4] Composed by Resnais out of a series of locations, Marienbad is a fantasy, a composite place in the film. Its resonance is as much an effect of its name, like Manderlay or Xanadu, as of its evocation of an enclosed, luxuriant world. In the film's narrative, Marienbad is only another of the places, the baroque hotels, where the characters may once have stayed. Yet the shots of the endless corridors and decorations, the statues and topiary trees in the garden, its reflecting lake, all conjure Marienbad as place, as film location, as obsession in the spectator's imagination.

As the film dissolves a sense of space, so it dissolves other certainties of time, memory and identity. Hence its difficulty and its fascination, which overtake us from the start. As Jean-Louis Leutrat writes beautifully about the titles sequence: 'the names in the *L'Année dernière à Marienbad* credits are presented in relief letters on a grey background, as on certain visiting or invitation cards. We are being summoned to a ceremony, or to a soirée' (Leutrat 2000: 8). Before seeing any of the film's images, we hear a voice, its words at first indistinct, gradually coming into focus, taking form and shape. The voice describes the setting, the décor – 'couloirs interminables', 'salons surchargés d'une ornementation d'un autre siècle' (Robbe-Grillet 1961: 24–5)[5] – which we will see in the opening shots of the film. Words precede images here, as if the extraordinarily tactile, sentient world of Marienbad – its stucco work, its encrusted chandeliers and frosted mirrors – is called up, imagined as a result of the words we hear narrated. The film then offers a series of tracking shots, each evolving out of another, allowing us some imaginary navigation of the palace described. The camerawork is reminiscent of *Toute la mémoire du monde*, or even *Nuit et brouillard*, but here the spaces seem purely ornamental. Resnais plays with detail, passing extraordinary filigree work, intricate metal flowers and foliage, imprinting in our mind image upon image, unending images, of an ornate and strangely lifeless world.

As the physical spaces of the film seem to be conjured out of its opening words, so is its central intrigue. Before the film settles on its investigation of the relations between three characters, a woman, a man who may be her sometime lover, and another who may be her

---

4 'Well, it was perhaps elsewhere [...] in Karlstadt, Marienbad, or Baden-Salsa – or even here, in this drawing room'.

5 'unending corridors'; 'rooms crammed with decorations from another century'.

husband, we hear echoes of their dialogue and story spoken by the formally dressed guests who make up the chorus of *L'Année dernière à Marienbad*. These guests act with little of their own volition but function as part-animate props in the story; in evening dress, they watch a play in whose dialogue we hear echoes of the words which have opened the film and a man saying to a woman: 'je m'avançais à votre rencontre'. After the close of the play we see the figures in social conversation and hear fragments of their dialogues – 'Nous nous sommes rencontrés, déjà, autrefois...', 'Je ne me rappelle pas bien' (Robbe-Grillet 1961: 31).[6] These words seem here empty phrases, exchanged between the figures. The film shows the social language which circulates, the social code which constructs identities and social interchange (recalling the repetition and circulation of phrases more broadly in the *nouveau roman*). Yet what is significant is the way the film settles on such an exchange, allowing it to gather meaning in repetition, as this nexus of words, a man's memory, a woman's denial, becomes the attachment on which their impossible love and the film's possible plot is fixed. It is as if the man and the woman, named only X and A in Robbe-Grillet's screenplay, slowly emerge out of the social group in the grand hotel. At first they are merely part of its groupings of guests, almost indistinguishable from the others around them, but their story slowly takes form, as if summoned by the very setting, as if conjured as one potential history and intense narrative within this ritualised, petrified world. The challenge of the film is to allow this history to seduce its viewers, to allow it to become sentient and passionate, built as it is out of echoes, out of mere fragments of dialogue.

In interview, Resnais sums up the film: 'Dans un palace international, un étranger rencontre une jeune femme et lui raconte l'histoire d'amour qu'ils ont vécue l'année dernière. La femme nie, l'homme affirme, s'entête. Qui a raison?' (*Premier Plan* 1961: 81).[7] Resnais identifies a question the film asks, a question which is continually modified but never resolved. The continued exchanges between the couple work precisely to undo any certainty we reach at

---

6 'I was going forward to meet you'; 'We have already met, in the past...', 'I don't remember clearly'.

7 'In an international palace, a stranger meets a young woman and tells her the love story they lived the previous year. The woman denies this, the man confirms it and persists. Who is right?'.

any particular stage in the film. Uncertainty, indeed, is crucial to understanding the film's effect (and is sustained as motif in the image of the game which is played several times over in the film, but never explained or resolved).

As it explores uncertainty, *L'Année dernière à Marienbad* is specifically a film about sexual difference, about the role of fantasy in supporting desire and about the disturbing action and contact that can be created through language. Speaking about the film, Resnais has said: 'peut-on jamais savoir, en effet, si l'on projette sur l'autre ses propres phantasmes ou si l'on "reçoit" mal les phantasmes du partenaire?' (*Premier Plan* 1961: 81).[8] Žižek, following Lacan, looks at the role of fantasy in desiring relations. He argues, quoting Lacan: '"there is no sexual relationship", no universal formula or matrix guaranteeing a harmonious sexual relationship with one's partner' (Žižek 1997: 7). If this is the case, then to engage with the other 'every subject has to invent a fantasy of his or her own, a "private" formula for the sexual relationship – for a man, the relationship with a woman is possible only in as much as she fits his formula' (Žižek 1997: 7). Fantasy, for Žižek, constitutes our desire and provides its coordinates. Within a fantasy, a woman becomes desirable; she is also thus in some ways familiar or knowable for the man because she is part of his fantasy. Fantasy makes her desirable, but it also protects the man against the unknowability of the female other. As Žižek writes: 'fantasy is the screen by means of which the subject avoids the radical opening of the enigma of the Other's desire' (Žižek 1997: 31).

In *L'Année dernière à Marienbad*, as we have seen, a man approaches a perhaps unknown, beautiful woman and sets out to persuade her (and himself) that he knew her last year. His words construct her as always already known: 'Vous êtes toujours la même. J'ai l'impression de vous avoir quittée hier' (Robbe-Grillet 1961: 46); 'Vous êtes toujours aussi belle' (Robbe-Grillet 1961: 48).[9] The first approach to the woman is avoided by this claim that she is familiar. The words which claim her as familiar, already known, establish the relation between them whether or not it existed previously. When the woman denies having known the man the previous year, she can deny their

---

8 'can one ever know, in fact, whether one projects one's own fantasies onto the other or whether one "receives" one's partner's properly?'.

9 'You are still the same. I have the impression that I left you only yesterday'; 'You are still as beautiful'.

past acquaintance but in so doing finds herself already entangled in their present dialogue. More than a strategy to approach her, however, the man's insistence that he has known her previously reveals this as the fantasy which supports his desire for her. She is to be desired in the present because she has been known in the past. The present relations will gather pathos, beauty and meaning through their recall and repetition of events, possibly imagined, the previous year. The man's prior success with this woman, fantasised as such, bolsters his current attempts to seduce her with language. This fantasy of prior acquaintance is protective, then, but only so far. As Resnais reminds us, fantasies of self and other may not be reciprocal and may open doubt and intrigue between lovers.

The woman at first simply denies that they have known each other the previous year. The man says to her, several times: 'Mais vous ne semblez guère vous souvenir' (Robbe-Grillet 1961: 49).[10] She seems at first almost to indulge his fantasies as she listens to him, yet she replies: 'Je ne crois pas qu'il s'agisse de moi. Vous devez vous tromper' (Robbe-Grillet 1961: 58).[11] After an elaborate excursion into the imagination, as he recalls their conversations the previous year, their idle questioning of the meaning and pose of a statue of a couple in the gardens, she replies: 'Je vous répète que c'est impossible. Je n'ai même jamais été à Frederiksbad' (Robbe-Grillet 1961: 74).[12] We may wonder whether the man's fantasy involves not merely the encounter with a woman he has known the previous year, but also the woman's denial of this encounter so that he may, with lingering insistence, return to her again and again to construct new scenarios which may jog her memory, all the while entrapping her in a series of narratives which will gradually become familiar to her. In this sense, the woman's resistance, her refusal of the pleasure of recognition, themselves rarefy the desire now constructed between them. Ironically, it will be in the moments when the woman appears to start to share some memory, or fantasy, of the past, that the relation between them begins to become more disturbing to the man and his fantasy less protective. Here we encounter issues about the woman, as much as the man, as desiring subject and about the horror they will begin to construct between them. Where, for Deleuze, *Hiroshima mon amour*

10 'But you barely seem to remember'.
11 'I don't think it can have been me. You must be mistaken'.
12 'I repeat that it is impossible. I have never even been to Frederiksbad'.

shows two protagonists constructing a memory for two, *L'Année dernière à Marienbad* explores what it means to construct a fantasy for two.

The unnamed heroine of *L'Année dernière à Marienbad* is played, in her first screen role, by Delphine Seyrig. Resnais had seen her in New York, in a production of an Ibsen play, and chose her for the part. Seyrig recalls: 'Dans *Marienbad*, je devais être une "dame" très sophistiquée. C'était un rôle pour Grace Kelly, pas pour moi. Je me sentais tout à fait étrangère au milieu de grands palaces qui est décrit dans le film. Je ne pouvais pas "faire semblant" d'être A. Il fallait donc que je compose le personnage' (*L'Arc* 1961: 66).[13] This composition of the character is supported by her very careful visual construction. Seyrig is dressed by Chanel in the film and wears an extraordinary series of dresses: sleeveless black dresses, both short and long, pale, lustrous dresses with raised, gilded, tactile fabric, a gauzy white dress with fluttering and fragile drapes, a black dress with intricate lace mantilla over her shoulders, and most expressively, the white feathered peignoir she wears in her bedroom, which is matched by a black plumed evening cloak in which she screams in the gardens, close to the end of the film, a deathly Queen of the Night. In these chiaroscuro garments, each perfectly tailored, sculpting Seyrig's body, veiling yet revealing its shape, she is a fashion icon (Brigitte Bardot later asked Chanel to dress her in the style of Marienbad). In each shot Seyrig is perfectly made up, her eyelashes with thick mascara so they appear like dark flowers or insects. Her hair, bobbed and swept back, gives her the androgynous sensuality of a Lee Miller or Man Ray image. Critics have cited Louise Brooks, in particular *Pandora's Box*, as inspiration for Seyrig's sleek, self-possessed image. Her feline qualities are recalled in many of the poses, quizzical, sensuous, sphinx-like, that Seyrig adopts in the film. Resnais works with her body and gestures, fashioning her so she is infinitely pliable, silky, unsettling, impassive. Even her voice is languid, liquid, gilded in these scenes, as she appears both maternal and sensual, reassuring her suitor that she has no memory. Graham Parkes suggests, indeed: '"A" might well stand for anima, since the actress (Delphine Seyrig)

---

13 'In *Marienbad*, I had to be a very sophisticated "lady". It was a role for Grace Kelly, not for me. I felt entirely unfamiliar with the milieu of grand palaces which is described in the film. I could not "pretend" to be A. So I had to make up the character'.

projects so well the statuesque softness, mysterious and somehow timeless, that anima characteristically evokes' (Parkes 1994: 50).

Seyrig here embodies a filmic image of the eternal feminine; she is compared by one critic to Garbo. For Sacha Vierny, the film's cinematographer, Seyrig's face and silhouette, the way she was lit in the film, helped to recall earlier cinema, Hollywood and a golden age of French cinema. This sense of Seyrig's image as iconic, a sense of her beauty, the self-indulgent loveliness of many of the film's images of her, do not dominate in current readings of the film, however. She is usually read as hysterical (see Benayoun 1980: 98), in discussions which focus on her 'convulsive attitudes' (Brunius 1962: 153), on her laughter and screaming, on her attempt to merge with the mirror images in her pale bedroom. Robbe-Grillet has described her as a 'belle prisonnière peut-être encore vivante de cette cage d'or' (Robbe-Grillet 1961: 13).[14] Certainly her husband, if such he is, suggests he has brought her to this hotel to convalesce.

Naomi Greene aligns Seyrig's character with the heroine of *Hiroshima mon amour* and other Resnais protagonists, writing: 'Resnais's women, in particular, display what Kai Erickson describes as the classic symptoms of trauma – that is, the "continual reliving of some wounding experience"' (Greene 1999: 32). The critic T. Jefferson Kline has further pursued an original reading of the film following its implications in this respect. For Kline, as for Greene, "Resnais's work ... portrays sensitively the attempts of his characters, more often than not women, to come to grips, through the work of the imagination, with the complexities of their past' (Kline 1992: 69). Kline draws out the importance of an allusion in *L'Année dernière à Marienbad* to Ibsen's play *Rosmersholm* (a poster for a play named *Rosmer* is seen in the corridors of the opening of the film). Kline reminds us that Freud made a reading of the incest motif in *Rosmersholm*. To understand the place of *Rosmer* in *Marienbad*, Kline reads the woman herself as incest survivor imperfectly recalling her traumatic past and living that out in her relation to her lover, and in particular in what he describes as her 'repetition compulsion with respect to abusive relationships' (Kline 1992: 78).

An image of a woman as hysteric and survivor seems apt with regard to the heroine of *Hiroshima mon amour*, in contrast to her

---

14 'beautiful prisoner, still perhaps living in this golden cage'.

impassive, patient Japanese lover, it is more arguable with reference to *L'Année dernière à Marienbad*. If there is madness or delusion in the film, the mad subject might be just as properly the lover, manically intent on embroiling this perhaps unknown woman in a story of their shared past. Or, indeed, as I shall outline, another reading might see the trauma of the film not preceding the encounter between the man and the woman – as Kline's reading of the heroine as incest survivor necessarily suggests – but more disconcertingly produced by that encounter. Resnais and Robbe-Grillet may be seen to stage a *folie à deux* (shared insanity) of which both X and A, and to some extent the spectator as well, are victims.

Where at the start of the film the man and the woman appear as two separate, autonomous individuals, the effect of *L'Année dernière à Marienbad* as it continues is to make us increasingly uncertain about the limits of the subjectivity and desire of these lovers. This effect is in part created by our uncertainty over the status of the images viewed. As the man speaks, recalling his memories of last year in Marienbad, images appear on the screen. They do not always entirely match his descriptions of the past and they do not offer a coherent continuity of memory. Where at first certain markers seem to be used to indicate whether the images are, supposedly, memory images or images from the present encounter (in the first 'memory' image Seyrig's dress is pale, for example, where in the 'present' it is dark) any such systematisation collapses (she will go on to appear indiscriminately in the same pale and dark dresses in both 'memory' and 'present' images). We become aware that there is no layering of past and present, that the 'memory' images are perhaps conjured in the imagination, choreographed, often on the basis of the very material of the present. The similarity between the 'memory' and 'present' images, pursued to the extent that quickly we have no sense of how to categorise any image we see, forces attempts to see the images chronologically to break down (as Sarah Leperchey writes: 'l'on renonce vite à démêler le réel de l'imaginaire' (Leperchey 2003: 29)).[15] Instead we may come to understand the film as built out of a vertiginous series of virtual images, each a variation on the encounter between the man and the woman. These are not 'memory' images but mental images, pictures of their encounter as it is or might be, or

---

15 'one quickly gives up trying to distinguish the real from the imaginary'.

might have been, conjured in the imagination out of the words the man speaks.

Resnais has said in interview: 'on ne sait jamais si les images sont dans la tête de l'homme ou dans la tête de la femme. Il y a tout le temps un balancement entre les deux' (*Premier Plan* 1961: 86).[16] Critics have tried to analyse this *balancement* to understand the moves of the film between subjective viewpoints. Brunius, in an early review, writes: 'While the bulk of the film follows the Narrator's recollections, some sequences follow *her* mental processes and show events as *she* imagines them, even confronting their different memories of the same object' (Brunius 1962: 123). Such a reading keeps in play the sense that something did happen last year in Marienbad, and is recalled by the narrator. Yet Brunius slips from memory to imagination as he speaks of the woman imagining, rather than remembering, the scenes viewed. Haim Callev sees Resnais's cinema as representation of mental rather than memory images and seeks to identify the source of the images viewed in the individual protagonist's consciousness. With respect to images of sexual violence which I shall come on to discuss, he writes: 'Obviously hers would be the fantasy of rape acceptance, presented with the fast tracking shots through the white over-exposed corridors' (Callev 1997: 224). He continues: 'Similarly hers would be the fantasy of murder. Her body falls in four alternative positions, as if she [were] trying to choose and visualise the most graceful position for the moment of her death' (Callev 1997: 224). With respect to the film's narrative, there may, however, be reasons not to align these images with the woman's fantasy or imagination alone.

As intimated above, I suggest that the film plays with the possibility that these are shared images that the lovers conjure between them. This collaborative act, ironically, brings its own fear and trauma. I have suggested that the man elaborates a fantasy which allows him to desire the woman. In that fantasy he has known her and loved her in a previous year and he tries to persuade her to remember this, whilst always being faced by her gracious amnesia and denial. Her seeming willingness to accept this role of amnesiac, to return to scenes of false recall and denial, seems to suggest that this fantasy is erotic for her also, that this scenario constructs the man himself as

16 'one never knows if the images are in the man's head or in the woman's. There is throughout a movement between the two'.

desirable to her. Yet the fear and power of the film, despite its reputed glacial lifelessness, come in the way this joint fantasy of non-reciprocity and forgetting develops between the couple. Their relation moves to the next stage as, after a period of the woman's erotically satisfying denial of the man, she now appears to start to remember. The intimation comes in a dialogue between the couple in a dark night-time scene in the hotel's bar. The darkness of this scene is rapidly interrupted by a series of sudden shots of the woman's bedroom. As Penelope Houston writes, 'An initial hint of secession comes in those hallucinatory shots of her room, a series of flashes, each almost imperceptibly longer than the last, from the sombre darkness of the hotel bar to this blinding white room, as yet bare and unfurnished by imagination' (Houston 1961–62: 27). For Houston, the woman is ceding to the man's persuasion (for Robbe-Grillet indeed, 'Tout le film est en effet l'histoire d'une persuasion: il s'agit d'une réalité que le héros crée de sa propre vision, par sa propre parole' (Robbe-Grillet 1961: 12)).[17] The woman seems to start to satisfy her lover's desire by remembering. To quote Houston again: 'We are watching a conviction gradually taking shape on the screen, spreading out, acquiring an independent form, drawing in nourishment from the air around it like a Japanese flower dropped into a bowl of water' (Houston 1961–62: 27).

We may wonder how the woman's apparent recall, or adoption, of subjectivity in the fantasy they construct between them changes and distorts the man's fantasy, disrupting its protective value. The shots of the bedroom come at first as so many rapid intrusions, hallucinatory flashbacks recalling the involuntary memories of *Hiroshima mon amour*. One reading would suggest that these images are traumatic moments of recall. The scenes gradually lengthen, interrupting the scene in the bar until we remain long enough in this pale mental image to see the man become visible within the shot, within the room, in the lower left hand side of the frame. The woman's response is visceral; we see three repeated shots of her in the bar in the present recoiling from him. The threat the man seems to embody suggests force or sexual violence. Certainly this is the affect of these shots and of some that follow. But these need not simply be seen as returning

---

[17] 'The whole film is in fact a story of persuasion: it is about a reality that the hero creates from his own vision, his own words'.

repressed memories. If they are the woman's mental images, rather than recall the past she might anticipate here what might happen as she pursues this fantasy relation with X. What threatens her here is perhaps the presence of this man – of his image – in the space of her room, her privacy, her fantasy. It is arguably their *folie à deux* which threatens her. Is she not suddenly afraid that her own fantasy of herself as impervious, indulgent but amnesiac, will not protect her forever from the radical opening of the man's desire for her?

The man as well is unsettled by his appearance in her bedroom and by the turn their dialogues are taking. That she now appears to have some memory disrupts the fantasy of her amnesia and opens her again as unknowable and threatening. That they may in turn have shared an intimation of his once or future threat to her is also all the more disquieting; this very sense of his threat opens questions again. Has the fantasy of his persuasive language, his seduction of A through the imagination, protected him from his wish more physically to take possession of her? Does she confront the possibility that she may desire his threat or violence? Does he in turn fantasise her desire to be raped? The white bedroom is now the rarefied locus of their desire for each other. The man speaks the words: 'je pénètre à nouveau dans votre chambre' (Robbe-Grillet 1961: 119).[18] We see shots of the room, again uncertain from whose perspective they are seen. The woman now retreats into denial: 'Non, je ne connais pas la suite. Je ne vous connais pas. Je ne connais pas cette chambre, ce lit ridicule, cette cheminée avec son miroir...' (Robbe-Grillet 1961: 121). He turns on her saying: 'Quel miroir? Quelle cheminée? Que dites-vous?' (Robbe-Grillet 1961: 121).[19] The room has nowhere been described, merely remembered or imagined. Her words, while attempting denial, show that she is party to the memory or fantasy of her bedroom, which he has entered, making her afraid. What is fearful here is the woman's receptivity, her continued engagement in a fantasy in which she is erotic victim. This is disturbing for her, and indeed for her lover.

As the fantasy plays out, he continues to enter her room, but in this imaginary act he still does not gain possession or knowledge of her, he merely renders her more vulnerable, more fragile in their shared

18 'I enter into your room once more'.
19 'No, I don't know what happens next. I don't know you. I don't know this room, this ridiculous bed, this fireplace with its mirror...'; 'What mirror? What fireplace? What are you saying?'.

images. Now she wears the floating gauzy frock which seems to tremble as she moves, now the glorious feathered peignoir which renders her part animal, part languishing fetish. His entries into her room can be seen as so many mental rehearsals for a scene which is at once central to the film and absent from it, creating a further conundrum for the viewer. In the screenplay the fantasy climaxes in a brutal rape. Robbe-Grillet writes:

> X apparaît en premier plan, vu de dos. Assez rapide et brutale scène de viol. A est basculée en arrière, X lui maintenant les poignets (d'une seule main) sous la taille .... A se débat, mais sans résultat aucun. Elle ouvre la bouche comme pour crier; mais X, penché sur elle, introduit aussitôt dans cette bouche, en guise de bâillon, une menue pièce de lingerie fine qu'il tenait dans l'autre main. (Robbe-Grillet 1961: 156)[20]

Resnais refused to shoot the scene. In its place in the film we see repeated blanched shots of the woman, arms outstretched, widely smiling, the camera each time approaching her rapidly. Roy Armes notes that 'the brilliant white scene of A welcoming X over and over again with open arms ... is a pure invention of the director' (Armes 1980: 8). He argues indeed that the absent rape scene would fit the film's pattern of symmetry far better. It seems a deft choice to rehearse the rape, as it were, and to erase the scene itself: in the first place because it avoids violence to Delphine Seyrig and explicit violence on screen; also because it thus tantalises the viewer, not allowing us to know whether the rape which seems implied, though not viewed, has come to dominate and embody the fantasy relations between X and A. We are protected from the fear that the woman fantasises her own rape – though this is dizzily intimated in Resnais's tracking shots of her with open arms, receiving the man into her embrace.

As the film progresses, the man himself is increasingly unsettled in his role as the woman's seducer and he will in turn have recourse to her patterns of denial. While he has insisted on the presence and reality of the past and their memories, he now begins to cast doubt on the memories they fantasise between them, saying: 'Non... Non... Je

20 'X appears in the foreground, seen from behind. A fairly quick and brutal rape scene. A is tipped backwards, X holding her wrists (with one hand) behind her back ... A struggles, but without any effect. She opens her mouth as if she is going to scream; but X, leaning over her, quickly gags her with a small piece of her underwear he had in his other hand'.

ne me souviens plus... Je ne me souviens plus moi-même' (Robbe-Grillet 1961: 140) and 'Non, non, non!... C'est faux!... ... Ce n'était pas de force' (Robbe-Grillet 1961: 157).[21] In this sense she wins in his game as he too comes to deny the past. Yet she herself is victim of this, if she is seen to imagine and choreograph her own rape.

The end of the film offers no resolution. At one point in their dialogue, the man has said to her: 'Mais vous demeuriez toujours à une certaine distance, comme sur le seuil, comme à l'entrée d'un lieu trop sombre, ou inconnu...' (Robbe-Grillet 1961: 111).[22] This image of the woman reflects how she is seen early in the film, often at the edge of the frame, or at the doorway between the rooms of the baroque palace. His words also have resonance for the end of the film where we see a night-time shot of the palace, an imposing black façade, viewed from afar, with only a few windows lit. Against this image we hear the man's words about the gardens at night: 'Il semblait, au premier abord, impossible de s'y perdre... au premier abord... le long des allées rectilignes, entre les statues aux gestes figés et les dalles de granit, où vous étiez maintenant déjà en train de vous perdre, pour toujours, dans la nuit tranquille, seule avec moi' (Robbe-Grillet 1961: 172).[23] This end envisages no exit from their shared fantasy, instead an entry into its darkest most hidden space as they have approached the opening of each other's desire. This desire seems to gel finally in violence, madness and death. Resnais has commented on the terror of making the film, on the impression of touching on things which completely outstripped him (Benayoun, Ciment and Pays 2002: 184). In the last shots we have seen of her, the woman wears her black-feathered cloak; as she screams in the night, as she has previously in her room, her pale face contorted resembles a death's head. While this is the parting image of the woman, it has resonance for the film as a whole.

Questions of death have haunted readings of *L'Année dernière à Marienbad*. The opening lines from the play within the film intimate

---

21 'No... No... I no longer remember... I no longer remember myself'; 'No, no, no!... It's not true!... ... It wasn't by force'.
22 'But you would always remain at a certain distance, as if you were on the threshold, at the entrance to a place too dark, or unfamiliar...'.
23 'At first it seemed impossible to get lost there... at first... along the straight paths, between the statues with their fixed poses and the granite flag stones, where you were now already getting lost, forever, in the tranquil night, alone with me'.

that this may be a ghostly drama played out by 'fantômes sans nom' (*Premier Plan* 1961: 10), served by 'domestiques immobiles, muets, morts depuis longtemps sans doute' (Robbe-Grillet 1961: 31).[24] Resnais relates: 'Plusieurs spectateurs m'ont dit que cette femme n'existait pas, qu'elle était morte depuis longtemps, que tout se passait chez les morts' (*Premier Plan* 1961: 86).[25] For Peter Cowie, 'X may be Orpheus and A his Eurydice, with M representing Death. Resnais's avowed love of Cocteau and of *Orphée* could support this' (Cowie 1963: 145). Such readings emphasise the timeless aspect of the film, and its echoes of myth and fairy tale. Resnais neither accepts or dismisses readings of his film as death encounter; they are merely part of the 'infinité de solutions' the film offers (*Premier Plan* 1961: 13). He specifies: 'On peut dire ainsi qu'il s'agit de la quête de l'autre ou d'un prince charmant arrivant au château pour réveiller sa "belle" endormie, d'un envoyé de la Mort qui vient chercher sa victime un an après ou simplement d'une femme qui a eu une aventure et hésite entre son mari et son amant' (*Premier Plan* 1961: 81–2).[26]

A further way in which the film plays between life and death is more in keeping with its erotic theme. As in *Nuit et brouillard* and *Hiroshima mon amour*, Resnais is concerned here with life and lifelessness, flesh and stone and the difficulty at times of distinguishing between them. Actors in *L'Année dernière à Marienbad* are often petrified and rendered living statues in the film; further, as Leutrat specifies, 'if the humans are "turned into stone" (by their immobility, poses, rigid gestures, etc.), the statue itself is animated by the shots of it taken from different angles' (Leutrat 2000: 50). Resnais instantiates a hesitation between life and death, in the stifling corridors of his baroque palace, in its garden, laid out like a cemetery. Yet his interest in a sentient world petrified is evidence also of his concern with the tactile. For Monaco, '*Marienbad* is a magnificently tactile film: an opera of statues' (Monaco 1979: 63) and, as Benayoun reminds us,

24 'nameless phantoms'; 'servants who were motionless, silent, doubtless long dead'.

25 'Several viewers have said to me that this woman did not exist, that she has been long dead, that everything was happening in the realm of the dead'.

26 'infinity of solutions'; 'One can say thus that it is about the quest for the other or about prince charming arriving at the castle to wake his sleeping beauty, or about a messenger of Death coming a year later to seek his victim or simply about a woman who has had an affair and cannot decide between her husband and her lover'.

Resnais wished his film to be examined like a statue (Benayoun 1980: 92). This mode of consuming the film, of observing it in three dimensions and touching its surface, is in keeping with Robbe-Grillet's admission that the spectator may choose to appreciate rather than interpret the film, seeing it more sensually as 'un film qui ne s'adresse qu'à sa sensibilité, qu'à sa faculté de regarder, d'écouter, de sentir et de se laisser émouvoir' (Robbe-Grillet 1961: 18).[27]

Resnais's work has been compared with that of the Surrealist artists. Robert Benayoun, in particular, explores pictorial resonances, picking up on the ways in which Seyrig in feathers and dramatic poses recalls the erotic, collaged women of Max Ernst's *Une Semaine de bonté*. Speaking elsewhere of the film, he compares Resnais's fantasmagorical setting to the paintings of Magritte, finding his Marienbad: 'nocturne dans le diurne, diurne dans le nocturne (comme dans ces tableaux de Magritte où les demeures de minuit s'inscrivent sous des cieux d'aube)' (Benayoun 1980: 85).[28] We may wonder whether it is indeed Magritte or more properly Delvaux whose name, and images, should be summoned. Michael Worton has remarked recently on the difference between Delvaux and Magritte, one bringing an excess and the other an evacuation of eroticism. It is the excess, not the absence, we find in *L'Année dernière à Marienbad* embodied in the figure of Delphine Seyrig, herself reminiscent of Delvaux's luminous, lunar, marmoreal and hypnotic women. Resnais and Robbe-Grillet's diurnal/ nocturnal palace of dream and fantasy is peopled and animate, erotic, as we find, 'derrière chaque buisson',[29] further images of X and A in interminable, languishing dialogue.

Yet more than the Surrealist artists, inspired by, but objectifying, their female muses, Resnais works in *L'Année dernière à Marienbad* to make the woman at least in part, and in disturbing inter-relation with X, a subject of her own desire. Thinking about silence, in an essay 'Muteness Envy', Barbara Johnson explores the sexual politics of nineteenth-century representations of women: 'numerous are the Parnassian poems addressed to silent female statues, marble venuses and granite sphinxes whose unresponsiveness stands as the mark of

---

27 'a film which is only addressed to one's senses, to one's faculty of looking, listening, feeling and being moved'.
28 'nocturnal in the day and diurnal in the night (like in those paintings by Magritte where midnight dwellings are etched beneath dawn skies)'.
29 'behind every bush'.

their aesthetic value' (Johnson 1998: 132). She shows how the ideal woman is petrified and how men turn to statues to understand something of sexual pleasure: 'In his efforts to collect reliable testimony from women about their pleasure, Lacan finally turns, astonishingly, to a statue, thus writing his own Parnassian poem: "You have only to go and look at Bernini's statue [of Saint Theresa] in Rome to understand immediately that she's coming, there is no doubt about it"' (Johnson 1998: 134). In turn, Johnson suggests that there are 'two things women are silent about: their pleasure and their violation. The work performed by the idealization of this silence is that *it helps culture not to be able to tell the difference between the two*' (Johnson 1998: 137). In a film whose aesthetic depends on the statue, on frozen motion and marmoreal timelessness, Resnais's heroine remains contrarily febrile, moving, sentient, though vulnerable. She is never the statue whose pose reveals her pleasure. Resnais refuses to allow her to be tied up (as in Robbe-Grillet's fantasy) but instead allows her to move freely. The bind of this liberty, however, is that we see her choose to play out her fantasy as she opens her arms to X, as she herself faces her own imbrication in fantasy, her own inability to tell the difference between her pleasure and her violation.

Readings of the film's sexual politics point to some of the problems with the scenario Robbe-Grillet and Resnais create between them. Robbe-Grillet says of X: 'il lui offre un passé, un avenir et la liberté' (Robbe-Grillet 1961: 13).[30] For Weyergans: 'Le film serait donc l'histoire d'une femme qui se libère, ou qui a des velléités de se libérer (puisqu'elle rêve de cette libération)' (quoted in Zissler, Massuyeau and Verpillat 1961: 13).[31] For me, there is no liberation at the end of *L'Année dernière à Marienbad*, though there may be an act of transgression, and movement into the unknown. What is radical about the film is not its liberation of A, about which I am doubtful, but its gradual intimation that she, like the heroine of *Hiroshima mon amour*, may seek a love which devours and deforms her, that she may be an actor and not an object in the relation that is generated by the dialogue between lovers. This is disturbing to X, disrupting his authorship, letting him be fantasised as rapist by his lover. Yet it is also,

---

30 'he offers her a past, a future and liberty'.
31 'So the film would be the story of a woman who sets herself free, or who has the impulse to set herself free (since she dreams of this liberation)'.

surely, disturbing to A – and to viewers – who see her participation in a fantasy by which she is destroyed.

As Leutrat remarks: 'the film's deviations are as complex as those of the human heart' (Leutrat 2000: 9). For Robbe-Grillet: '*Marienbad* est une histoire assez opaque comme nous en vivons dans nos crises passionnelles, dans nos amours, dans toute notre vie affective. Par conséquent, reprocher au film de ne pas être clair, c'est reprocher aux passions humaines d'être toujours un peu opaques' (Labarthe and Rivette 1961: 12).[32] For Resnais: '*Marienbad* décrit les hésitations, les affolements, les angoisses, et aussi les grands moments de bonheur qui accompagnent toute passion. On se demande si on ne rêve pas, on imagine le meilleur ou le pire. J'étais donc en plein réalisme psychologique' (*L'Arc* 1961: 96).[33] For me, *Marienbad* is radical in its approach to the problem of the sexual relation. Rather than perpetuating a view of the male subject of desire and his female object, *L'Année dernière à Marienbad* explores the play of desire between two individuals, their fatal contamination of one another as their imagined narrative unfolds, their fear of each other's difference, violence and unknowability. Neither is a free player in this game, both have lost, and are lost, at the end.

A question remains here about *L'Année dernière à Marienbad*. How could Resnais turn from the political engagement of *Hiroshima mon amour* to the closed, sepulchral world of this baroque palace? Resnais himself contemplates this as he says: 'Et faire ce film au moment où je crois, justement, qu'on ne peut faire de film, en France, sans parler de la guerre d'Algérie. D'ailleurs, je me demande si l'atmosphère close et étouffante de *L'Année* ne résulte pas de ces contradictions' (*Premier Plan* 1961: 45).[34] *L'Année dernière à Marienbad* is certainly a film which

---

32 '*Marienbad* is a fairly opaque story like those we experience in the crises of our passions, in our love affairs, in our whole emotional life. And so, reproaching the film for not being clear is the same as reproaching human feelings for always being rather opaque'.

33 '*Marienbad* describes the hesitations, the turmoil, the anxiety, and also the great moments of happiness which accompany any passion. One wonders if one is dreaming, one imagines the worst or the best. So I was really in the realm of psychological realism'.

34 'And I was making this film at a time when I think that, rightly, one could not make a film, in France, without speaking about the Algerian war. Indeed, I wonder whether the closed and stifling atmosphere of *L'Année* does not result from those contradictions'.

plays with a timeless past, leading Bersani and Dutoit, ever critical of this phase in Resnais's filmmaking, to describe the film as 'a decadent period piece' (Bersani and Dutoit 1993: 190). Yet some of the concerns and tropes of Resnais's earlier engagements with trauma, pain and death return in *L'Année dernière à Marienbad* in various transposed forms. A historically situated reading of the film is difficult. Yet in the echo chamber or padded cell of *Marienbad*, Resnais is still working through issues which will surface in his next film, for some a more political film, *Muriel ou le temps d'un retour*. In *Muriel*, Resnais will return to a man's horrified fascination with a woman suffering. He will explore again the uncertainties and vicissitudes of human inter-relation, the inability to know reciprocity, or to know, indeed, how far the other is known. *Muriel*, far more than *Marienbad*, is about Algeria and about contemporary history. Yet *Muriel*, as we shall see, offers no positive sense of the possibility of recall, or of testimony in film. It is without resolution or optimism. From *L'Année dernière à Marienbad*, indeed, Resnais's films are increasingly uncertain and indirect in their politics. He may still treat political issues in *La Guerre est finie* and even *Stavisky* but from *Marienbad* onwards we see his films moving intermittently, and with fits and starts, more towards surface and form, towards a numbing and a stifling of political reference and relevance. This may be a despondent response to the lack of political purchase of any film; or it may be a recognition that, as in *Marienbad*, what fascinates Resnais ultimately, what we glimpse in the mirror within the frame of his filmmaking, is the spectacle of inter-relation, of human performance and deception, fantasy, falsity and annihilation.

References

L'Arc: Alain Resnais, 31 (1961).

Armes, Roy (1980) 'Robbe-Grillet, Ricardou and *Last Year at Marienbad*', *Quarterly Review of Film Studies*, 5:1 (winter), pp. 1–17.

Benayoun, Robert (1980) *Alain Resnais: arpenteur de l'imaginaire* (Paris: Stock/Cinéma).

Benayoun, Robert, Michel Ciment and Jean-Louis Pays (2002) 'Ne pas faire un film sur l'Espagne, entretien avec Alain Resnais', in Stéphane Goudet (ed.), *Positif, revue de cinéma: Alain Resnais* (Paris: Gallimard [Folio]), pp. 162–87.

Bersani, Leo and Ulysse Dutoit (1993) *Arts of Impoverishment: Beckett, Rothko, Resnais* (Cambridge MA: Harvard University Press).

Brunius, Jacques (1962) 'Every year in Marienbad or The Discipline of Uncertainty', *Sight and Sound*, 31:3 (summer), pp. 122–7 and p. 153.
Callev, Haim (1997) *The Stream of Consciousness in the Films of Alain Resnais* (New York: McGruer Publishing).
Chekhov, Anton (1997) *The Plays of Anton Chekhov*, translated by Paul Schmidt (New York: Harper Collins).
Cowie, Peter (1963) *Antonioni, Bergman, Resnais* (London: The Tantivy Press).
Greene, Naomi (1999) *Landscapes of Loss: The National Past in Postwar French Cinema* (Princeton NJ: Princeton University Press).
Houston, Penelope (1961–62) '*L'Année dernière à Marienbad*', *Sight and Sound*, 31:1 (winter), pp. 26–8.
Johnson, Barbara (1998) 'Muteness Envy', *The Feminist Difference: Literature, Psychoanalysis, Race and Gender* (Cambridge MA: Harvard University Press), pp. 129–53.
Kline, T. Jefferson (1992) 'Rebecca's Bad Dream: Speculations on/in Resnais's *Marienbad*', *Screening the Text: Intertextuality in New Wave French Cinema* (Baltimore MD: Johns Hopkins University Press), pp. 54–86.
Labarthe, André S. and Jacques Rivette (1961) 'Entretien avec Resnais et Robbe-Grillet', *Cahiers du cinéma*, 21:123 (September), pp. 1–21.
Leperchey, Sarah (2000) *Alain Resnais: Une lecture topologique* (Paris: L'Harmattan).
Leutrat, Jean-Louis (2000) *L'Année dernière à Marienbad* (London: BFI Film Classics).
Monaco, James (1979) *Alain Resnais* (New York: Oxford University Press).
Parkes, Graham (1994) 'Phantasy Projections of the Multiple Psyche in *8½* and *Last Year at Marienbad*', *Film and Philosophy*, 1, pp. 42–54.
Premier Plan: Alain Resnais (1961), 10.
Robbe-Grillet, Alain (1961) *L'Année dernière à Marienbad* (Paris: Minuit).
Zissler, Albert, Michel Massuyeau and Frank Verpillat (1961) *FRAMO présente* L'Année dernière à Marienbad (Paris).
Žižek, Slavoj (1997) *The Plague of Fantasies* (London: Verso).

4

Muriel ou le temps d'un retour (1963)

In his study of *L'Année dernière à Marienbad*, Jean-Louis Leutrat writes: 'we are in the temporality of the eternal return' (Leutrat 2000: 61). The film with which Resnais would follow *Marienbad*, *Muriel*, bears the subtitle *Le Temps d'un retour* (the time of a return). The film marks a return for Resnais, who will work again here with Jean Cayrol. *Muriel* also shows Resnais returning to, and reordering, some of the material of his earlier films. More explicitly, *Muriel* is a film about the aftermath of events, about the return home (after war), about the possibility of return to the past in remembering or return to the present through forgetting. Cayrol has said: 'Ce qui m'intéresse, en général, ce ne sont pas les drames. C'est ce qui se passe après. Non pas l'aller, mais le retour' (*L'Arc* 1961: 10).[1] In *Muriel*, as Resnais multiplies narrative strands and repeated images, the viewer, reminded of *Hiroshima* and *Marienbad*, becomes increasingly uncertain about the possibility of experiencing or making sense of this return. For Sarah Leperchey, as we watch the film, 'il nous semble assister, plutôt qu'à une progression, à un perpétuel retour des choses' (Leperchey 2003: 68).[2]

Cayrol and Resnais first discussed the project in 1959 (Monaco 1979: 75), and Resnais began shooting three years later (between November 1962 and January 1963). The film won the Critics' Prize at Venice and Delphine Seyrig, appearing once more as Resnais's

---

1 'In general I am not interested in the events themselves but in what happens afterwards. Not the departure, but the return'.
2 'it seems as if we witness, rather than a progression, a perpetual return of things'.

heroine, won the 'Volpi' cup for best actress. Lamenting a generally weak year at Venice, Tom Milne wrote in *Sight and Sound*: 'Still, there was *Muriel ou le temps d'un retour*, to my mind a masterpiece, and Resnais's most intricate examination of the structures of memory' (Milne 1963: 177–8). *Muriel* has, nevertheless, divided critics. Alexander Walker commended the film only to morbid filmgoers wishing to see a talent in the last stages of decomposition. *Muriel* is a film which troubles its viewers and is, for a variety of reasons, hard to watch. Claude Ollier writes in *Cahiers du cinéma*: 'L'impression dominante que j'ai ressentie très vite a été celle d'une croissante angoisse, et même d'une terreur, absolument semblable à celle que j'ai ressentie en voyant *Marienbad*' (Kast 1963: 22).[3] Drawing on the anxiety conjured by the film, Jean-André Fieschi compares *Muriel* with Hitchcock, in particular *The Birds*: 'l'onirisme, et ce sentiment d'angoisse, de terreur feutrée, naissent ici aussi de l'accumulation des détails quotidiens, mais jusqu'à l'exaspération' (Kast 1963: 26).[4] *Muriel* is also unsettling for critics in the distance it maintains between the viewpoint of the spectator and that of the protagonists. For Marcel Mettey, we watch the characters like an entomologist observing insects (Mettey 1978: 168). For Alan Williams: 'Many critics consider *Muriel* to be Resnais's greatest film, though [general] audiences often find it hard to follow because of its jagged, Eisensteinian editing and highly elliptical screenplay' (quoted in O'Brien 2000: 49). It is only on repeat viewings, returns to the film, that we can begin to emerge from paralysis and succumb to the film's power. As Tom Milne writes, returning to review *Muriel* for *Monthly Film Bulletin* after seeing it first in Venice: '*Muriel* is not an easy film: one has to watch and listen with every nerve alert; and at each subsequent viewing it undergoes a strange, enchanting sea-change, apparently altering shape physically as one penetrates further into its enveloping beauty and warmth' (Milne 1964: 71).

Muriel is a film which plays on our nerves. Its subject, Algeria, is approached apparently more explicitly here for the first time in Resnais's filmmaking. As Marie-Claire Ropars writes: 'Filmed during

3 'The dominant impression which I felt almost immediately was one of growing anxiety, and even of terror, entirely similar to what I felt seeing *Marienbad*'.
4 'the dream-like quality, and this feeling of anxiety, of muffled terror, also arise here from the accumulation of everyday details, pushed to exasperating extremes'.

the Algerian war, *Hiroshima* cannot and will not refer to it' (Ropars-Wuilleumier 1990: 182). As we saw in the previous chapter, Resnais suggested that the claustrophobia of *Marienbad* might reflect a response to Algeria and to what might not be represented. At this time, Resnais signed the Free Algeria manifesto, together with Sartre and 120 other artists and intellectuals (Kreidl 1977: 88). The Algerian War ended in 1962; in its aftermath Resnais and Cayrol could succeed in making and showing *Muriel*, described by Kreidl as an overtly anti-OAS (Organisation de l'armée secrète) film. As Michel Marie writes:

> *Muriel* n'est en aucune façon un film qui s'efforce de tout dire sur la guerre d'Algérie. Mais il tente de revenir, au niveau de sa matière du signifié comme dans son projet idéologique, sur les silences du cinéma français pendant la période antérieure (1954–1962), et sur le rôle effectif qu'a joué le cinéma en tant qu'appareil idéologique à cette époque. En ce sens, *Muriel* désigne notamment *ce* dont ce cinéma parlait, *au nom de quoi* il parlait, et par voie de conséquence, *ce qu'il occultait*. (Bailblé 1974: 337)[5]

Emily Tomlinson casts more doubt on such a reading, however, noting for example that the Algerian novelist, Rachid Boudjedra, complains that *Muriel* is not a film about Algeria but a film where Algeria is something everyone tries to forget (Tomlinson 2002: 53).

The way in which Resnais approaches Algeria, in *Muriel*, is through the story of a woman tortured. This appears at first almost entirely obscured within the narrative and action of the film. *Muriel* is set in Boulogne-sur-mer in the autumn of 1962. Its events take place in the fortnight between Saturday 29 September and Saturday 13 October. We observe the lives of Hélène Aughain and her stepson Bernard. The narrative begins on an evening when Hélène's former lover, Alphonse, arrives to stay with her, bringing with him a young woman, Françoise, who he claims is his niece. Bernard, who is only in his early twenties, has recently returned from military service in Algeria. Indeed, Bernard's return is one of the major axes of the narrative. On his return to Boulogne and to Hélène, we find gradually

---

5 '*Muriel* is by no means a film which tries to say everything about the Algerian war. But it tries, in its means of signification as in its ideological project, to go back over the silences of French cinema of the period immediately before (1954–62), and over the effective role cinema played in this period as ideological apparatus. In this sense, *Muriel* indicates *what* cinema was talking about, *in which name* it was speaking, and as a consequence *what it was hiding*'.

that he has (metaphorically) brought Muriel with him, that he is unable to leave her behind.

The meanings which attach to the name Muriel are at first uncertain in the film. The name has, like Marienbad or Nevers, a totemic quality: it designates more than the woman Bernard appears to remember from Algeria. As O'Brien remarks: 'the signifier Muriel comes to stand for both the tortured woman and the act of torture itself' (O'Brien 2000: 56). Yet Muriel means more than this in the film, where the name, as signifier, seems to be linked to what Bernard misses, to what he desires. We first hear the name in an exchange between Bernard and Hélène. Bernard says to his stepmother: 'Je vais faire un tour, voir Muriel' (Cayrol 1963: 43). Hélène replies: 'Tu ne m'as jamais dit où tu avais rencontré ton amie, elle n'a pas un nom d'ici' (Cayrol 1963: 43). Bernard does not respond to Hélène directly, but says instead: 'Elle est malade en ce moment' (Cayrol 1963: 43); then he changes his mind and continues: 'Non, elle n'est pas malade' (Cayrol 1963: 43).[6] Tom Milne describes Bernard ambiguously as 'haunted by his military service in Algeria and by an unhappy affair with a girl called Muriel' (Milne 1963: 178). Bernard's visceral encounter with Muriel is by no means an affair, but we do not know this at this stage in the film. Muriel's name next returns as Alphonse looks through papers in Bernard's room. We glimpse the name in close-up images of the papers – Resnais seems to pass many documents fleetingly before our eyes. In these papers there are the words '5 mai: Muriel est morte au bout de 30 heures' (Cayrol 1963: 70).[7]

Naomi Greene writes: 'Unable to talk about the "real" Muriel, [Bernard] has invented, seemingly for the benefit of his stepmother, a "false" Muriel, a young woman who is, he says, his fiancée' (Greene 1999: 48). Bernard appears traumatised by Muriel's ordeal. As Cayrol specifies: 'Ce qu'il a pu voir, ce qu'il a dû faire l'a tellement blessé, qu'il reste comme halluciné, mais il se retient, fait silence, gardant tout en lui, ne communiquant pas ses terribles connaissances' (Cayrol 1963: 21).[8] Bernard is unable, or unwilling, to communicate

6 'I am going out to see Muriel'; 'You've never told me where you met your girlfriend, she doesn't have a local name'; 'She is ill at the moment'; 'No, she is not ill'.
7 '5 May: Muriel died after 30 hours'.
8 'What he has seen, what he has had to do has so wounded him that he is still reeling from it, but he holds himself back, keeps silent, keeping everything inside, not communicating his terrible knowledge'.

his experience and his subsequent grief. Françoise, later in the film, transparently criticises Bernard's reticence – 'Moi, je me plains quand je suis malheureuse, je le dis à tout le monde' (Cayrol 1963: 120)[9] – but the film itself is more doubtful about the possibilities of testifying, of bringing grief and guilt into the open. Cayrol continues to say of Bernard, 'sa mémoire se réfugie dans sa caméra, dans son magnétophone, dans ses armes, dans ses films' (Cayrol 1963: 21).[10] Resnais and Cayrol choose to reflect on memory and film as testimony by making Bernard himself an amateur filmmaker. He says of his own filming: 'J'accumule des preuves, c'est tout' (Cayrol 1963: 99).[11] Yet *Muriel* itself is uncertain about film as proof.

As well as the papers with Muriel's name, we see photographs from Algeria – as the film collages evidence, documents – and most importantly we see a film, footage with which Bernard has returned to France. The showing of this film, and the voice-over that accompanies it, are critical in *Muriel*. Naomi Greene describes the scene as 'a black hole at the centre of *Muriel*' (Greene 1999: 48); this black hole is the film's point of origin and point of (no) return. Critics concur on the scene's importance in the film, but interestingly mis-remember or mis-place its location in the film. For Alyssa O'Brien, the scene comes 'about a third of the way through the film' (O'Brien 2000: 53); for Greene, we see Bernard's film 'toward the end of *Muriel*' (Greene 1999: 48). In fact the scene is almost precisely at the film's centre. It forms shot 374 out of 773 and occurs 59 minutes through the two-hour film. If the scene is a black hole, it really is at the centre of *Muriel* structurally and temporally, as well as semantically. (For Benayoun, the scene is revelatory for the action of the whole film (Benayoun 2002: 135).)

We see three and a half minutes of footage; Resnais shot this in 8mm and blew it up to a grainy 35mm. The shots show scenes of military life in Algeria; they are as banal and generic as this description suggests. The screenplay emphasises that these are 'des images assez floues d'Afrique du Nord, très carte postale' (Cayrol 1963: 89)[12] (critics have also compared Resnais's muted colour shots

9 'I complain when I'm unhappy, I tell everyone'.
10 'his memory takes refuge in his camera, his tape recorder, his weapons, his films'.
11 'I'm gathering evidence, that's all'.
12 'quite hazy images of North Africa, like a postcard'.

of Boulogne to a postcard aesthetic; Françoise is herself seen looking at postcards in Prisunic). Bernard's images of soldiers in Algeria are in contrast, however, to the voice-over we hear. Deleuze, writing about modern cinema, has said: 'ce qui définit le cinéma moderne, c'est un "va-et-vient entre la parole et l'image" qui devra inventer leur nouveau rapport' (Deleuze 1985: 322).[13] Resnais has explored this disjuncture and creation of a new relation previously, in *Hiroshima mon amour* for example, where in the woman's voice-over we hear of recovery in Hiroshima, flowers growing out of the ashes and ruins, and see at the same time the most painful images of burnt children (Duras 1960: 28). In the radical opposition between word and image in *Muriel*, Resnais makes us question whether there is any relation at all between what we see and what we hear.

Bernard's film seems for some moments to take over *Muriel*, to engulf our viewing experience. Rather than locate us in Bernard's workshop, in a particular viewing scenario, the film chooses initially merely to confront us with images and the words which accompany them. Bernard speaks the words, but it is only at the end of the scene that he is identified visually as the source of the voice-over. The words Bernard speaks tell of Muriel's torture. She was an unknown woman in Algeria ('Personne n'avait connu cette femme avant' (Cayrol 1963: 89)). As Bernard first encounters her she seems between life and death: 'Elle avait l'air endormie, mais elle tremblait de partout' (Cayrol 1963: 89). Bernard continues: 'On me dit qu'elle s'appelle Muriel. Je ne sais pas pourquoi, mais ça ne devait pas être son vrai nom' (Cayrol 1963: 89–90).[14] This signifier may only be falsely attached to the woman who is the film's centre and origin. Yet it is under this name that Bernard speaks of her horrific ordeal. I quote his voice-over at length to give a sense of its duration and impact:

Il fallait qu'elle parle avant la nuit.

Robert s'est baissé et l'a retournée. Muriel a gémi. Elle avait mis son bras sur ses yeux. On la lâche, elle retombe comme un paquet.

C'est alors que ça recommence. On la tire par les chevilles au milieu du hangar pour mieux la voir. Robert lui donne des coups de pied. Il

13 'what defines modern cinema, is a "movement backwards and forwards between words and images" which must invent their new relation'.
14 'No one had known this woman before'; 'She looked as if she was asleep, but she was trembling all over'; 'They told me she was called Muriel. I don't know why, but that can't have been her real name'.

prend une lampe-torche, la braque sur elle. Les lèvres sont gonflées, pleines d'écume. On lui arrache ses vêtements. On essaie de l'asseoir sur une chaise, elle retombe; un bras est comme tordu.

Il faut en finir. Même si elle avait voulu parler, elle n'aurait pas pu. Je m'y suis mis aussi. Muriel geignait en recevant les gifles. La paume de mes mains me brûlait. Muriel avait les cheveux tout mouillés.

Robert allume une cigarette. Il s'approche d'elle. Elle hurle. Alors son regard m'a fixé.

Pourquoi moi?

Elle a fermé les yeux, puis elle s'est mise à vomir. Robert a reculé, dégoûté. Je les ai tous laissés.

La nuit je suis venu la voir. J'ai soulevé la bâch... Comme si elle avait séjourné longtemps dans l'eau... comme un sac de pommes de terre éventré... Avec du sang sur tout le corps, dans les cheveux... des brûlures sur la poitrine. Les yeux de Muriel n'étaient pas fermés. Ça ne me faisait presque rien, peut-être même que cela ne me faisait rien du tout.

Le lendemain matin avant le salut aux couleurs, Robert l'avait fait disparaître (Cayrol 1963: 90)[15]

The words which describe the torture of Muriel accumulate physical and sensory details – her swollen lips, the sweat in her hair, her vomit and her blood. The viewer may respond to these triggers but the scene is still hard, perhaps impossible, to picture adequately. It seems to have no relation to the images we view on screen, though the evocation of Muriel's physical, suffering presence may recall the images of dead and dying bodies, man-handled like so many objects, in *Nuit et*

15 'It was necessary for her to speak before nightfall. Robert bent down and turned her over. Muriel groaned. She had put her arm over her eyes. They let go of her, she falls lifeless. It is then that it starts again. They drag her by her ankles into the middle of the hangar to see her better. Robert kicks her. He takes a torch and points it at her. Her lips are swollen, foaming. They tear off her clothes. They try to sit her on a chair, she falls off; one of her arms seems to be broken. They have to bring this to an end. Even if she had wanted to talk, she wouldn't have been able to. I set about it as well. Muriel was moaning as she was struck. The palms of my hands were burning. Muriel's hair was all wet. Robert lights a cigarette. He goes up to her. She screams. Then she fixed her eyes on me. Why me? She closed her eyes, then she started to vomit. Robert recoiled, disgusted. I left them all. In the night I came to see her. I lifted the tarpaulin. It was as if she had been left underwater... like a split sack of potatoes... With blood all over her body and in her hair... burns on her chest. Muriel's eyes were not shut. It hardly affected me at all, perhaps it even had no effect on me at all. The next morning before the salute to the colours, Robert had had her removed'.

brouillard. As Greene writes: 'the voice-over recounts the episode blow by blow, but the scene itself is never witnessed' (Greene 1999: 48).

It could be said that, as Resnais refused to film Robbe-Grillet's projected rape of the woman in *L'Année dernière à Marienbad*, so he declines to film the torture of Muriel. The film could in this way escape a voyeuristic imaging of a woman being severely hurt. Yet the voice-over itself is already graphic in its description of Muriel; Resnais showed previously, in *Nuit et brouillard*, that his filmmaking would encompass images of horror, however opaque or inadequate they might remain as representations of trauma. Naomi Greene argues that the absence of images of torture can be interpreted 'as a reflection, an indictment, of the harsh restrictions imposed by French censorship at the time of the Algerian war' (Greene 1999: 48–9). Following this line of argument, *Muriel* draws attention to these images as absent – in the film and more broadly in France in the early 1960s. For Alyssa O'Brien, *Muriel* depends on spectator participation such that the viewer is called on to relieve her anxiety by filling the gaps, by finding what is absent; this leads, as she suggests, to the recognition that 'in filling in the gaps, the spectator is forced to participate in a scene of torture' (O'Brien 2000: 53). I am less sure that Resnais calls on us to supplement the film in our viewing experience; rather *Muriel* seems to disenable us as viewers, to deprive us of knowledge and pleasure, to awaken doubts. If the absence of images, of proof, of Muriel, holds political force read as comment on France's climate of censorship and non-disclosure, it also holds less laudable meanings as the figure of Bernard is examined further.

Bernard's character at first seems to conjure sympathy. Cayrol says of his motives in creating Bernard: 'J'avais été très frappé par la gêne des garçons qui revenaient de l'armée: ils étouffaient littéralement, comme si l'expérience qu'ils avaient vécue là-bas était incommunicable. C'était un secret trop lourd pour eux. Je voulais montrer cela aussi' (*L'Arc* 1961: 11).[16] In the voice-over with which he accompanies his film, Bernard appears to denounce himself, his own involvement in the torture of Muriel and his own lack of feeling and numbness as it took place. As we learn after the film showing, Bernard is speaking

---

16 'I had been very struck by the difficulties of the young men coming back from the army: they were literally suffocating, as if the experience they had lived over there could not be put into words. It was too heavy a secret for them. I wanted to show that as well'.

to an addressee, an old man named Jean. As Bernard reaches the end of his account, Jean asks about Robert, Bernard's companion in the army: 'Mais où il est maintenant ce gars-là?' (Cayrol 1963: 90); Bernard replies: 'Il se ballade à Boulogne, comme tout le monde' (Cayrol 1963: 90), to which Jean says in turn: 'Mais vous aussi!' (Cayrol 1963: 90).[17] Jean's words reinscribe Bernard's own guilt, which had been momentarily deflected onto Robert. Confronting Robert later, Bernard will further act out this deferral of culpability in a gesture which, for Leperchey, is redemptive: 'Ce qu'était Bernard a changé: il était un tortionnaire parmi les autres; mais, parce qu'il se dresse contre Robert, on peut désormais dire qu'il était le tortionnaire qui allait se révolter contre la torture' (Leperchey 2003: 79).[18]

Bernard may revolt against torture – as does the film *Muriel* – but we may still wonder how far he bears witness to Muriel's experience and really makes it known. In addition to the amateur film footage we see, there is an audio tape that Bernard has made somewhere in Algeria. He never willingly listens to this tape or plays it to others, but at a moment late in the film Françoise, accidentally or not, switches on the tape-player and lets its sounds – laughter – briefly be heard. Bernard violently pulls the tape from the machine and throws it across the room. For Leperchey, '[a]vec le bruit des rires diffusé par le magnétophone, tout le traumatisme de la guerre d'Algérie semble resurgir pour Bernard' (Leperchey 2003: 77).[19] This scene closely precedes Bernard's murder of Robert. The return of the sounds of the scene of torture appears to act as catalyst; it may catalyse action but again stifles memory and representation. As Marie-Claire Ropars reminds us: 'le film ne montre rien de ce que raconte Bernard quand il le projette, tandis que si la bande magnétique est l'enregistrement de la scène de torture, elle renvoie directement à ce qui s'est passé' (Bailblé 1974: 274). She points out further: 'Il faut d'ailleurs constater que la bande est arrachée par Bernard, et que le film s'achève donc sur

---

17 'But where is this lad now?'; 'He's walking around Boulogne, like anyone else'; 'But so are you!'.
18 'What Bernard was has changed: he was a torturer amongst others; but, because he rises up against Robert, one can say that from this point on he was the torturer who was going to revolt against torture'.
19 '[w]ith the sound of laughter broadcast by the tape recorder, all the trauma of the Algerian war seems to return for Bernard'.

la destruction de la seule trace éventuelle de l'histoire "Muriel"' (Bailblé 1974: 274).[20]

Muriel offers minimal, but sufficient, evidence that Muriel's torture did take place. Robert, encountering Bernard at large in the streets of Boulogne, says: 'Tu veux raconter Muriel? Muriel, ça ne se raconte pas' (Cayrol 1963: 110).[21] He places Muriel's story in the realm of the 'intransmissible', or more particularly in the realm of what will be repressed and silenced on return to France. Since Robert refuses to speak of Muriel, since the tape is destroyed and images are missing in Bernard's film – when Hélène enters Bernard's atelier and switches on his projector the images melt before her leaving a blank square of light – the only knowledge or testimony we have as viewers comes from Bernard's narration. Marie-Claire Ropars again observes brilliantly: 'D'une certaine manière, Bernard vit le passé historique sur le mode individuel, sur un mode qui est finalement très narcissique, celui de sa propre aventure et de son traumatisme personnel. Mais par le refus de toute image mentale, qui distingue *Muriel* d'*Hiroshima* et de *Marienbad*, l'écriture du film propose la critique de cette attitude' (Bailblé 1974: 297).[22] In depriving us directly of images of Muriel – proof of the torture – and of Bernard's mental images or memories, the film sets us doubly at a distance from events. Rather than cover the distance, we are left to wonder about Bernard's memories or imagining of Muriel. We may wonder about the correlation between Muriel as woman murdered in the torture ordeal in Algeria and Muriel the imagined fiancée of whom Bernard speaks to Hélène. Is the imagined love a way of keeping Muriel alive in memory, keeping her name circulating (Bernard turns in shock in the streets as a mother calls to a child named Muriel)? Does the creation of a romantic attachment to Muriel belie something

20 'the film shows nothing of what Bernard recounts when he shows it, whilst the audio tape is the recording of the torture scene and refers directly to what happened'; 'Further it must be noted that Bernard pulls out the tape, and that the film thus ends with the destruction of the only actual trace of the story "Muriel"'.
21 'You want to tell [the story of] Muriel? Muriel can't be told'.
22 'In a certain way, Bernard lives the historic past in an individual mode, in a mode which is in the end very narcissistic, relating as it does to his own adventure and his personal trauma. But by the refusal of any mental image, distinguishing *Muriel* from *Hiroshima* and *Marienbad*, the film's writing criticises this attitude'.

erotic, however twisted, in Bernard's retention of Muriel's story as his narrative of Algeria? Where Resnais and his crew may have pretended in jest that the woman from Nevers was fabricating her story, the stakes seem higher if we suggest that Muriel is Bernard's invention. Yet in watching *L'Année dernière à Marienbad* we may have become dubious about the truth of memory in Resnais's films, and their investment in (sexual) violence against women. Departing from my reading of *Marienbad*, it would be offensive to suggest any willed involvement in violence on Muriel's part; indeed her agency is what has been eradicated in the torture chamber and even in the film where she has no voice or image. Unlike A in *Marienbad*, who has some autonomy, Muriel is instead entirely Bernard's creation. Muriel may not be adequately represented, her experience may be seen as untouchable horror. Yet, as Resnais lets images screen rather than reveal events which have taken place, we might reckon too with the fear that Muriel may serve as a screen memory, as a memory reworked to hide us from something still more disturbing. Is the torture of Muriel the single hideous scenario Bernard has witnessed in twenty-two months in Algeria? Is it the ultimate in horror, the trauma by which he is possessed, or does Muriel as fantasy, put into words by Bernard, hide further horrors which go untraced?

Muriel, like *Marienbad*, is a vertiginous film allowing us no grasp, pulling back from any definitive statement. (For Bersani and Dutoit, who admire the film, '*Muriel* is constantly rushing away from a narrative centre never firmly established in the first place' (Bersani and Dutoit 1993: 190).) Through the puzzles of such a film, Resnais draws us into the difficulty of thinking about memory, knowledge and testimony. This effect is only enhanced when we begin to take into account the whole expanse of the film. Indeed despite the film's title, Muriel may at first seem a fairly minor part of its history. To consider the film further we need to return to Hélène and Alphonse, whose story takes up more screen time than Muriel's, yet is also inflected by it. I have used the image of a kaleidoscope in describing the effect of Resnais's filmmaking; kaleidoscope images are seen literally in *Muriel* and indicate the ways in which all the parts of the narrative reflect one another, yet continually diverge and differ. This double motion of reflection and distancing creates much of the film's puzzlement and dislocation.

The film opens with a jarring series of close-ups which fragment the room and objects they represent, like a Cubist painting. As Penelope Houston writes: 'Resnais does not let us take in the whole scene at a glance, as he could quite easily do, but breaks it into fragmentary details: the customer's hand on the door; Hélène's listening face; the hot water poured from the kettle; the apartment's confusion of furniture. The totality of the scene emerges only *after* the shots have been absorbed into our consciousness: and this, as it develops, is to be the film's method' (Houston 1963–64: 35). Indeed, we may question whether any totalities can be seen and known in *Muriel*. Resnais chops up the diegetic reality we perceive, disorienting us and making the viewing process self-conscious. Yet the reality he represents is also confusing, unexpected. Hélène as antiques dealer, as we see in this first scene, works from home, living amongst the objects she sells. Her domestic space is also a commercial space and inherently transactional and transitory. Bernard describes the apartment as 'une salle des ventes' ('an auction room') (Cayrol 1963: 62). The home, and the domestic, are unsettled and rendered uncanny. Alyssa O'Brien might be seen to align Resnais notionally with Perec or Godard as she sees *Muriel* as 'an aesthetic product that captures and comments on the alienation endemic to contemporary French society' (O'Brien 2000: 49). Susan Sontag speaks more specifically, in aesthetic terms, of the alienation of the viewer, arguing: 'When Resnais cuts abruptly, he pulls the viewer away from the story. His cutting acts as a brake on the narrative, a form of aesthetic undertow, a sort of filmic alienation effect' (Sontag 1963–64: 25). For Bersani and Dutoit, 'Hélène's apartment is a masterpiece of disorienting space' (Bersani and Dutoit 1993: 190). Alienation and disorientation are captured too through Hélène's actions and her restlessness. As the screenplay specifies: 'Hélène ne s'arrêtera de bouger, d'aller et de venir. On va la sentir mal à l'aise, elle s'occupe, se perd dans mille gestes, se trompe, revient comme si elle avait oublié quelque chose' (Cayrol 1963: 52).[23] The rhythm and disruption of her behaviour are again reflected and enhanced in the narrative construction of *Muriel*. As Hélène seems never to settle, so the film is increasingly restless. Resnais and Cayrol offer fairly intensive investigation of the evening of Saturday 29 September in the first act of the film, of Friday 5 and

23 'Hélène will not stop moving about, going to and fro. She will seem uneasy, she takes something up, loses herself with hundreds of small deeds, makes a mistake, comes back as if she had forgotten something'.

Saturday 6 October in the third act and Sunday 14 October in the fifth act. But the second and fourth act instead show time passing between the weekends (for Ropars, indeed, time is the focal point of *Muriel* (Bailblé 1974: 270)). The second and fourth acts each create a collage of temporally unmarked incidents which the viewer finds increasingly hard to arrange in any narrative order (Ropars compares this imaging of time passing to the end of *L'Education sentimentale*; we might also think of *To the Lighthouse*). As the screenplay specifies, the scenes are sometimes linked to the story and the characters, but they must also create a climate of panic (Cayrol 1963: 113). This sense of panic seems captured too in the aria which we hear several times in the film.

Through the intrusive cutting of the film, its restlessness, its challenge to order, its plangent music, *Muriel* appears to assault the viewer. This can certainly be read as reflection on modern alienation and on the unease of this post-war French community (indeed questions about the weight of memory and the heritage of the Second World War will surface again later in this discussion). But the unease and tension of *Muriel* also surely has something to do with the woman's torture at its centre, certainly before this story is told. Celia Britton argues that 'the violence of the visual fragmentation [is] an *echo* of the violence of the film's deepest theme'. She continues: 'The visual "morcellement" [splitting] of the jerky cutting – and also the many close-ups of parts of bodies – thus comes to look like *mutilation*' (Britton 1990: 38). Retaining Britton's sense that the film's assault and disorientation relate, through displacement, to its thematics of torture, I suggest that Resnais does not so much echo physical mutilation – which he has shown more viscerally in his earlier films – as intimate the psychological effects of torture on its victim.

In *The Body in Pain*, Elaine Scarry looks in detail at torture, controversially crossing national and cultural boundaries to argue for common human experience of pain. She emphasises that 'intense pain is world-destroying' (Scarry 1985: 29). She continues: 'Intense pain is also language-destroying: as the content of one's world disintegrates, so the content of one's language disintegrates; as the self disintegrates, so that which would express and project the self is robbed of its source and its subject' (Scarry 1985: 35). In the process of this annihilation of world, language and self, space and its objects are radically reduced and transformed. Scarry specifies: 'the world is reduced to a single room or set of rooms' (Scarry 1985: 40). Further, the objects in this world are voided of their regular function, 'the objects themselves, and with them the fact of civilization, are annihilated: there is no wall, no window, no door, no bathtub, no refrigerator, no chair, no bed' (Scarry 1985: 41). As these familiar objects become part of the paraphernalia of torture, instruments inflicting savage pain, we witness what Scarry describes as 'a return to and mutilation of the domestic' (Scarry 1985: 45). These words seem prescient for *Muriel*. I do not suggest that Resnais reflects Muriel's experience in the frantic domestic scenarios of the film; rather I suggest he creates an effect of inflection and contamination. The domestic scenes in *Muriel* (which on a first viewing appear alarmingly implausible) draw their urgency and affect from their proximity within the film to the history of Muriel. In this sense, with respect to her story, as a muted reflection of its psychological effects, the scenes become more resonant. Indeed, returning to Ropars's point above about the lack of subjective images from Bernard's point of view, we might nevertheless say that the memories and remains he has brought with him to Boulogne of his experience in Algeria and of Muriel's experience, colour the seemingly unrelated domestic scenes in his home town.

Here again the film works through patterns of reflection and difference. Boulogne is itself already a disrupted and alienated town; Cayrol specifies that he chose it as such to be the setting of *Muriel*. Comparing *Muriel* to *Hiroshima mon amour*, Deleuze writes: 'il y a deux mémoires encore, chacune marquée par une guerre, Boulogne, l'Algérie' (Deleuze 1985: 154).[24] Benayoun also makes a comparison between the films, describing Boulogne as a 'ville reconstruite, à la fois ancienne et moderne, où le passé et l'avenir précaire se mêlent inextricablement, comme Nevers et Hiroshima dans un film précédent' (Benayoun 2002: 132).[25] As she arrives in Boulogne, Françoise says: 'Ça a l'air tout reconstruit; c'est à cause de la guerre?' (Cayrol 1963: 49). Alphonse replies: 'Une ville martyre' (Cayrol 1963: 49). Hélène continues: 'Oui, il y a eu beaucoup de morts, de fusillés... Je ne me souviens du nombre...' (Cayrol 1963: 49).[26] Resnais builds a

24 'there are two memories again, each marked by a war, Boulogne, Algeria'.
25 'a rebuilt town, ancient and modern at once, where the past and a precarious future are inextricably mingled, like Nevers and Hiroshima in a previous film'.
26 'Everything looks rebuilt; is it because of the war?'; 'A martyr town'; 'Yes, there were many dead, people shot... I can't remember how many...'.

collage of Boulogne showing rapid shots (each only a second on the screen) of the city's landmarks: a café, the station, the casino, parts of the old town. These images flash by like so many slides. Significantly Resnais cuts between night and day shots: a shot of the Casino at night, followed by a day-time image of the old town gateway, is reminiscent of the cross-cutting between night-time Hiroshima (reconstructed) and day-time Nevers (remembered) close to the end of *Hiroshima mon amour*. Resnais returns briefly to his earlier film to create a collage of Boulogne, now finding different, disjunctive images in a single setting. Again he uses a type of creative geography, responding to the town as location which bears its past, in ruins, and its present in rebuilt, anodyne spaces. (As Monaco says of the film: 'it situates its examination of the world of the mind in a geographical place which has its own concrete significance and which serves, in addition, as the locus for states of mind' (Monaco 1979: 74).) *Muriel*'s Boulogne may recall the editing of urban images in *Hiroshima mon amour*, but the later film is without the disturbing pleasure in Hiroshima as rebuilt oblivious space, manifested in Resnais's dazzling images of the city lights at night, water, façades and moving urban spaces. Boulogne is resolutely drab, though shown in colour. The town as 'ville-martyr' is barely tracked by Resnais's moving camera; instead the urban location is known through a kaleidoscopic series of images, often figuring the chance encounters which take place in the (small) town. This is a location of interwoven connections, of banal yet disrupted domesticity. It is represented in the figure of the 'maison qui glisse' ('slipping house') (Cayrol 1963: 102) which appears in an anecdote told by Hélène's sometime lover de Smoke. The building is built on the cliff, on uncertain foundations. As de Smoke says: 'Elle est neuve, elle est vide, et on attend qu'elle tombe' (Cayrol 1963: 102).[27]

Boulogne is the town to which Bernard returns, but it is also the town recalled by Hélène and Alphonse. They have spent nights here previously, at the Folkestone Hotel, now destroyed. They have had a love affair in 1939, but, apparently through a misunderstanding it dissolved. From Boulogne, Hélène summons Alphonse as a revenant, to attempt to recall her past. As Leperchey says, in *Muriel*: 'une mise en interaction constante anime les deux histoires, celle d'Hélène avec

---

27 'It is new, it is empty and we are waiting for it to fall down'.

Alphonse et celle de Muriel avec Bernard' (Leperchey 2003: 60).²⁸ Hélène admits to Alphonse that she has feared he was wounded in the war: 'J'avais tellement peur que vous ne soyez défiguré par la guerre, une blessure, je ne sais... Je vous voyais toujours dans mes rêves, la tête dans l'ombre. Comme si vous vouliez cacher votre visage' (Cayrol 1963: 63).²⁹ She fears finding in Alphonse's physical form the wound or trauma that Bernard appears to have suffered psychologically. Yet Alphonse as revenant is hopelessly banal; his stories of his past, his time in North Africa, are invented to screen the reality of his bankrupt restaurant in France, his desertion of his wife. Alphonse obfuscates at every step; Cayrol describes him improvising his existence. His manoeuvres involve lies and a willed removal from the past (measures which seem all the more insidious in the context of the more serious subjects the film treats). He says in conversation with Hélène: 'Nous n'allons pas revenir sur le passé' (Cayrol 1963: 67); she replies, with due logic: 'Mais vous êtes ici pour cela' (Cayrol 1963: 67).³⁰ Resnais and Cayrol question: 'Que veut Hélène? Que recherche-t-elle? Conquérir Alphonse? Boucler sa propre vie? Confronter ses souvenirs? Y faire naître un avenir ou s'en délivrer? Elle l'ignore elle-même, comme Alphonse ignore pourquoi il est venu' (Resnais and Cayrol 1963: 51).³¹

The authors and protagonists give away little sense of the motivations behind the plot. This uncertainty about motivation hovers behind the trivial puzzles, and minor irritants, of the film. Why does Alphonse bring his 'niece' with him on his trip to see Hélène? Why does Hélène invest so little in her role as hostess that she goes out to the casino, without Alphonse, each night? Both might be seen to deflect attention from the encounter between them, adopting indifference in their inter-relation (Alphonse will gradually begin to play the part of suitor to Hélène). We can try to make sense of their lack of

---

28 'constant interaction animates the two stories, the story of Hélène and Alphonse, and that of Muriel and Bernard'.
29 'I was so afraid that you would be disfigured by the war, a wound, I don't know... I always saw you in my dreams with your head in shadow. As if you wanted to hide your face'.
30 'We are not going to go back over the past'; 'But that's what you are here for'.
31 'What does Hélène want? What is she looking for? To win over Alphonse? To complete her own life? To confront her memories? To let a future emerge there or to free herself from it? She doesn't know herself, as Alphonse doesn't know why he has come'.

connections, but this does not remove the ways in which the actions in the film can seem at times baffling, and should perhaps remain unexplained to retain their true effect (a further example comes with the figure of the man Bernard meets on the cliff who asks him à propos of nothing whether he can find a sire for his goat (Cayrol 1963: 83)).

Where Alphonse might be seen to dissimulate, to hide his past, Hélène is all the more mystifying. Cayrol poses the question of Hélène in the following terms: 'Peut-on chercher refuge dans les grands moments privilégiés de sa propre existence? Voilà ce qu'elle peut se demander' (Cayrol 1963: 17).[32] Her encounter with Alphonse seems to destroy this refuge, to bring her in contact more properly with the passage of time. Indeed the film might be said to be concerned with the dangers of idealising and revivifying the past. Houston expresses this strongly as she says in a review of the film: 'The past is a kind of stimulus which sees us through the present; and is as fraught with danger as most stimulants' (Houston 1963–64: 34). The questions Hélène and Alphonse pose to one another go unanswered. He asks: 'Que suis-je encore pour vous?' (Cayrol 1963: 77); 'Pourquoi n'étiez-vous pas venue au rendez-vous au Globe d'Or?' (Cayrol 1963: 81). Hélène, more meditative, says: 'Je me demande ce que je fais de ma vie' (Cayrol 1963: 93) and finally: 'Alphonse, est-ce qu'on va en finir avec ce passé?' (Cayrol 1963: 119).[33]

A further disturbing effect of *Muriel* arises specifically from Resnais's return to the actress of *L'Année dernière à Marienbad*. Only two years separate the films, yet the seductive image of inscrutable femininity seems to have disappeared. We gain an inkling of Hélène's former attraction and playfulness; when Alphonse questions her about why she failed to come to their various rendez-vous, she replies: 'Je disparaissais pour vous devenir indispensable, c'était idiot' (Cayrol 1963: 77)[34] (words reminiscent of *Marienbad*). But Hélène's past with Alphonse is over twenty years distant (the summer of 1939 compared to 1962 Boulogne). Delphine Seyrig seems to cover these twenty years

---

32 'Can one seek refuge in the great heightened moments of one's own existence? This is what she might be asking herself'.

33 'What am I still for you?'; 'Why didn't you come to meet me at the Globe d'Or?'; 'I wonder what I am doing with my life'; 'Alphonse, are we going to finish with this past?'.

34 'I was vanishing to make myself indispensable to you, it was foolish'.

in the mere two which separate *Muriel* and *Marienbad*. In the later film she plays '[une] femme perdue, éperdue, facilement hagarde, cheveux gris, voix sourdement vibrante d'inquiétude' (Mettey 1978: 163).³⁵ Seyrig forsakes the glamour of *Marienbad*, and Chanel, for a more disturbed, if banal, role in *Muriel*. Hélène's clothes are ill-fitting and age her; her life seems entirely unkempt as she returns to the Casino to lose money each night, shamelessly borrowing from her friends. Seyrig's brilliant performance recalls at moments the phrasing and artifice of *Marienbad*, but here her words seem strained, stripped of seductive power. She moves stringently between moments of social pretence, glimpsed in Hélène's extraordinary professional façade, and moments when the hollowness and falsity of this role are evident. Resnais films Seyrig here frequently with her glance cast aside as she stares into space or beyond her interlocutor. A jolt is felt for the viewer who moves from A to Hélène; this filmic connection works to emphasise the extent of the latter character's disarray.

Hélène seems lost in the past; there is no catharsis, redemption or reconnection for her in her resurrected relation to Alphonse. At the very end of the film, she arrives at the old station in Boulogne, asking about the train to Paris. The station employee, to whom Hélène has spoken at the start of the film as she comes to meet Alphonse, says now, 'il ne s'arrête plus ici maintenant. On le prend à la nouvelle gare, ça change' (Cayrol 1963: 138).³⁶ With a dizzying sense of the escalation of time we see that this has changed in the mere two weeks of the film's diegesis. Hélène attempts to return to the same place, only to find it missing. This reflects on her failed attempt to re-find Alphonse and the failure of return in the film altogether.

Yet there is one further way in which the film appears, as it were, to come full circle. This is in the connection between Hélène and Bernard which necessarily links the two parts of the narrative, the story of Muriel and the (failed) love story between Hélène and Alphonse. Hélène is Bernard's stepmother, not his real mother. Bernard has come into Hélène's life in catastrophic manner, during the war; it is a bombing which catalyses Hélène's mariage to Aughain, Bernard's father. She explains to Alphonse: 'La pluie tombait du toit sur le petit lit de Bernard, encore épouvanté. Aughain m'a regardée: je

---

35 '[a] lost woman, distraught, easily pushed over the edge, with grey hair and a voice quivering with muted anxiety'.

36 'it doesn't stop here now. You take it at the new station, things change'.

les ai emmenés tous les deux chez moi... Bernard ne voulait plus me quitter' (Cayrol 1963: 78–9).[37] This scene is revisited between Hélène and Bernard at the end of the film as she rushes to his atelier, fearful that he has committed suicide. Bernard says to Hélène: 'Tu te souviens du plafond crevé...? La neige tombait sur mon lit' (Cayrol 1963: 137). She replies, correcting his memory: 'Non, c'était la pluie... Tu avais les cheveux tout blancs à cause du plâtre' (Cayrol 1963: 137).[38] This scene might show the vicissitudes of memory, sensory impressions misplaced as one character corrects and aligns the memory of another. We see Bernard and Hélène here, echoing Deleuze, creating a memory for two. Yet this scene is telling in other ways too. We see the trauma behind Bernard's (filial) love for Hélène. This has brought her into his life, and he has clung to her. This is central to their relationship in Boulogne, the 'ville-martyr' of which they are proper citizens. Perhaps this trauma, Boulogne, also subtends Bernard's response to Algeria. We learn nothing in the film of Bernard's mother, victim we may guess of the bombing he survives. Perhaps Muriel also screens, and reveals, the body of this missing mother, whose absence is likewise denied by the presence of Hélène.

Muriel is by no means complacent, or confident of the possibility of testimonial or political filmmaking; the torture may only be registered indirectly. Critical of the film, Tomlinson argues that history becomes '"traumatized", compulsively acted out, but not "worked through"' (Tomlinson 2002: 55); Resnais 'fixat[es] on a break-down of language which precludes informed exchange with either the past or the racial "other"' (Tomlinson 2002: 67). In its colliding fragments of narrative, the film is doubtful about memory and representation of the past: any literal trace of the torture scene is destroyed; Bernard's investment as witness to Muriel's torture may be erotic or painfully narcissistic. In the narrative with which this history intersects, Hélène appears through the course of the film gradually to lose the relic from her past she has retained, her love for Alphonse, in her attempt to relive something of its passion. Memories of the past are shown again to be ever distorted through subjective recall, to be

37 'The rain was falling through the roof onto the little bed where Bernard lay terrified. Aughain looked at me: I took them both home with me... Bernard no longer wanted to leave me'.

38 'You remember the hole in the ceiling...? Snow was falling on my bed'; 'No, it was rain... Your hair was all white because of the plaster'.

intransigent, resistant. Bernard leaves at the end of the film, further reiterating the film's warnings against return and repetition: 'Tu sais, je vais m'en aller. Je te dis au revoir. Je ne pense pas que je pourrai revenir' (Cayrol 1963: 137).[39] The film ends in desolation, in an empty search and blind movement onwards. This again may be read as an inflection of its subject. *Muriel* shows, through Bernard's failures, that it can never reach or trace the pain at its centre. Hence the film's pessimism, its erosion of sensuality at every turn, its refusal of release or reprieve.

Resnais will not return to the horror of *Muriel*, though violence and memory distortions still haunt his work; his next film, better liked by the public, was *La Guerre est finie*.

References

L'Arc: Alain Resnais, 31 (1961).
Bailblé, Claude, Michel Marie, Marie-Claire Ropars (1974) *Muriel* (Paris: Editions Galilée).
Benayoun, Robert (2002) 'Muriel, ou les rendez-vous manqués', in Stéphane Goudet (ed.), Positif, *revue de cinéma: Alain Resnais* (Paris: Gallimard [Folio]), pp. 130–6.
Bersani, Leo and Ulysse Dutoit (1993) *Arts of Impoverishment: Beckett, Rothko, Resnais* (Cambridge MA: Harvard University Press).
Britton, Celia (1990) 'Broken Images in Resnais's *Muriel*', *French Cultural Studies*, 1:1, pp. 37–46.
Cayrol, Jean (1963) *Muriel* (Paris: Seuil).
Deleuze, Gilles (1985) *Cinéma 2: L'Image-temps* (Paris: Minuit).
Duras, Marguerite (1960) *Hiroshima mon amour* (Paris: Gallimard [Folio]).
Greene, Naomi (1999) *Landscapes of Loss: The National Past in Postwar French Cinema* (Princeton NJ: Princeton University Press).
Houston, Penelope (1963–64) 'Resnais's *Muriel*', *Sight and Sound*, 33:1 (winter), pp. 34–6.
Kast, Pierre (*et al.*) (1963) 'Les Malheurs de *Muriel*', *Cahiers du cinéma*, 149 (November), pp. 20–34.
Kreidl, John Francis (1977) *Alain Resnais* (Boston MA: Twayne Publishers).
Leperchey, Sarah (2000) *Alain Resnais: Une lecture topologique* (Paris: L'Harmattan).
Leutrat, Jean-Louis (1994) *Hiroshima mon amour* (Paris: Nathan).

---

39 'You know, I'm going to go. I'll say goodbye. I don't think I'll be able to come back'.

Mettey, Marcel (*et al.*) (1978) '*Muriel*', *Image et Son*, 331 bis (hors série) (September), pp. 159–68.

Milne, Tom (1963) 'Venice', *Sight and Sound*, 32:4 (autumn), pp. 177–8.

Milne, Tom (1964) '*Muriel ou le temps d'un retour*', *Monthly Film Bulletin*, 31:364 (May), pp. 70–1.

Monaco, James (1979) *Alain Resnais* (New York: Oxford University Press).

O'Brien, Alyssa J. (2000) 'Manipulating Visual Pleasure in *Muriel*', *Quarterly Review of Film and Video*, 17:1 (March), pp. 49–61.

Resnais, Alain and Jean Cayrol (1963) '*Muriel ou le temps d'un retour*', *L'Avant-scène du cinéma*, 30 (October), pp. 51–5.

Ropars-Wuilleumier, Marie-Claire (1990) 'How History Begets Meaning: Alain Resnais's *Hiroshima mon amour*', in Susan Hayward and Ginette Vincendeau (eds), *French Film: Texts and Contexts* (London and New York: Routledge), pp. 173–85.

Scarry, Elaine (1985) *The Body in Pain* (New York: Oxford University Press).

Sontag, Susan (1963–64) '*Muriel ou le temps d'un retour*', *Film Quarterly*, 17:2 (winter), pp. 23–7.

Tomlinson, Emily (2002) *Torture, fiction, and the repetition of horror: ghost-writing the past in Algeria and Argentina* (PhD dissertation, University of Cambridge).

5

La Guerre est finie (1966), *Je t'aime je t'aime* (1968), *Stavisky* (1974)

Between 1964 and 1976 Resnais made three films: *La Guerre est finie*, *Je t'aime je t'aime* and *Stavisky*; he also contributed a section to Chris Marker's collaborative *Loin du Viêt-nam* (1967) and worked on a number of projects which did not come to fruition (Gilbert Adair speaks of 'a rare phantom filmography' (Adair 1977: 120)). The three major films completed differ from each other fairly widely in form and content, and each film seems to be an investigation of one of the various directions Resnais's cinema might take. The non-completed projects – most famously an adaptation of a popular series *Les Aventures de Harry Dickson*, but also projects about the Marquis de Sade and H.P. Lovecraft, and a film of B movie clichés, *The Monster Maker* – are likewise (virtual) experimentations of this kind (see Monaco 1979: 145–66).

Critics have remarked on the change in Resnais's films from *La Guerre est finie* onwards. Tom Milne writes in *Sight and Sound*: 'with *La Guerre est finie* ..., it is as though some timid night creature had finally emerged from its lair, still a little wary perhaps, but ready to be recognised as an ordinary mortal, amused, tender and capricious, rather than the remote intellectual paragon born of Duras, Robbe-Grillet and ... Cayrol' (Milne 1966: 196). Yet *Je t'aime je t'aime*, not a critical success at the time of its release and a highly demanding film, again undoes this new image of Resnais. After faltering years at the end of the 1960s and the start of the 1970s, reeling as it were from the (non-)reception of *Je t'aime je t'aime* – Monaco conjures an image of Resnais in New York, impoverished, trying to develop film projects, eating cheap food in China Town – he would go on to make *Stavisky*, a film which again confounded critics but found popular success.

Linking *La Guerre est finie* and *Stavisky* is the work of screenwriter and novelist Jorge Semprun, who, after working on the first film with Resnais and going on to work with Costa Gavras, returned to Resnais. Semprun has spoken of his pleasure in working with Resnais: 'c'est une expérience d'une telle rigueur, d'une telle richesse que ce doit être, sans doute, difficile ensuite de s'adapter à quelqu'un d'autre' (Pays 2002: 188).[1]

La Guerre est finie (1966)

Jorge Semprun published his first novel, *Le Grand Voyage*, in 1963. Semprun, Spanish by birth, joined the Spanish communist party at the age of 18 in 1942. The following year he was arrested by the Gestapo and sent to the camp at Buchenwald where he remained until 1945. He continued his communist work after the war in exile in France, working with the resistance against Franco's regime in Spain. *Le Grand Voyage* is a testimony to his experience of deportation. A stringent and innovative work, it disrupts chronological sequence in its narrative in a manner very likely to appeal to Resnais. While the main trajectory of the narrative relates to the journey of the title, the protagonist's agonising time in a railway wagon on the way to the camp, this is cross-cut by sparse reflections on the camp itself and more numerous detailings of the return to freedom. This structure allows the camps to exist nowhere and everywhere within the narrative – the horror of the camp is conveyed in anticipation and in retrospect but left all but a fissure or absence within the story itself. Semprun signals his interest in exploring mental states, the conjuring of a future and the tentative escape from reality in dream and imagination. His work is grounded in political terms, his hero pragmatic and a realist. Yet as novelist Semprun is concerned with the ways in which subjective perceptions layer and deepen a relation to external reality.

Having read *Le Grand Voyage*, Resnais approached Semprun in 1964 and suggested that they work on a film together. Semprun recounts: 'Au départ, on s'était dit avec Alain qu'on ne parlerait pas de

[1] 'it is an experience of such rigour, and such richness, that it certainly must be difficult to adapt yourself afterwards to someone else'.

l'Espagne. Mais l'idée première, le pourquoi de l'entreprise, qu'Alain m'a soumise, c'était de faire un film politique' (Pays 2002: 190).² Nevertheless Spain becomes the subject of *La Guerre est finie*. Resnais had already engaged with the Spanish Civil War in *Guernica*. By the 1960s, the question of Spain, and political opposition to Franco's regime, had a long heritage. Part of the narrative of *La Guerre est finie* concerns the identity and questioning of a Spanish revolutionary (Diego) who wonders about his present tactics. Despite the title, *La Guerre est finie*, the film questions rather whether the war might ever be over. In choosing this title, Resnais and Semprun are citing *Le Grand Voyage* where the protagonist uses the phrase: 'maintenant que la guerre est finie' ('now the war is over') (Semprun 1963: 92). The film pursues this conjecture (indeed, for Semprun 'd'une certaine façon, Diego pourrait être le personnage du *Grand Voyage* vingt ans après' (Pays 2002: 194)).³

Resnais and Semprun worked on *La Guerre est finie* between January and April 1965. The film is set at Easter 1965, from 18 to 20 April. It was the first French/Swedish co-production, with Swedish actress Ingrid Thulin (who worked with Ingmar Bergman) playing Diego's partner Marianne. The exteriors were shot in France, while the interiors were shot in a studio in Stockholm. The film, like various of Resnais's early works, would cause some international disquiet. Penelope Houston recounts the fate of the film at Cannes: 'As so often, the film everyone most wanted to see was the film the Festival had rejected. Resnais's *La Guerre est finie* couldn't be shown officially for fear of offending the Spanish Government' (Houston 1966: 125). Nevertheless, *hors festival*, the film would win a clutch of prizes, including the Prix Louis Delluc in January 1967. In interview Resnais is stoical about Cannes and positive about the film's politics: 'Mais j'ai l'impression que la sortie du film et son retrait de la compétition à Cannes confirment son contenu et lui donnent d'ailleurs un retentissement dont il n'aurait sans doute pas bénéficié autrement'

---

2 'At the start, Alain and I said that we would not talk about Spain. But the first idea, the question behind the project, as Alain presented it to me, was to make a political film'.

3 'in some ways, Diego could be the character from *Le Grand Voyage* twenty years on'.

(Benayoun, Ciment and Pays 2002: 167–8).⁴ The film immediately received critical accolades. For Jean de Baroncelli, writing in *Le Monde*: '*La Guerre est finie* est un film d'une dignité parfaite, d'une hauteur et d'une noblesse de sentiment absolument irréprochables. Ce n'est ni un pamphlet ni un réquisitoire, mais une pure tragédie' (cited in Mettey 1970: 57).⁵ For Marie-Claire Wuilleumier, writing in *Esprit*, *La Guerre est finie* is 'sans doute le film le plus communicable de Resnais, et, par là même, le plus accompli' (cited in Mettey 1970: 61).⁶

Although *La Guerre est finie* began as a political project, Resnais is equivocal about whether the film is itself properly *engagé*. Semprun explains this qualm away: 'Pour moi, évidemment, c'est un film "engagé", mais il [Resnais] a une notion très exigeante de l'engagement et il y a la modestie de son attitude' (Pays 2002: 203).⁷ Rather than offer lessons in militancy, Resnais offers insight into the doubts, hesitation and commitment of an individual. Showing us the work of a committed communist, as it is lived, dreamed and imagined, arguably carries responsibilities. In a film which is concerned with the imagining and anticipation of reality, it seems all the more important that facts and historical data are verifiable. Resnais insists on the veracity of the film's historical and political moment. Accused of inventing the call for a general strike in Spain for the purposes of the film, Resnais insists: 'Le journal qui appelait à la grève générale est authentique, c'est lui que j'ai filmé' (Mettey 1970: 59).⁸ It is from this basis in data and documentation that the film can depart into the subjective reality of its protagonist, Diego.

Diego is played by Yves Montand (Resnais has been criticised for not choosing a Spanish actor). For Benayoun, Diego is Resnais's

4 'But it is my impression that the release of the film and its withdrawal from competition at Cannes confirm its content and also give it an effect which it doubtless would not have benefited from otherwise'.
5 '*La Guerre est finie* is a film film of perfect dignity, of an absolutely impeccable loftiness and nobility of sentiment. It is neither a tract nor an indictment, but a pure tragedy'.
6 'without a doubt Resnais's most communicative film and, as such, the most accomplished'.
7 'For me, of course, it is a "committed" film, but he [Resnais] has a very demanding notion of commitment and he is being modest as well'.
8 'The newspaper with its call for a general strike is authentic, it is the one that I filmed'.

most positive character; he is like Bernard but more mature (Benayoun 1980: 131). For Prédal, however, all Resnais's heroes are eaten up by anxiety (Prédal 1996: 115), and Diego is no exception. But Diego works to convert his anxiety into activity, adopting the role of revolutionary and various disguises (he is known under the names Diego, Carlos, Domingo, Francisco, Rafael, 'René Sallanches' and, at the end, 'Gabriel Chauvin'). The film opens as Diego returns to France from a clandestine trip to Spain, on a borrowed passport. Diego is stopped at the border and asked his telephone number in Paris; the number is then called. The phone is answered by Nadine Sallanches, daughter of the man who has loaned Diego his passport. Nadine plays along and speaks to Diego as if he were her father. He tells her he will come round that evening. Diego successfully enters France. He has come to warn Juan, a fellow member of the communist group, that he is in danger in Spain. But Juan has already left for Barcelona. Diego reports to the group on the situation in Madrid and on recent arrests. Another member of the group, Ramon, is to go to Barcelona to contact Juan; Ramon dies suddenly, however, and Diego takes his place, travelling back to Spain at the end of the film. It is clear that the police are searching for him. In the few days' interlude in Paris, he meets Nadine and observes her activist friends; he also rejoins his partner Marianne, who will herself apparently leave for Spain, by a different route, at the end of the film.

Diego is the consciousness of the film, yet in certain voice-over passages he is addressed as 'tu'. For Mettey, this use of the second person allows a certain distancing and objectivity. Perhaps too it suggests how far Diego is a self-conscious actor, observing himself and the role he is playing. He views himself from outside as another; he observes himself acting and consciously plans his future. *La Guerre est finie* is distinctive indeed in its use of flashforwards, revealing in particular Diego's anticipation of events before they take place. Certain moments of the future imagined relate to events which will later take place in the film. There is always some difference between anticipation and actuality, nevertheless Resnais has said: 'Il m'intéresse, quand on voit les scènes, qu'elles correspondent à une sensation de "déjà-vu", qu'elles soient un peu annoncées. Je crois que tous les personnages du film sont présentés une fois en imaginaire avant de l'être en réel' (Benayoun, Ciment and Pays

2002: 181).[9] Appropriately the visual style of the virtual and actual scenes is continuous; at certain points the viewer may be uncertain about what is 'imagined' and what is 'real'.

Haim Callev looks closely at the mental images in the film, examining for example images close to the start where Diego in the car, about to cross the border, imagines his immediate future. Callev comments on how disconcerting these shots are for the viewer so early in the film, yet proceeds to familiarise us with them as he breaks them down in his reading. In studying the stream of consciousness in Resnais's films and offering a structural analysis of the ways in which this is conveyed, Callev leaves no space for hesitation or indeterminacy. Whether or not we are supposed to try to determine the status of each shot viewed in *La Guerre est finie*, uncertainty, in spectatorial response, may be valued as it reflects some of the thematic and emotional effects of the film. Demeure writes in *Positif*: 'Mais ce qui fait alors l'extrême valeur de *La Guerre est finie*, c'est que ces incertitudes procèdent non plus seulement d'une méthode traduisant des préoccupations personnelles à l'auteur, mais de la réalité même qu'il a choisi de dépeindre' (Demeure 2002: 159).[10] The uncertainty of the political situation is rendered indirectly through spectatorial uncertainty. For John Ward, 'Diego lives in a maze of illusions out of which he is trying to thread his way to some kind of reality' (Ward 1968: 89). For Milne, '*La Guerre est finie* drives straight forward, altogether harder and more sharply cut' than Resnais's earlier films, yet 'with Diego's premonitory flashes – a train missed, an arrest, a death – lending an urgent edge of fear' (Milne 1966: 196). He comments in particular on the effect of imagined shots of Ramon's funeral close to the end of the film: 'Imagining Ramon's funeral in Paris, Diego receives an intimation of his own death (flash shot of a cemetery standing dreamlike on the edge of the sea)' (Milne 1966: 196). As Milne indicates, the shots acquire a poetic and premonitory quality; imagining the future, Diego also exposes to us his fears (and his desires), perpetual shadows of the future.

9 'It interests me when one sees the scenes that they correspond to a feeling of "déjà-vu", that they are anticipated. I think all the characters in the film are presented once as imaginary figures before they appear in reality'.
10 'But then what makes the greatest strength of *La Guerre est finie* is that these uncertainties no longer only result from a methodology which translates the author's personal preoccupations, but from the very reality he has chosen to depict'.

Houston comments that Resnais is not concerned with memory in *La Guerre est finie*, 'rather he is concerned with chance and fatality – the other side of the Resnais coin, the Hitchcock side, which sees a story not in terms of what happened, but of what might happen' (Houston 1966: 125). In this sense, Resnais opens up the possibility of numerous choices, destinies which move off in different directions. On his return to Paris, for example, Diego goes to look for a woman in an HLM outside the city. When she is not at the address he visits, he says simply (echoing *L'Année dernière à Marienbad*): 'c'était peut-être ailleurs'.[11] Just as in the reality of Paris there are numerous estates which resemble each other – with the anonymous modern architecture which interests Resnais in *Hiroshima mon amour* or *Muriel* – so there is the sense that Diego's life has numerous possible paths, trajectories, constructions.

Two paths that Resnais maps out more clearly form part of Diego's affective life. Resnais recounts in interview:

> Un critique anglais a fait quatre lignes sur le film, et il disait: '*La Guerre est finie* a été fait pour prouver que, si on est un révolutionnaire espagnol, on fait l'amour avec beaucoup plus de lyrisme que les autres', etc. Cela m'a fait rire sur le moment, mais, dans le fond, il est vrai que, dans la situation de danger permanent, dans l'appréhension d'être arrêté et jeté en prison d'un moment à l'autre, il y a aussi quelque chose d'exaltant dans les difficultés soudaines de l'amour' (Benayoun, Ciment and Pays 2002: 181).[12]

Implicitly he aligns *La Guerre est finie* with the resurgent eroticism, in the face of risk and death, of *Hiroshima mon amour*. On the evening of his return to Paris, Diego visits and makes love with Nadine Sallanches and then later goes home to his partner Marianne, in turn to perform again and make love with her. His amorous encounters take up a good part of the centre of the film. For Kreidl, *La Guerre est finie* is 'one of the first films made about sexual politics' (Kreidl 1977: 144). For Mettey, the film testifies to Diego's virility. Another reading

---

11 'it was elsewhere perhaps'.
12 'An English critic wrote a few lines about the film and said "*La Guerre est finie* was made to prove that, if one is a Spanish revolutionary, one makes love with more lyricism than others" etc. It made me laugh at the time, but, really, it is true that in a situation of permanent danger, fearing being arrested and thrown into prison at any moment, there is also something exhilarating in the unexpected troubles in love'.

might see Diego as a more Stendhalian hero, undecided between two women, one more youthful and impetuous, one more maternal and serene. Nadine and Marianne are even perhaps two alternatives, two virtual lovers between whom Diego, in his imaginings, fails to choose.

It is with respect to Nadine that *La Guerre est finie* offers its clearest example of a flashforward or anticipatory set of shots (for Callev, the sequence is 'a riveting cinematic experience, disclosing the euphoria inspired by the grace of attractive young women in Diego's consciousness' (Callev 1997: 50)). Before he meets her, Diego imagines Nadine and we see a series of momentary shots of different young women, anonymous at first, seen from behind, but becoming clearer and more identifiable as Diego's fantasies take hold. These images of young women are anchored as variations on Nadine. Intercut with the sequence we see imagined anchoring shots of the road sign for the 'rue de l'estrapade' ('strappado' street, 'strappado' referring to torture by hoisting to a height and letting fall to the length of the rope) and the house number '7'. The rhythm and motion of the images – the young women are always moving – are reminiscent of the fleeting imagined shots of Delphine Seyrig in *L'Année dernière à Marienbad*. The viewer is party to Diego's (erotic) anticipation, his anxiety and desire as he conjures virtual images of Nadine which are quickly displaced in the film by the seemingly actual presence of Geneviève Bujold, playing the young woman.

Resnais creates a seductive image of Bujold, with her long dark hair and large eyes. In different ways she resembles both Nita Klein in *Muriel* and Sabine Azéma in *La Vie est un roman*. Nadine is also attractive because she has saved Diego at the frontier. Her pretence that she is his daughter offers a fantasy of paternal/filial love through which their desire exists. Nadine kisses Diego, initiating a series of increasingly poetic and unrealistic shots. Resnais repeats images of touch and tactile contact, familiar from *Hiroshima mon amour*, as we see hands on skin and Diego's sensory attention to Nadine. As we see the opening of her legs, the overexposed shots are bleached to white. For a critic in *Monthly Film Bulletin*, 'Resnais depicts their love as a dream, their bodies bleached white like some vision of the sublime' (D.W. 1966: 164).

If the love with Nadine is depicted as a dream, love with Marianne is not by contrast a reality; instead it seems a variation on the first encounter, another way of living and filming an erotic attachment.

Marianne, played by Ingrid Thulin, blonde in contrast to Bujold, is nearer to Diego in age. She is working on a book project of images of the city (allowing shots of her apartment covered in photographs). Resnais admits that he has been criticised for not making Marianne herself a political activist (Benayoun, Ciment and Pays 2002: 182). Diego and Marianne make love on his return to Paris. We see small erotic details: Marianne undoes her hair and is seen naked. Diego and the camera close in and caress her skin; he kisses her feet and we see a close-up shot of her face and pleasure. The mood of the scene is less ecstatic than the over-exposed love-making with Nadine, but it is no less tender.

The deepest feelings in the film come at its close, again in shots of Diego and Marianne. The shots depict departure, and not love-making. We see Diego in a car and a close-up on his face (a similar close-up has been used at the start of the film to indicate the transition from actual to virtual images). In a dissolve we see an image of Marianne, reminiscent of *Marienbad*, moving forwards towards us, towards Diego. Although readings of the film have not put Marianne's actuality in doubt, the editing suggests that the image of Marianne we see here might be Diego's imagining of the future, or indeed an actualisation of his desire. Images of fantasy and of the future have been in the film in part associated with women dreamed or imagined. Marianne here, moving towards Spain to take her place at Diego's side, might be another figment of his imagination. Such a reading might thread doubt into the apprehension of harmony most have found at the end of *La Guerre est finie*.

Diego is a sensitive lover, or at least imagines himself as such, yet the sexual images of the film perpetuate a dynamic of desire where the man seems active and in control. This is reflected in the very circulation between women in the film. But if the film's treatment of desire, in the two love-making scenes and in the image of merger at the close, is struck with uncertainty – if these are fantasies of Nadine and Marianne – we find *La Guerre est finie* disrupting and disquieting its ageing revolutionary, its subject of action and desire. Uncertainty thus opens more effectively the readings and meanings of even this, purportedly Resnais's most accessible, straightforward film.

Loin du Viêt-nam (1967) and *Je t'aime je t'aime* (1968)

In his short piece for Chris Marker's cinematic essay, *Loin du Viêtnam*, Resnais invents a character, Claude Ridder, who will reappear, played by a different actor, in his next film, *Je t'aime je t'aime*. The first Ridder is played by Bernard Fresson (who took the part of the German soldier in *Hiroshima mon amour*). Jacques Sternberg, who wrote the screenplay for *Je t'aime je t'aime*, describes Ridder's part in the earlier film, saying that he wanders around his apartment, voicing ideas in any order to a bemused, immobile young woman (Sternberg 2002: 123). Monaco sees Ridder in direct contrast to Diego in *La Guerre est finie* (Monaco 1979: 116). Rather than offering another film about the uncertainties of political action, Resnais returns to Duras's point about the impossibility of making a film about Hiroshima. For Monaco, 'the film [*Loin du Viêt-nam*] is mainly about the impossibility of making a film about Vietnam from and in France' (Monaco 1979: 116). For Prédal, Resnais's segment contains an implicit criticism of the project as a whole (Prédal 1996: 113). In *Je t'aime je t'aime* Resnais retains the figure of the confounded young man, but is less political in his aim. As Suzanne Liandrat-Guigues writes, the second Ridder, played by Claude Rich, is as indecisive, but less loquacious (Liandrat-Guigues 2002: 218).

Je t'aime je t'aime has been the least successful of Resnais's films commercially (Monaco 1979: 121) (for Prédal it is a testing and stifling film (Prédal 1996: 175), for Kreidl it is told 'lethargically' (Kreidl 1977: 155)). Resnais collaborated with Jacques Sternberg, a writer of science fiction, whom he met at a mutual friend's house. Sternberg's script sometimes creates a self-conscious 'Resnais' film where Ridder is asked, for example, 'Où étiez-vous l'année dernière à cette époque?'[13] (*L'Avant-scène* 1969: 18), Ridder is even seen phoning the talking clock. The film was shot in and around Brussels in the autumn of 1967 and was shown in Paris at the end of April 1968. Timing was unfortunate due to the imminent events of May '68. The film was not shown at the Cannes festival, itself shortened in solidarity with the striking students and workers. In any case, as Suzanne Liandrat-Guigues writes: 'En 1968, l'heure n'était pas à ce type d'interrogation'[14]

---

13 'Where were you last year at this time?'.

14 'In 1968, it was not the right time for this type of interrogation'.

(Liandrat-Guigues 2002: 215). In 2002, however, the reissued film was shown at the Cannes film festival; a large dinner was held in Resnais's honour and articles paying tribute to the film appeared in *Positif*. The film was still playing in Paris cinemas in 2003.

In *Je t'aime je t'aime* Resnais and Sternberg offer an analysis of memory and destiny, in the guise of a science fiction film. Claude Ridder has made a suicide attempt. The film opens in the clinic as he is recovering from the physical after-effects. As he leaves the clinic he meets several scientists from the Crespel laboratories, who ask him to take part in an experiment. They explain that he has been chosen at random; yet Ridder's survival of suicide makes him the ideal subject (as one of the scientists says: 'Il est rare de voir quelqu'un revenir d'aussi loin. C'est précisément ce que nous cherchons' (*L'Avant-scène* 1969: 13)).[15] They explain, too, the nature of their experiments, saying that they are studying time. Ridder is compliant and agrees to enter their surreal time machine, where only mice have travelled previously. They prepare for him to be cast back one year, exactly, to 4 o'clock on 5 September 1966, to relive a minute of his past. The machine, or Ridder himself, malfunctions, however, and Ridder becomes caught as moments from his past proliferate. He is missing in the past; when he does return to the machine his reappearances are so brief that he cannot be rescued or extracted by the scientists. This infernal, fractured return to his past is only terminated when he re-encounters the moment of his own suicide. He is released from memory only to die on the lawn, outside the laboratory.

One of the difficulties for the viewer is that the returning memory scenes come seemingly at random and with, initially, no apparent narrative, psychological ordering or motivation. Resnais has claimed to be influenced by the automatic writing of the Surrealists; in his investigation of consciousness he might be aligned with Woolf or Joyce. Deleuze considers the film in the context of his work on the time-image, writing: '*Je t'aime je t'aime* malgré l'appareil de sciencefiction, c'est la figure du temps la plus simple, parce que la mémoire y concerne un seul personnage' (Deleuze 1985: 153).[16] Yet *Je t'aime je t'aime* confronts us with the mind of the other as alien. It is only with

---

15 'It is rare to see someone come back from so far. It is precisely what we are looking for'.
16 '*Je t'aime je t'aime* despite the science fiction device is the simplest figure of time, since in it memory is that of a single person'.

patience, as the film proceeds, that we come to know some complicity and intimacy with Claude. To view the film we have to accept all that we do not know on a first viewing; we gradually build our sense of Claude's past from the disordered fragments which return. The difficulty of the film comes almost exclusively, indeed, from its editing and deliberate disorder. Visually the film is far less textured and experimental than some of Resnais's earlier works. It has only 334 shots. Each scene, or moment from the past, is shot in a single take, usually with Ridder in frame (Cieutat 2002: 119). Jebb notes: 'There is not a mix or a dissolve in the whole picture and only rarely does the camera move within a shot' (Jebb 1971: 162). Callev reports that Resnais also edited a chronological version of the material, without the time-travel narrative (Callev 1997: 184).

On making *L'Année dernière à Marienbad*, Resnais commented: 'Quand on arrive près du *Phoque* de Brancusi, on peut l'aborder par n'importe quel côté ... De même, je rêvais d'un film dont on ne saurait laquelle est la première bobine' (Bounoure 1974: 103).[17] More than in *Marienbad* it is in *Je t'aime je t'aime* that he might be seen to have realised this aim as the returns to the past, and Claude's returns to the present, seem deliberately without order. This randomness, or serendipity, is further enhanced in Sternberg's vision: 'L'idéal pour moi aurait été de faire un film élastique, qui aurait duré douze ou vingt-quatre heures. Les gens seraient entrés et sortis quand ils voulaient, ça n'avait pas d'importance puisque l'histoire pouvait être prise par n'importe quel bout' (*L'Arc* 1961: 28).[18] What we see in the film is only a small part of a man's stock of memories, and indeed of the potential film Sternberg would have us imagine. Resnais and Sternberg seek to defy narrative ordering and by this token to suggest that Ridder's memories themselves come unbidden. Yet the film does not merely provide this sense of randomness, it offers at least two explanatory frameworks within which we can make sense of the memory disorder. The first relates to trauma, the second to death.

17 'When one gets close to Brancusi's *Seal*, one can approach it from any side .... Likewise, I was dreaming of a film where one would not know which is the first reel'.
18 'For me the ideal would have been to make an elastic film, which would have lasted twelve or twenty-four hours. People would have come in and gone out when they wanted to without it mattering because the story could be started wherever'.

Inevitably the viewer will be interested in the content of Ridder's memories. His first return is to a seaside scene where he is on holiday with his girlfriend Catrine. This scene offers submarine images, allowing Resnais, like Woolf, to suggest some sense of memory and consciousness as fluid, as expressed through marine depths. Catrine asks Ridder what he has seen underwater and he replies: 'Deux serpents de mer, quelques requins, des méduses géantes'[19] (*L'Avant-scène* 1969: 21). (Resnais here anticipates the marine images he will use in *On connaît la chanson*). In the faltering of the time machine, *Je t'aime je t'aime* also returns later to this same scene and we find Catrine's question, and Ridder's reply, repeated several times over. For Deleuze, aquatic imagery, imagery of the swamp, is significant and linked to Catrine as a figure of maternity or eternal femininity: 'Toutes sortes de régions sont ainsi brassées dans la mémoire d'un homme qui saute de l'une à l'autre, et semblent émerger tour à tour d'un marécage originel, universel clapotement incarné par la nature éternelle de Catrine' (Deleuze 1985: 153–4).[20]

Catrine seems the cradle of Ridder's memory as he returns to this seaside. For Resnais, 'c'est un tamis, la mémoire – et il s'agit de savoir pourquoi certaines choses passent à travers le tamis et pas certaines autres' (*L'Avant-scène* 1969: 11).[21] As we pass through the film we gradually learn more about the return of Ridder's consciousness to Catrine. She has represented that figure of unknown female beauty that is familiar in Resnais's films; for Thirard, '*Je t'aime je t'aime*, c'est, comme son titre l'indique, une toute simple histoire d'amour, de celles mille fois racontées' (Thirard 2002: 213).[22] Catrine is the film's lost object of desire, but Ridder also has interest in other women, including a fantasy figure who appears in his bathroom, wishing to be bathed by him. As menace underlies desire in *Marienbad*, we find in *Je t'aime je t'aime*, as Resnais suggests: 'le thème que l'on tue toujours ceux qu'on aime – même si on ne les tue pas physiquement' (*L'Avant-*

---

19 'Two sea snakes, some sharks and giant jellyfish'.
20 'All sorts of regions, stirred up like this in the memory of a man who moves from one to the other, seem to emerge in turn from the original swamp, a universal lapping of the waves embodied in the eternal nature of Catrine'.
21 'memory is a sieve – and it's a question of knowing why certain things pass through this sieve and not others'.
22 '*Je t'aime je t'aime* is, as its title indicates, a very simple love story, one of those told thousands of times'.

scène 1969: 11).²³ For Strick, 'Catrine ... represents both the impulse and the interruption for the flow of his existence' (Strick 1971: 165). In a scene with his female friend Wiana, Ridder accuses himself of Catrine's murder: 'J'ai tué Catrine à Glasgow, il y a deux mois. En janvier, j'étais parti à l'improviste avec Catrine et je suis revenu seul' (*L'Avant-scène* 1969: 28).²⁴ When Wiana finds this impossible to believe, he replies: 'Tu as raison, je suis incapable de tuer qui que ce soit ... mais tu as tort, je l'ai pourtant fait' (*L'Avant-scène* 1969: 28).²⁵ We learn, in scenes intercalated through the film, that Catrine has died asphyxiated in their hotel bedroom in Glasgow. Ridder recounts variations on the scene: perhaps he noticed that the fire had gone out before he left the room for the evening; perhaps the fire only went out after he had left Catrine peacefully sleeping; perhaps Catrine herself was suicidal. Uncertainty about events remains in the film, although Ridder's own suicide is unequivocal (if not immediately effective). As with *La Guerre est finie*, we might relinquish trying to determine the 'truth' of the events, but find interest instead observing Ridder hesitating between explanatory narratives and moments of self-inculpation. Immediately before his confession to Wiana, we learn in the screenplay that Ridder is in the state of mind of someone who has survived a traffic accident: unhurt but distraught (*L'Avant-scène* 1969: 28). Ridder is, in other words, a survivor of trauma, the trauma of Catrine's death. His love story with her has the discontinuities, the repetitions and shock intrusions of post-traumatic memories. The shattering of the narrative in this sense might be read as expressive and as reflective of the very disorder of Ridder's state of mind.

Yet the film is multi-faceted, crystalline and self-reflecting in Deleuze's sense (for Deleuze himself the film is made up of 'des alternatives indécidables'²⁶ (Deleuze 1985: 157)). So many virtual images of Ridder's past might be seen to return again for other reasons. Perhaps we are not asked to choose between these possibilities but to open them out as alternative, virtual readings of the film.

23 'the theme that one always kills those one loves – even if one doesn't kill them physically'.
24 'I killed Catrine in Glasgow, two months ago. In January I left unexpectedly with Catrine and I came back alone'.
25 'You are right, I am incapable of killing anything ... but you are wrong, I still did it'.
26 'impossible choices'

Resnais has admitted that one of the obsessions behind the film is death; Mag Bodard, the film's producer, writes: 'J'ai senti que *Je t'aime je t'aime* permettait d'aborder cette autre rive, et c'est pour ça que j'ai eu envie de le faire' (Bodard 2002: 127).[27] Strick describes the film as 'the kind of yarn in which key moments of a man's life are permitted to unreel before our eyes at the instant of death' (Strick 1971: 166). For Bounoure, the film is fatalistic, the return to the past leading inevitably to the present moment of death (Bounoure 1974: 85). Resnais's film might be a dream as Ridder is dying, a montage of the moments which pass, in review, through his shattered, dying mind. In the time-scale of the narrative it takes him a month to die (his suicide, listening to Misterioso by Thelonius Monk, is dated 5 August 1967; his death, after two hours in his past, takes place on 5 September 1967 on the lawn outside Crespel). This time-lag speaks of his delayed response, of his unwillingness to relinquish the past and his life. The excursion through the chosen scenes brings him effectively to a point of no return, his suicide, which, as it is relived and represented, proves finally fatal. In this sense the film bears vivid comparison to Chris Marker's *La Jetée*, a further film ostensibly of time travel which, with much pathos, shows a man return to the past to encounter the moment of his own death.

Resnais's following two films, *Stavisky* and *Providence*, though different from *Je t'aime je t'aime*, and from each other, both represent a protagonist who is dying or already dead. For Prédal, in a resonant phrase, '[l]es héros de Resnais voient leur existence les lâcher, s'éparpiller en morceaux sous leurs yeux' (Prédal 1996: 139).[28] Death, its denial, and the arbitrary paths towards extinction will continue to concern Resnais into the 1980s. Yet *Je t'aime je t'aime* ends more lightly with a close-up image of a mouse which, unlike Ridder, has survived travel in time. The head of the operation at Crespel has told Ridder earlier in the film: 'La souris B est un pionnier. ... Elle a revécu une minute dans son passé' (*L'Avant-scène* 1969: 18).[29] Ridder questions how they know that the mouse has successfully moved through time. Tacit proof comes in the film where, on the beach with

---

27 'I felt that *Je t'aime je t'aime* allowed one to approach this other shore, and that is why I wanted to do it'.
28 'Resnais's heroes see their existence leave them, dispersed in pieces before their eyes'.
29 'Mouse B is a pioneer. ... It has relived a moment from its past'.

Catrine back in 1966, at 4pm, the time when all the time-travel experiments take place, a mouse suddenly appears on the beach. Humorous and unlikely time-travel narrative, fractured history of individual trauma and death, filmic experiment, *Je t'aime je t'aime* shows some of the potential lines of development of Resnais's art as he moves away from more historically rooted subjects.

Stavisky (1974)

After *Je t'aime je t'aime*, Resnais was absent from the screen for five years. *Stavisky*, with which he reemerges, marks a new interest in the ways in which nostalgia, rather than traumatic memory, distorts the past. Nostalgia is manifested not in the subject matter of the film, but in the manner of representation, in particular in a concern for art deco design and motifs. This will recur in *Mélo*, in his documentary *Gershwin* and in his latest film, the musical *Pas sur la bouche*. Nostalgia for the 1920s and 1930s might be witnessed in the décor and costume design of other films of the 1970s, for example *The Conformist* (1970) or *The Great Gatsby* (1974). Resnais makes a film that is of its decade and yet also, in its colours, its textures, its grand sensuality, of another decade imagined and artificially reconstructed.

With *Stavisky*, Resnais returned to work with Semprun. *Stavisky*, a French/Italian co-production, which owed 80 per cent of its finance to star Jean-Paul Belmondo, proved one of Resnais's most successful films at the box office. It fared no better than *Je t'aime je t'aime* with critics, although the later film was criticised for different reasons. Frédéric Vitoux writes: 'Ses censeurs lui ont tout d'abord reproché de n'être pas strictement un film politique, un film sur l'affaire Stavisky. Après quoi, ils lui ont fait grief d'être un film superficiel, décoratif et mondain' (Vitoux 2002: 222).[30] *Stavisky* represents the life of Serge Alexandre, or Stavisky, between 24 July 1933 and his suicide, or murder, on 8 January 1934. The film also flashes forward to the Commission of Enquiry held at the Palais Bourbon in April 1934. Serge Alexandre was a French-Jewish financier of Russian origin; as Naomi Greene writes: 'Stavisky, who floats fraudulent bonds and

30 'Its critics at first accused it of not being a strictly political film, a film about the Stavisky affair. After this, they reproached it for being a superficial, decorative and worldy film'.

believes that everything and everyone can be bought, is the quintessential capitalist' (Greene 1999: 55). Resnais's film pays particular attention to Stavisky's last fraudulent venture, the selling of the fake 'bons de Bayonne' (false cash vouchers produced by the Crédit Municipal of Bayonne). The uncovering of this fraud led directly to Stavisky's death; the two in turn had an extraordinary impact on the French state. Jonathan Rosenbaum explains:

> The revelation of his crime resulted in the downfall of two ministries. The Radical Socialist premier Camille Chautemps was forced to resign after right and left extremists accused him of crooked deals with Stavisky; then his successor Daladier also had to step down after using force to repress the bloody riots staged by extremists (mainly royalists) in February 1934 (Rosenbaum 1973–74: 25).

Greene places Resnais's work in *Stavisky* on a level with his earlier, more evidently engaged political films. She argues that 'this reconstruction itself is built around the "traces" of the past like those seen in previous works' (Greene 1999: 52). For Greene, as we have seen, the shadows or obfuscations of Resnais's work, all that is not said, reflect a climate of censorship and a concern to give a faithful impression of this. The Stavisky affair, as treated by Resnais, offers reflections in particular on French anti-semitism (this is visualised for example in a tracking shot which circles around Stavisky, immediately after the character Borelli has said: 'on ne se méfie jamais assez des métèques, des apatrides, des Juifs!' (*L'Avant-scène* 1975: 47).[31] The film also attempts a broader perspective on Stavisky's era through the inclusion of a parallel narrative of Trotsky in political exile in France.

Stavisky opens indeed with Trotsky's arrival at Cassis. Trotsky and his wife remain liminal figures in the film, though the contrast between their history and that of Stavisky is significant. Resnais says in interview: 'J'ai tourné la séquence Trotski après la séquence Stavisky. Il s'agissait pour moi d'opposer, aussi simplement que possible, sans chercher de symbolisme, deux mouvements' (Beylie 1974: 39).[32] Frédéric Vitoux picks up on this opposition between, as he puts it, the exile who still seeks some analysis of the political

---

31 'one is never wary enough of different races, exiles, Jews!'.
32 'I filmed the Trotsky episodes after the Stavisky ones. I felt it was a question of setting two movements in opposition, as simply as possible, without looking for symbolism'.

situation and the adventurer-criminal who seeks to avoid reality. (Vitoux 2002: 224–5). The screenplay itself draws attention at one point to the precise connection between these two opposed strands of narrative, in this way indicating the broad reverberations following Stavisky's death. Granville, a young follower of Trotsky, says to Erna, a German-Jewish refugee in France: 'Sans Stavisky, pas de 6 février. Sans l'émeute fasciste du 6 février devant laquelle Daladier capitule, pas de gouvernement d'union nationale. ... Sans gouvernement d'union nationale, pas d'expulsion de Trotski. Donc, sans Stavisky...' (*L'Avant-scène* 1975: 50).[33] The film works, like *Hiroshima mon amour*, through paralleling and opposition; it shows the unexpected connection between two histories (just as the word Hiroshima is in the papers as the French woman arrives in Paris, escaping Nevers). Through the Trotsky narrative in *Stavisky*, Resnais allows the film broader reach, embracing an era, not an individual destiny. The film hints at the other virtual narratives that might have been traced, allowing Stavisky's story to be ghosted by other histories. Resnais is not primarily interested in *Stavisky* as historical film but as film of proliferating representations.

Resnais saw a waxwork model of Stavisky in the Musée Grévin when he was a child. He says: 'J'ai voulu voir Stavisky comme peut le voir un enfant de douze ans. C'est l'âge que j'avais à l'époque' (Bounoure 1974: 90).[34] Resnais shows nostalgia for the 1930s of his childhood, for Stavisky as a representation. Indeed representation is arguably key to Stavisky's success and identity. For Prédal, Alexandre Stavisky is continually acting, representing himself (Prédal 1996: 19). Vitoux writes of the film that it offers a portrait of the part Stavisky was playing, rather than the man he really was (Vitoux 2002: 224). Resnais says in interview that Belmondo was the only French actor who could convey the character's magnetism and theatricality (Beylie 1974: 41). Theatricality is literally a theme in the film. Stavisky owns a theatre and attends rehearsals for a play in Paris, helping Erna Wolfgang by taking the role of the ghost in *Intermezzo* while she reads

33 'Without Stavisky, no 6 February. Without the fascist riots of 6 February which cause Daladier to capitulate, there would be no government of national unity. ... Without the government of national unity, Trotsky would not have been expelled. So, without Stavisky...'.

34 'I wanted to see Stavisky as a child of twelve can see him. That was how old I was at the time'.

her part. Stavisky is at the theatre with Arlette, watching *Coriolanus*, when Borelli comes to tell him that the affair of the 'bons de Bayonne' has been uncovered. Indeed the film makes links between Stavisky's role as *faussaire* (forger) and swindler and his more theatrical, hedonistic interest in performance and self-representation. For Deleuze, the many alternative facets Stavisky presents make him a quintessentially cinematic figure (Deleuze 1985: 173).

Tony Rayns identifies the effect of the multiple identities and deceptions in *Stavisky*, writing of Resnais: 'his ultimately bleak masterpiece is a perfectly lucid tangle of dreams, memories and ideas, composed of lies and truths from the lips of drowning men' (Rayns 1975: 162). For Prédal, in *Stavisky* Resnais stays on the surface, offering intimations, but no depth (Prédal 1996: 64). Certainly *Stavisky* pays loving attention to surfaces and texture; further, though, it is through the accumulation of such sensory images that the film achieves its depth and resonance, its emotional impact on the viewer. Bounoure asks Resnais why he used images of snow, an ermine and a white carnation; Resnais replies: 'Je ne sais pas... Je n'approche d'un film que sensuellement' (Bounoure 1974: 90).[35] The film, which is carefully stylised and constructed visually, abounds in images of white fur and feathers (Arlette's glamorous white garments), in images of white flowers (Stavisky orders Arlette a mountain of white flowers, lilies, orchids, camelias and roses (*L'Avant-scène* 1975: 26)), in images of snow (where Stavisky retreats to Chamonix). This luxurious, glacial, Mallarméen world is reflected, or finds its source, in Arlette's dreams (Bounoure aludes to Mallarmé more broadly (Bounoure 1974: 69)). Arlette tells Stavisky that she has had the same dream again. He asks: 'Toujours les mêmes mots?'; she replies: 'Les mêmes... l'hermine, les orchidées... Ta voix dans mon oreille...' (*L'Avant-scène* 1975: 26).[36] At the end of the film, immediately before Stavisky's death, we see rapid images from Stavisky's perspective: Arlette sleeping in a bed surrounded by white roses, the ermine poised to disappear down a hole in the snow. The latter image of the white, furred living creature against the snow seems peculiarly resonant. It offers a sense of hesitation between life and death, as it seems febrile in the cold, sentient yet reminiscent of Arlette's

35 'I don't know... I only approach a film through the senses'.
36 'Always the same words?'; 'The same... the ermine, the orchids... Your voice in my ear...'.

elaborate stoles. The ermine's disappearance down the snow hole bespeaks closure, insertion and completion – Stavisky's story closed. The image, merely sensory, acquires meaning as it recalls Arlette's dream, as it threads together the images of fur and pallor in the film, as it arrives arbitrarily (like the white mouse in *Je t'aime je t'aime*) in Stavisky's eye-line, as he is dying. Through such webs of connection, as we are party to the mental images of his protagonists, yet largely unaware of their sense, Resnais generates a seemingly unexplained, yet resonant, emotional response.

The same sensual, mnemonic effects are created through Resnais's filming of buildings and architecture in the film. To introduce Stavisky as character Resnais films the Hôtel Claridge at Biarritz. (Prédal comments on Resnais's ability to project his characters' psychology onto their surroundings (Prédal 1996: 28).) The camera moves slowly down the façade of the building, gradually surveying its material substance (frequently the tracking shots in *Stavisky* work along the vertical axis). We return to images of the hotel at various moments in the film, Resnais's patient, moving camerawork creating a sense of love and nostalgia for this sumptuous façade, this image of slightly faded glamour and luxury. Resnais's filming of the hotel has drawn comparisons with *Marienbad*. Different, more morbid, stone and sculptural images also draw Resnais's attention in *Stavisky*, notably an image of a stone pyramid from the Parc Monceau in Paris. This is viewed twice in the film, seemingly without motivation. Prédal comments: 'Resnais insère dans ses histoires des plans absolument inexplicables par rapport à la diégèse' (Prédal 1996: 74).[37] He continues: 'Tel est, par exemple, le lent travelling avant sur le petit tertre funéraire du parc Monceau dans *Stavisky*. Resnais explique que, la première fois, le plan évoque l'enfance d'Alexandre qui s'est déroulée dans ce parc; la seconde fois, la même image souligne la mort venant frapper le personnage' (Prédal 1996: 74).[38] In a different interview, Resnais says, however: 'Il m'a semblé qu'une telle image,

37 'Resnais inserts in his stories shots which are absolutely inexplicable with relation to the diegesis'.
38 'One such, for example, is the slow forwards tracking shot towards the little funerary monument in the Parc Monceau in *Stavisky*. Resnais explains that, the first time, the shot evokes Alexandre's childhood which he spent in this park; the second time, the same image emphasises death coming to strike the character'.

irrationnelle je vous l'accorde, concrétisait bien ce climat de mystère' (Beylie 1974: 39).[39] The pyramid might have symbolic meaning with relation to the film as a whole; for Monaco: 'The pyramid became the metaphorical emblem of the film for Semprun and Resnais: Stavisky was the peak of a structure of fraud that reached deep into the bowels of French society' (Monaco 1979: 170). Yet we might also, as with the ermine above, see the image as one which triggers mnemonic responses in the viewer. It is certainly a funerary image, at once of white lifeless marble and of outdated, nostalgic commemoration. The image, following Resnais, speaks of both Stavisky's childhood and his imminent death, it may be a memory image for Stavisky recurring, reminding him of, yet screening him from his fate.

Stavisky is a beautifully macabre film; for Kreidl, 'the theme of death haunts the entire film' (Kreidl 1977: 166); for Dawson, 'even the flowers ... are as redolent of death as of romanticism' (Dawson 1974: 38). Prédal writes that Resnais felt that the last weeks of Stavisky's life were a type of burlesque, very black and very sinister nonetheless (Prédal 1996: 190). Resnais manages too to convey something of the pathos and melancholy of Stavisky's approach to death. In Père-Lachaise at night, he is seen lying on a tomb, recalling his father's suicide. (Resnais speaks of his own love of visiting cemeteries, particularly the cemetery in Nice and cemeteries in Italy (Beylie 1974: 41).) His father killed himself in protest and shame on learning of Stavisky's first arrest. If Stavisky's own death is a suicide, he shadows his father. The funerary image from the Parc Monceau seems the emblem of this more reflective, poetic and painful cast to the film, as Resnais and Semprun make Stavisky a dreaming and mourning son, as much as a man trapped.

Rayns describes *Stavisky* as 'a post mortem on a vanished era and an analysis of the disarray afflicting the French Left' (Rayns 1975: 162). For Milne, in the film, 'one finds the bankrupt society excoriated so mercilessly in *La Règle du jeu*' (Milne 1975: 186). Resnais, as melancholic, recreates an era with painstaking care. He wanted to make the film in black and white, but his distributor refused; he still used 'only setups and shot angles that were possible in the early thirties' (Monaco 1979: 180). As Vitoux remarks, Resnais's *mise-en-*

---

39 'It seemed to me that an image like this, irrational I admit, worked well to materialise this climate of mystery'.

scène, in particular in the scenes between Arlette and Stavisky, recalls 1930s cinema (Vitoux 2002: 227). Arlette herself, played as a mannequin or idol by Anny Duperey, is seen as movie star icon; Beylie describes her as a pearl and compares her to Seyrig in *Marienbad*, but also to Dietrich and Garbo (Beylie 1974: 46).

The film retains a wonderment and fascination with the image of the era. *Stavisky* contains poetic, lyrical shots of Stavisky and Arlette walking on the beach in evening dress, and also of Trotsky and his wife similarly walking by the sea. These images recall the shots of nostalgia and denunciation in Marguerite Duras's *India Song*. Resnais depicts a world destroyed; he reflects on its politics yet also, with equanimity, captures its rare moments of beauty.

References

Adair, Gilbert (1977) 'Providence', *Sight and Sound*, 46:2 (Spring), pp. 120–1.
L'Avant-scène du cinéma: Je t'aime je t'aime, 91 (April 1969).
L'Avant-scène du cinéma: Stavisky, 156 (March 1975).
Benayoun, Robert (1980) *Alain Resnais: arpenteur de l'imaginaire* (Paris: Stock/Cinéma).
Benayoun, Robert, Michel Ciment and Jean-Louis Pays (2002) '"Ne pas faire un film sur l'Espagne": entretien avec Alain Resnais', in Stéphane Goudet (ed.), Positif, *revue de cinéma: Alain Resnais* (Paris: Gallimard [Folio]), pp. 162–86).
Beylie, Claude (1974) 'Alain Resnais, Jorge Semprun et *Stavisky*', *Ecran*, 27 (July), pp. 37–47.
Bodard, Mag (2002) 'Une part de mon héritage', *Positif*, 495 (May), pp. 127–9.
Bounoure, Gaston (1974) *Alain Resnais* (Cinéma d'aujourd'hui 5) (Paris: Seghers).
Callev, Haim (1997) *The Stream of Consciousness in the Films of Alain Resnais* (New York: McGruer Publishing).
Cieutat, Michel (2002) '*Je t'aime je t'aime*: L'écho du temps, l'écho du coeur', *Positif*, 495 (May), pp. 117–19.
Dawson, Jan (1974) '*Stavisky*', *Film Comment*, 10:5 (September–October), p. 38.
Deleuze, Gilles (1985) *Cinéma 2: L'Image-temps* (Paris: Minuit).
Demeure, Jacques (2002) 'De Guernica à Barcelone, toute la mémoire du monde ou presque', in Stéphane Goudet (ed.), Positif, *revue de cinéma: Alain Resnais* (Paris: Gallimard [Folio]), pp. 153–61.
Greene, Naomi (1999) *Landscapes of Loss: The National Past in Postwar French Cinema* (Princeton NJ: Princeton University Press).
Houston, Penelope (1966) 'Festivals 66: Cannes', *Sight and Sound*, 35:3 (summer), pp. 125–7.
Jebb, Julian (1971) '*Je t'aime je t'aime*', *Sight and Sound*, 40:3 (summer), pp. 162–3.

Kreidl, John Francis (1977) *Alain Resnais* (Boston: Twayne Publishers).
Liandrat-Guigues, Suzanne (2002) 'Une minute ordinaire', in Stéphane Goudet (ed.), Positif, *revue de cinéma: Alain Resnais* (Paris: Gallimard [Folio]), pp. 215–19.
Mettey, Marcel (1970) '*La Guerre est finie*', *Image et son*, 244, pp. 49–72.
Milne, Tom (1966) '*La Guerre est finie*', *Sight and Sound*, 35:4 (autumn), pp. 196–7.
Milne, Tom (1975) '*Stavisky*', *Sight and Sound*, 44:3 (summer), pp. 186–7.
Monaco, James (1979) *Alain Resnais* (New York: Oxford University Press).
Pays, Jean-Louis (2002) '"Un film expérimental": entretien avec Jorge Semprun', in Stéphane Goudet (ed.), Positif, *revue de cinéma: Alain Resnais* (Paris: Gallimard [Folio]), pp. 187–206.
Prédal, René (1968) *Alain Resnais* (Paris: Lettres Modernes [Etudes Cinématographiques]).
Rayns, Tony (1975) '*Stavisky*', *Monthly Film Bulletin*, 42:498 (July), pp. 161–2.
Rosenbaum, Jonathan (1973–74) '*Stavisky*', *Sight and Sound*, 43:1 (winter), p. 25.
Semprun, Jorge (1963) *Le Grand Voyage* (Paris: Gallimard [Folio]).
Sternberg, Jacques (2002) 'Resnais le conciliant', *Positif*, 495 (May), pp. 120–3.
Strick, Philip (1971) '*Je t'aime je t'aime*', *Monthly Film Bulletin*, 38:449 (June), pp. 165–6.
Thirard, Paul Louis (2002) 'Un film d'auteur', in Stéphane Goudet (ed.), Positif, *revue de cinéma: Alain Resnais* (Paris: Gallimard [Folio]), pp. 208–14.
Vitoux, Frédéric (2002) 'La double mort d'Alexandre Stavisky', in Stéphane Goudet (ed.), Positif, *revue de cinéma: Alain Resnais* (Paris: Gallimard [Folio]), pp. 222–8.
W., D., (1966) '*La Guerre est finie*', *Monthly Film Bulletin*, 33:394 (November), pp. 164–5.
Ward, John (1968) *Alain Resnais or the Theme of Time* (London: Secker & Warburg/British Film Institute).

6

Providence (1977)

At the start of *Providence*, the camera moves slowly towards a stone sign or marker bearing the inscription 'Providence' in curving, antiquated letters. The sign is entwined with foliage. The film cuts to images of trees in near darkness, the camera moving through their shadow. The films opens with markers of obscurity, with a tracking camera taking us deep into foliage, undergrowth. This opening, which moves to a shot where a glass is shattered, has led to comparisons with *Citizen Kane* (for example Maillot 2003). *Providence* is a film which is self-conscious about cinema as medium; for Van Wert, it is 'a meta-film, a film about the making of films, a work of art about the fabricating of art works' (Van Wert 1979: 179). Dirk Bogarde, who stars in the film (and whom Resnais had previously imagined casting as the Marquis de Sade), compares Resnais's world to that of Visconti or Losey. Others make comparisons across media, comparing images in *Providence* to Surrealist paintings and conjuring the names of Breton, Magritte, Delvaux and de Chirico (Claude Beylie in *L'Avant-scène* 1977: 7). *Providence* is a composite and oneiric piece, condensing and displacing a broad range of influences, yet moving beyond an interrogation of art itself towards a reckoning with fantasy and disturbed, veiled intimations of the real (horror, the inexpressible, annihilation). It is the last of Resnais's films which offers such a stretching, grandiose engagement with an imaginary universe and a suffering mind.

Providence was Resnais's first English-language film. The script was written by David Mercer, a British playwright who has worked for the stage and for television. It was the producer Klaus Hellwig who first suggested Mercer to Resnais; Resnais read Mercer's plays and agreed to work with him. Mercer's script, precisely written and carefully played by the film's two major actors, Bogarde and John Gielgud, brings dry humour, with a deep sense of the bizarre, to Resnais's repertoire (he acknowledges that audiences are uneasy about laughing in his films (Jousse and Nevers 1993: 25)). As Monaco suggests: 'It's an ethereal one, but *Providence* is Resnais's first wholehearted comedy' (Monaco 1979: 202). Monaco, however, voices reservations about *Providence*, writing: 'The one weakness in *Providence* – and it may be fatal for some viewers – is that the story-outside-the-story is nearly as fatuous as the story within the story' (Monaco 1979: 195). In resumé, Resnais's film may sound improbable or ephemeral; yet in its form and in the fears it addresses, I suggest, against Monaco, that it is far more profound, and one of Resnais's finest films.

Pierce addresses the ways in which the form of the film is entwined with its meaning: 'One hesitates to try to impose order on *Providence*, its chaos being germane to the nightworld of creation, fractured consciousness, and deathbed pillaging of the soul Resnais constructs' (Pierce 1980: 251). Clive Langham (John Gielgud), the dying novelist who is the subject of the film, whom critics have aligned with Resnais, cites criticisms of his own imaginary work, viz.: 'the search for style has often resulted in the want of feelings'. Langham argues back, in terms resonant for Resnais: 'Style is feeling. Its most elegant and economic expression'. Resnais himself speaks of what he sees as a paradox where his films are criticised as being too cerebral where he himself sees them as entirely instinctive (Benayoun 2002b: 239). In an interview about *Providence* he further specifies that he sees his films as 'un réceptacle de l'imaginaire ou de l'inconscient du spectateur' ('a receptacle for the imagination or the unconscious of the spectator') (Benayoun 2002b: 239). *Providence* is a film which leaves the viewer to make connections, to roam widely in its composite, collaged locations, in its layering of subjective perceptions and alternative versions of events. It is a film which makes meaning through its style – sepulchral, menacing, ironic, elegiac – and through its disjunctive editing, allowing us to explore misapprehension, confusion and false association through the very form of the film.

Providence is in two parts: one longer, initial night section and one shorter day part. The anchor of the film is the (imaginary) novelist Clive Langham, a figure who is compared in the film to Graham Greene. We follow Clive through the night as he wrestles with pain from his intestines and rectum (he is dying of cancer). The film we view at this stage is largely a film in Langham's mind and is made up of nightmare scenes and seemingly more conscious scenes of literary creation where Langham develops a plot for a novel peopled by his children: Claud (Dirk Bogarde) a prosecution lawyer, Sonia (Ellen Burstyn) Claud's wife, Helen (Elaine Stritch) Claud's mistress, and Kevin Woodford (David Warner) Clive's illegitimate son. The second part of the film, located the day after this night of agonising pain, hallucination and creativity, shows Clive awakening in the garden of his country house. His children come to celebrate his seventy-eighth birthday, bringing gifts and eating a meal on the lawn in a nostalgic, yet still unsettling, English pastoral scene. Both parts are haunted by Molly, Clive's wife, who is seen only in photographs and a brief flashback to her suicide. She is played, like Helen, by Elaine Stritch.

In interview, David Mercer suggests that in the first section of *Providence* there are three levels of reality: that of nightmare, that of literary creation and the imagination, and that of the material reality of the elderly writer (Benayoun 1980: 262). If we accept this, the first level is represented from the very opening of the film by a series of shots which evoke anxiety: a helicopter hovers over a church façade, the helicopter is then seen closer to, its propeller heard more clearly. The space of nightmare in the film is a space of surveillance and entrapment. Most substantially in evoking nightmare the film draws on images of deportation. In dark recurring shots we see figures herded into a stadium and waiting behind wire. At other moments there is mention of terrorist bombs and the demolition of buildings. This stratum of reality is constantly disquieting, constantly evocative of historical fears. Naomi Greene suggests that Resnais's shots recall the deportation of the Jews during the Occupation and she links the image of the stadium to the Vél d'Hiv (the location, pictured by Resnais in *Nuit et brouillard*, where many French Jews were assembled before deportation to the camps). For Greene, describing *Providence*, 'the spectacles brought to life by Resnais's cinema ... bear the imprint of historical anguish' (Greene 1999: 62). Farnsworth casts his net more widely and sees Resnais's film referring to and evoking a range of historical situations and horrors: 'Soldiers move either through a jungle-like forest, suggesting Vietnam, or through city-scapes, suggesting IRA terrorists or British counterterrorists – or ... the Pinochet counterrevolution in Chile of a few years before' (Farnsworth 2002:

103). For Prédal, the bombs, the search-parties, the helicopter, the explosions are, whilst historically resonant, more timeless images of anxiety (Prédal 1996: 116). Certainly the film draws on the scenarios, the structures which in the twentieth-century imagination speak of threat, dehumanisation and death. Yet it does not conjure specific ghosts of the past, nor engage effectively with particular situations, showing instead how those horrors become a conduit, even a concrete form for the expression of anxiety and terror. The film depends on the sense that these scenarios will be pregnant with pathos and fear for the viewer as well, that we will share their cultural context and menace. We are called to respond to the emotional impact, the physical forms of these scenes without being able to locate them. We have lost the voice-over of *Nuit et brouillard*; Resnais's historical evidence is now scrambled, invented, unlocatable. Indeed, dislocation and contamination are created in the relations between Mercer's different levels of reality.

Nightmare reality, the stuff of Clive's dreams, has been located as the menacing, anonymous world of the stadium and surveillance. Yet from the very start this world is in part imbricated with Mercer's second layer of reality, the world of literary creation. In the opening sequences of the film, we cut from the helicopter to shots in the woods where soldiers can gradually be seen advancing through the trees. They are tracking an elderly man, a man so hirsute he seems to be turning into a werewolf. This scene pursues the emotions of the helicopter shots, again playing on fears of surveillance and capture. The film cuts to the wide façade and steps of a building (reminiscent of *Marienbad*) and close-up shots of the helicopter viewed from below. It cuts then to Claud Langham by a window in a courtroom. His first words are, ironically, 'Surely the facts are not in dispute'. The film cuts again to images of the elderly man tracked and we discover improbably that these images of an army patrol and an old man sacrificed illustrate the case Claud is fighting in court: he attempts to prosecute the old man's (mercy) killer. The tale of the man murdered, Claud's court case, takes shape as the second stratum of reality in the film, the level of literary creation. Langham imagines and constructs a novel indicting his son in professional and amorous terms. What is telling is the proximity between the nightmare world and the literary world. The film intercuts these two worlds liberally; it pursues emotions and sensations across their boundaries. Later, the characters of the novel, Clive's children, will themselves be seen incarcerated in the camp of his nightmares. The film depends on this running across lines of demarcation, this constant displacement and reinvention in different contexts.

Marsha Kinder, comparing *Providence* to Robert Altman's *Three Women*, sees Resnais's film 'dissolving the boundaries between fantasy and ordinary reality' (Kinder 1977: 11). She argues: 'Both films use dream structures that contain inset dreams, but which move fluidly into conscious artistic creation' (Kinder 1977: 11). Diane Shoos seeks further to align literary creativity and dream in the film. She writes: 'Resnais's film is indeed concerned with the writer and dreamer's "creation", not only in the sense of the production of fiction or dreams, but also in terms of the continual definition and redefinition of the subject itself in and by the flux of different signifying operations' (Shoos 1989: 5). Shoos works to show how the literary strand of the film is dominated by the structures of dream. In the literary strand of the film, Clive's voice is heard at times over the shots. Ambiguously he both directs the characters' actions, yet also responds to them. The film suggests some symbiotic relation between creator and created script. Much of the film is made up of these hallucinated scenes, scenes of his novel conjured unedited by Clive, midway between conscious creation and involuntary viewing. The characters are his creations, yet he speaks to them as if they were wilful children. Their status is ambiguous since they are a composite: they are dream figures, created characters and also individuals who are part of Clive's proximate reality. Their identities are dizzyingly unstable, where divisions between the characters, and divisions between Clive and the characters are uncertain. Indeed, once or twice in an act of ventriloquism Clive's voice escapes his characters' lips, reminding us of his creative presence.

The most obvious permeable boundaries are those between Clive and Claud his prosecuting son, making the film, as more than one critic has commented, an oedipal drama. In keeping with this, uncertainty remains about any distinction between Helen, Claud's mistress (who is dying), and Molly, Clive's wife (who commits suicide when terminally ill). Both characters are played by Elaine Stritch, and a framed photograph of her as Molly is seen close to the start of each section of the film. The identities of Molly and Helen become more interchangeable as the film proceeds, as their names are confused, as

Claud eats prawns and drinks white wine with Helen, as Clive has with Molly. In his use of the same actress to play Helen and Molly, Resnais leaves us wondering whether Claud supposedly chooses a mistress who resembles his mother or whether Clive's imagination or unconscious explore a love between Claud and a woman who may resemble and recall or may indeed be Molly, his mother.

Shoos argues that: 'the frequently noted "projection" of Clive's characteristics onto his family is strikingly similar to the operations of condensation and displacement, overlapping strategies of what Freud called the "dreamwork"' (Shoos 1989: 8). She continues: 'Much as dreams employ elements from past and present experience and recombine them, causing them to lose their temporal specificity, the narrative of *Providence* is a complicated weave of the different elements of Clive's life, one in which time and place are displaced along with characters and events' (Shoos 1989: 9). Here what seems crucial is that Resnais's film imitates and expands upon the strategies of the "dreamwork", condensation and displacement. This in itself does not necessarily imply, however, that all or part of what we see is literally intended to be Clive's dream. Haim Callev, developing a reading of Resnais's films as explorations of stream-of-consciousness filmmaking, argues indeed for a more lucid and vigilant Clive. Callev writes: 'Creative ideas keep flowing through his mind in a process of free association and keep mixing with diverging mental images reflecting his scruples and his fears' (Callev 1997: 187). Callev argues that a *sleepless* night is the anchoring reality of the film.

The film itself may resist our attempts to categorise and control its images. Perhaps *Providence* calls us not to identify and interpret its images (as dream or waking reality) but to respond to their ambiguity, to their polyvalence. This seems signalled in the contamination and continuity between the various levels of reality identified at the outset by Mercer. This becomes all the more apparent when we consider the third stratum Mercer identifies, that of the lived physical reality of Clive, and the way it is perceived by night and by day.

Clive's lived reality is first glimpsed in the nocturnal section, though there is delay in showing us his face and thus identifying the film's images with his conscious or unconscious mental reality. His image appears some twenty minutes into the film. Against the dark background of his bedroom, his illuminated face seems the work of an artist with broad brushstrokes; Gielgud appears like a late Velázquez or a Francis Bacon. Clive is a Shakespearean figure, a Lear or a Prospero. His house is his island, peopled with shadows of his imagination. We see the material details of Clive's life, his constantly poured glass of Chablis, his deep red, ornate enclave. He alone appears embodied, material, in the nocturnal section of the film. By day, by contrast, he is visited by Claud, Sonia and Kevin, his other son. Where the night section is dominated by dream or created, subjective images, the day section is seemingly dominated by material reality – the house, the garden, the social exchanges between Clive and his children.

Initially in the day section, Claud and Sonia, and Clive's feelings towards them, seem far more benign than in the night section. In their acting styles, their levity, in the sunlit setting, the characters seem entirely distinct from their nocturnal avatars. Yet, as Pierce points out, 'there is residue from the night world: Sonia does seem selfless, Clive cannot help projecting onto his sons – mild, weary Claud is the threat, Kevin the joy' (Pierce 1980: 257). The two realms of the film, the two sections into which it is divided, do not remain distinct but seep into one another. It is through this effect that Resnais and Mercer work most carefully to question our (and film's) perceptions of reality.

In interview, cited by Callev, Resnais speaks in material terms of Clive's experience at night: '[Clive] feels that way especially at night: the 5 a.m. mentality. This is often the moment when one dies or takes medication. What is inoffensive in daytime becomes extremely painful at night. It is also the moment when all the scruples, angers and suffering assail you' (Callev 1997: 197). Resnais roots Clive's experience in a physical and temporal reality, a reality of insomnia and waking dreams when the body and mind are most vulnerable. *Providence* allows us to witness the perceptions (distorted and fused), as well as dreams and creations, of this fragile time. The film also aligns these with the perceptions of daytime reality, allowing us to perceive, eerily, both their difference and yet their similarity. Clive at night constructs Claud as his accuser: Claud is perceived to blame Clive for Molly's suicide. Claud in the day benignly says to his father about Molly's suicide: 'It seemed to me logical at the time. I didn't blame you'. For Monaco, the film explores 'a quasi-paranoid, irreconcilable dichotomy between one's image of oneself and one's image of the self as perceived by others' (Monaco 1979: 196). Resnais says, in words which recall earlier discussion of *L'Année dernière à Marienbad*: 'L'une des questions que pose le film est, si vous voulez, celle-ci: est-ce que nous sommes ce que nous pensons être, ou est-ce que nous devenons ce que les autres font de nous dans leurs jugements?' (Benayoun 2002b: 238).[1] The film illuminates the discrepancies between the characters' perceptions of themselves, the perceptions of others and the misapprehension and transformation which can result from their interaction. But with and beyond this reflection on inter-personal relations, the film questions perception per se.

Returning to the discrepancy between Clive's and Claud's reckonings with their own and each other's perception of Molly's death, we realise that there is no easy sense that the diurnal speech is the truth and the nocturnal fear a delusion. Since the structure of the film shows the night-time or nightmare reality first, its intimations must always shadow our reception of the day-time scene. In representing a reality of the mind and of perception in *Providence*, Resnais depends on proliferating versions. Our perception of Clive's guilt over Molly's death (either literal, imputed or self-imposed) is leavened and further altered by Claud's contrary claims. We see the panoply of emotions, their tremor, their oscillation, around a single event or memory. The second part of the film supplements the first by altering its affect, by denying its sometimes hostile and paranoid proof but not by eradicating these altogether. The parts of the film open *Providence* up as a series of reflecting realities which, wound together, may offer something of the hesitance and doubt of mental process.

In this sense, *Providence* may be seen as a precursor to the work of David Lynch in films such as *Lost Highway* (1997) and *Mulholland Drive* (2001). In the bipartite structure of *Lost Highway*, Žižek finds that 'we get the opposition of two horrors: the fantasmatic horror of the nightmarish *noir* universe of perverse sex, betrayal and murder, and the (perhaps much more unsettling) despair of our drab, "alienated" daily life of impotence and distrust' (Žižek 2000: 13). In much the same way in *Providence* we find not an idyll and its obverse, but two horrors or two fantasies, two differing reflections on reality. (For Laura Rascaroli, by contrast, in an equally tenable reading, both parts of *Providence* are part of a dream and the entire film resembles

1 'One of the questions the film asks is, if you like, this one: are we what we think we are, or do we become what others judge us to be?'.

'an inner stage traversed by projected images, fragments of Clive's personality, and by ghosts from his past' (Rascaroli 2002: 53).).

In showing these shadow realities and how they infest our thoughts and investment in relations with others, Resnais and Mercer do not move away from reality and realism but transform our modes of perception. Pierre Maillot describes Langham's world as 'touffu, confus, diffus' ('involved, confused and diffuse') (Maillot 2003: 42). He continues, playing on the usual sense of the 'real' and the Lacanian sense of the 'Real' (that which escapes representation, as the true horror that must be screened): 'C'est le monde où l'imaginaire et le réel se mêlent et s'engendrent de la façon la plus féconde, la plus troublante, la plus poétique mais aussi la plus réaliste, mieux encore la plus réelle' (Maillot 2003: 42).[2] In interview, David Mercer cites Francis Bacon saying: '"Je peux bâcler un portrait extrêmement ressemblant de la nature, mais je préfère *atteindre les nerfs*"' (Benayoun 2002c: 257).[3] This touching of nerves is also achieved by Resnais and Mercer in *Providence*.

Clive Langham is, throughout the film, a subject in pain. (For Prédal, the typical Resnais hero is an 'écorché vif' ('a man skinned alive') (Prédal 1996: 117).) Resnais has frequently treated subjects who are between life and death, his films drawing poignancy from the awful hesitation between the two states. As well as locating itself temporally in a waking night, a time of low resistance and insomnia, *Providence* spends time with Clive as he reckons with his physical pain and his resistance to dying. For Bersani and Dutoit, 'death in *Providence* is imagined as an explosive dispersal, a terrifying breaking out of the frame of the self, a centrifugal blast into nature, perhaps into the cosmos' (Bersani and Dutoit 1993: 203–4). He argues that 'because Clive is dying, the aphoristic mode can be thought of as his defence against self-dissolution' (Bersani and Dutoit 1993: 203). Indeed the fragility and mutability of the identities of the various characters in *Providence* serve to set them in contrast to Clive attempting to shore up his ego and choreograph the reality around him. Resnais certainly moves towards a more metaphysical reckoning with death in his films. But in *Providence* there is also a very real sense that death, or dying, is configured as a material, sensory reality.

2 'It is the world where the imaginary and the real mingle and beget one another in the most fertile, troubling, poetic but also realist, or better still real manner'.
3 'I can knock up an extremely life-like portrait but I prefer *to touch people's nerves*'.

The corporeality of the body's demise is signalled in the vicious pain and the illness – rotting guts – from which Clive suffers. Clive's fears of death are further figured in several shots of a post mortem which work, in Farnsworth's terms, to 'concretiz[e] the putrefaction of death' (Farnsworth 2002: 103). In pictorial shots, a corpse is seen on a dissecting table (Maillot compares the lighting of the scene to Rembrandt's *Anatomy Lesson* (Maillot 2003: 44n)). Clive's identification with the corpse is established in his voice-over as he states: 'he wants to cut me up'. We have seen the greying, fur-infested man killed in the forest by Kevin Woodford. The body transforming with age is replaced by the seemingly quiescent corpse. Clive nevertheless disrupts the repose of the corpse as he speaks as if with its voice. This illusion of continued sentience is pursued as the pathologist cuts through the rib cage laying open the man's internal organs. The rebarbative movements of the dissecting knife cause the corpse, a frail and dessicated body, to move, as if flailing on the table (recalling again the bodily horror of the late shots in *Nuit et brouillard*). The image of the post mortem returns again, a further intercut shot, in the diurnal sequence, as it is also recalled more incongruously as Clive carves a cold chicken. Resnais seeks a physical form in which to represent fear of dying and he allows this to create effects – of shock, of recognition, of revulsion – for the viewer.

With the permeable membrane that seems to separate Clive from the other characters in *Providence*, it is perhaps apt that Clive's own fear of dying brings back thoughts of his terminally ill and suicidal wife. Molly does not appear until late in the film. Indeed, Diane Shoos argues powerfully: 'Molly's physical absence from the dream narrative, coupled with her overdetermined indirect representation in the characters of Sonia and Helen, indicates that she is the central object of repression' (Shoos 1989: 10). Molly is recalled, and desired, in the figure of Helen Wiener, also played by Elaine Stritch, yet she is at first only seen in the film as a photographic image. This framed photograph appears like a blot, a death's head image, within the frame and within Clive's enclave. In the diurnal sequence Resnais creates a finely composed shot where we see within the frame, in Clive's right and left hands respectively, a hand-mirror in which his own face appears and the photo frame, holding Molly's portrait. The living and the dead are weighed up and equated. Clive's moment of self-portraiture is always already doubled and complemented by the image, mental and physical, of his dead wife. Imaging within the frame of Resnais's filmmaking reunites them. Yet, as Shoos points out, the film, however mnemonic and wish-fulfilling, does not reanimate Molly. The only live-action moment in which she is glimpsed is in a sudden flashback to Clive's discovery of her dead or dying, in another pictorial shot, where the blood-red bath water is in stark contrast to the black and white of the rest of the frame. Molly is inert in the film, a dead body that cannot be reanimated. *Providence* in this way shadows the thematics of *Muriel*, with a dead woman at its centre. Like Bernard in *Muriel*, Clive hesitates between desiring and mourning Molly. He offers a eulogy to her corporeal form, describing her breasts as a 'biological triumph'. Yet the wife he suddenly glimpses in memory is the woman near death who has opened her veins.

Farnsworth comments that, as often in Resnais's work, 'motifs of tomb-like structures occur throughout the film' (Farnsworth 2002: 103). The material world is for Resnais one of mourning and petrification, cross-cut with aesthetic beauty. One further way in which the film intersperses dream and the imagination, and privileges the material world, within a sombre, even melancholy perspective, is in the filming of places and locations. In 1974, Resnais and Semprun published a book named *Repérages*, which presents a collection of Resnais's potential and actual film locations. Semprun quotes Resnais saying in interview: 'le Leica est bien commode. Je m'en sers comme d'un bloc-notes où j'inscris pêle-mêle les images les plus diverses. Elles me serviront ensuite à matérialiser l'histoire, à fabriquer une autre réalité avec des matériaux pris un peu partout' (Resnais and Semprun 1974).[4] The black and white photographs in the book cut between location shots in Hiroshima and Nevers, shots taken in London in preparation for the unmade film about Harry Dickson, shots in New York and its suburbs. In these disparate places Resnais finds similar, congruent structures. In interview he has said: 'J'aime beaucoup dans chaque ville choisir le seul quartier qui me rappelle une autre ville. Il y a à Londres des coins qui rappellent New York, et à Bruxelles des endroits qui me font penser à Rome. Le

---

4 'the Leica is very handy. I use it like a note pad where I record the most diverse images as they come to me. These then help me to let the story take form, to create another reality with material gleaned from all over'.

Providence du film est en somme une capitale des capitales' (Benayoun 2002b: 249).[5]

Haim Callev comments on the geographical fluidity of the film: 'In the repertory of landscapes in Clive's mind, locations from various parts of the world serve interchangeably to suit his imaginative needs' (Callev 1997: 189). While named for a New England town, *Providence* is located in a disparate, imaginary location. Some markers identify the location of both nocturnal and diurnal sequences as England, yet this is by no means clear. In the nocturnal sequence, the geography of the location of Clive's book is uncertain and evolving, evoking again the condensation and displacement of dreams. The urban images used in the film were variously shot in the USA and in Europe: in Providence, Albany and Holyoke and in Brussels, Louvain, Antwerp and Limoges. It is primarily Claud who we see out in this composite city. He drives past elaborate Flemish townhouses, their architectural style evoking Symbolist art, while he is filmed in his car as a figure escaped from *film noir*. As he continues his move through the city the shots of mansions and their moving façades give way to dark wood clapboard houses and American Gothic mansions, again dark or red brick, before the city morphs once more to resemble any concrete and glass metropolis. As with the images of terror and fear – the helicopter, the camps – Resnais composes an imaginary urban space, an invisible city, a city of citations and nightmare resonance. Benayoun comments: 'on peut penser que Providence, qui est aussi une ville de Rhode Island, est la capitale d'Hiroshima, de Nevers, de Boulogne, de Marienbad, de "Crespel" et de Barcelone' (Benayoun 2002a: 230).[6] Resnais's composite city is constructed between as well as within his films, so that we can begin to imagine and map a space which reinvents the urban and inflects it with the spaces of dream and the imagination. The urban space of *Providence* is also a threatened, menacing space. It has in its precincts the camp in which Clive will find not only strangers but his own family.

Providence also, in contrast, conjures an elegiac world of material

---

5 'In every city I like to choose the only district which recalls another city for me. In London there are areas which recall New York, and places in Brussels which make me think of Rome. So the Providence of the film is a capital made up of capitals'.

6 'one can think that Providence, which is also a town in Rhode Island, is the capital of Hiroshima, Nevers, Boulogne, Marienbad, "Crespel" and Barcelona'.

PROVIDENCE (1977)   143

luxury (closer to the world in which Bogarde moved in films by Losey and Visconti). Claud's house variously opens at its back, in imagination, onto the seashore of New England and also of Cap Ferrat, where the characters have eaten seafood with white wine. Inside, Claud's house seems like a theatre set. Referring to the theme of adultery in the film, Kinder argues: 'The glamorous décor of Claud and Sonia's bedroom – with its lavender walls, crystal lamps, and satin chaise – helps fulfill Clive's wish of preventing the action from descending into vulgarity' (Kinder 1977: 17). The characters whose agonies we watch or imagine are living in cocooned surroundings. Clive himself is living and dying in an extraordinary mansion, an Englishman's castle with rolling resplendent gardens and views over the landscape, an image from a Henry James novel. This house, this ornate outmoded world, is also a reflection of Clive and his imagination. It is from this house, or rather its gardens, that we acquire one of the most extraordinary perspectives of the film.

Close to the end, as the family are dining at their table in the gardens, the camera rises from their social circle and seems, for some moments, to leave them behind, out of the frame. We follow instead an extraordinary 360° panoramic shot over the gardens and the surrounding verdant landscape. Critics differ in the way they respond to and read this shot. For Rascaroli, it signals the film's self-enclosure: 'Despite its deceiving journeys in space, the film never moved very far, but simply circled around itself, constructing the space of a return' (Rascaroli 2002: 57). For Shoos: 'The peace and contentment of the afternoon are summarized in the last few minutes of the film in a slow 360° pan which records the beautiful, pastoral surroundings ... and reassures us that there are no more nightmare visions to be found here' (Shoos 1989: 11). Riley and Palmer, too, find at the end 'a unity that is at once both aesthetic and moral' (Riley and Palmer 1981: 219). For Maillot: 'Resnais, dans un panoramique de 360 degrés porte un regard apaisé sur le monde'[7] (Maillot 2003: 47). Pierce comments, by contrast: 'It is late afternoon, the sun is low, and we are all too conscious of night's coming and the inevitability of Clive's descent back into hell to fight the raging demons of his fragmentary past' (Pierce 1980: 257). Adair writes, with still more melancholy: 'And, as the camera tracks gently away from the house in a 360-degree crane

7 'In a 360° shot, Resnais surveys the world with satisfaction'

over the English countryside's almost pre-Raphaelite greenness, why do we feel that, his pains at an end or the Chablis given out, *he has died in the night?*' (Adair 1977: 121). To substantiate such a reading, we might refer, too, to Žižek's reading of another 360° shot, in Kieślowski's *La Double Vie de Véronique* in the scene where Weronika encounters Véronique in the town square in Krakow. Zizek questions: 'is this camera's circular movement not to be read as signalling the danger of the "end of the world", somehow like the standard scene in science-fiction about alternative realities, in which the passage from one to another universe takes the shape of a terrifying primordial vortex threatening to swallow all consistent reality?' (Zizek 2001: 84). While the shot in *Providence* is infinitely more stately, more tranquil than the vortex to which Zizek refers, it still is reminiscent of this ominous, transfiguring move beyond coherent, fixed perception.

The film ends with the children leaving Clive, at his request, neither touching him nor bidding him farewell. They disappear, like ghosts, from the banquet, withdrawing into the palatial home, the extraordinary stone and carceral space which anchors the film. Clive is left alone, in repose at the end with his life now evacuated. A parting low-angle shot shows the façade of the house with dark windows, lightless and empty.

While *Providence* is an intensely personal drama, Resnais tends at moments to privilege not his characters but the spaces which precede them and which they later leave. In *Repérages*, Semprun speaks of the absence of human figures in early photography (a result of the long exposure times first necessary). He writes: 'Les photos d'Alain Resnais nous replonge dans cette angoisse originelle. Ce malaise, cet inconfort, cette remise en question: l'absence de l'homme vécue par l'homme' (Resnais and Semprun 1974).[8] In the urban shots in *Providence*, which look forward to images at the end of *Mon oncle d'Amérique*, in the perfectly smooth 360° shot of the landscape, Resnais shows us spaces without human presence. We can align these with the emotions and reactions of the protagonists we have known, but the connection is always imaginary, one we create. In filming unpeopled spaces with his moving camera, Resnais brings stylisation and abstraction into the film, spaces in which our emotions

---

8 'Alain Resnais's photos cast us back into this original anxiety. This unease, distress and questioning come from man's experience of man's absence'.

are suddenly undirected, spaces in which we can roam but in which we know no security. Matching horror with horror, he counters thus the brute entrapment and entropy of Clive Langham's world and of his body, which the novelist himself has attempted to escape or ignore in his involvement with an imaginary world.

As he dismisses his children, Clive Langham speaks of the 'strange and marvellous afternoon' he has spent with them. These same adjectives attach easily to Resnais's film. Lines of dialogue in the film return, emotions are repeated and rehearsed; rather than faltering, Clive's mind, if it is here that as viewers we exist, darts onwards with another flow of wine, another displacement and hidden connection. The film has the labile properties of a dream, constantly shaping and reshaping itself. At moments it cuts to the quick, yet shows too the veils of fiction and denial which may obscure too brutal knowledge. After *Providence*, Resnais will still not let death rest; the theme recurs in his films of the 1980s, but in more muted and shadowy forms.

References

Adair, Gilbert (1977) '*Providence*', *Sight and Sound*, 46:2 (spring), pp. 120–1.

L'Avant-scène du cinéma: Providence, 195 (November 1977).

Benayoun, Robert (1980) *Alain Resnais: arpenteur de l'imaginaire* (Paris: Stock/ Cinéma).

Benayoun, Robert (2002a) 'Un rêve de la morale', in Stéphane Goudet (ed.), Positif, *revue de cinéma: Alain Resnais* (Paris: Gallimard [Folio]), pp. 230–7.

Benayoun, Robert (2002b) 'Un divertissement macabre: Entretien avec Alain Resnais', in Stéphane Goudet (ed.), Positif, *revue de cinéma: Alain Resnais* (Paris: Gallimard [Folio]), pp. 238–52.

Benayoun, Robert (2002c) 'Atteindre les nerfs: Entretien avec David Mercer', in Stéphane Goudet (ed.), Positif, *revue de cinéma: Alain Resnais* (Paris: Gallimard [Folio]), pp. 253–8).

Bersani, Leo and Ulysse Dutoit (1993) *Arts of Impoverishment: Beckett, Rothko, Resnais* (Cambridge MA: Harvard University Press).

Callev, Haim (1997) *The Stream of Consciousness in the Films of Alain Resnais* (New York: McGruer Publishing).

Farnsworth, Rodney (2002) *The Infernal Return: The Recurrence of the Primordial in Films of the Reaction 1977–1983* (Westport CT: Praeger).

Greene, Naomi (1999) *Landscapes of Loss: The National Past in Postwar French Cinema* (Princeton NJ: Princeton University Press).

Jousse, Thierry and Camille Nevers (1993) 'Entretien avec Alain Resnais', *Cahiers du cinéma*, 474 (December), pp. 22–9.

Kinder, Marsha (1977) 'The Art of Dreaming in *Three Women* and *Providence*: Structures of the Self', *Film Quarterly*, 31 (fall), pp. 10–18.

Maillot, Pierre (2003) 'Un face-à-face transatlantique: Resnais/Welles', *Contre Bande: Alain Resnais*, 9, pp. 39–48.

Monaco, James (1979) *Alain Resnais* (New York: Oxford University Press).

Pierce, Constance (1980) 'Night for Day: Toward Reality in Resnais's *Providence*', *Literature/Film Quarterly*, 8:4, pp. 251–7.

Prédal, René (1968) *Alain Resnais* (Paris: Lettres Modernes [Etudes Cinématographiques]).

Rascaroli, Laura (2002) 'The space of a return. A topographic study of Alain Resnais's *Providence*', *Studies in French Cinema*, 2:1, pp. 50–8.

Resnais, Alain and Jorge Semprun (1974) *Repérages* (Paris: Chêne).

Riley, Michael M. and James W. Palmer (1981) 'Providence', *Literature/Film Quarterly*, 9:4, pp. 218–32.

Shoos, Diane L. (1989) 'Language and Repression in Alain Resnais's *Providence*', *Film Criticism*, 13:3 (spring), pp. 3–12.

Van Wert, William F. (1979) 'Meta-film and point of view in Alain Resnais's *Providence*', *Sight and Sound*, 48:3 (summer), pp. 179–81.

Žižek, Slavoj (2000) *The Art of the Ridiculous Sublime: On David Lynch's* Lost Highway (Seattle: University of Washington/Walter Chapin Simpson Center for the Humanities).

Žižek, Slavoj (2001) *The Fright of Real Tears: Krzysztof Kieślowski between Theory and Post-Theory* (London: British Film Institute).

7

Mon oncle d'Amérique (1980), *La Vie est un roman* (1983), *L'Amour à mort* (1984), *Mélo* (1986), *I Want to Go Home* (1989)

In 2003, MK2 released a *Coffret Collector: Alain Resnais* containing DVDs of the five feature films Resnais made during the 1980s. This was arguably a period of echoes for Resnais, of repeating patterns yet increasing uncertainty in the direction of his filmmaking. From his extraordinary reckoning with parallel lives and human behaviour in *Mon oncle d'Amérique*, he moves to a tightly interwoven yet farcical drama about history and education in *La Vie est un roman*, two delicate chamber pieces about love and death, *L'Amour à mort* and *Mélo*, and a burlesque yet melancholy film about an American cartoonist, *I Want to Go Home*.

Mon oncle d'Amérique (1980)

Resnais describes *Mon oncle d'Amérique* as a film about the central nervous system and human behaviour (Benayoun 2002b: 275). He creates a work which is experimental, tracing several personal destinies as case studies or human experiments. The catalyst for the film was a meeting between Resnais and the behaviourist Henri Laborit. Resnais recounts that a pharmaceutical laboratory had invited Laborit to make a short film about a memory-enhancing product. Laborit had seen *L'Année dernière à Marienbad* and had found in the film a perfect reflection of thought processes. He approached Resnais to make the short film with him, but the project failed through lack of money. Resnais in return suggested that they might collaborate on a longer project and found a producer willing to back them. Resnais had already read a number of Laborit's works and he set about reading Laborit's volume on behaviour. Script-writer Jean Gruault was commissioned to write a script drawing on Laborit's work; it was at this stage that a possible documentary was transformed into a feature film. *Mon oncle d'Amérique* was Gruault's first and most successful collaboration with Resnais; they would go on to make *La Vie est un roman* and *L'Amour à mort*. Gruault had also worked extensively with Truffaut, writing the script to *Jules et Jim* (1962) and also to Truffaut's later films *L'Enfant sauvage* (1969) and *La Chambre verte* (1978), which in their different ways anticipate some of the themes of *Mon oncle d'Amérique* and *L'Amour à mort*.

Speaking about his own creative process, Resnais says he sometimes thinks of himself as a small boy with his toy box, trying to fit one set of shapes with another (*L'Avant-scène* 1981: 6). *Mon oncle d'Amérique* is, as this image suggests, a film of playful composition and rearrangements. The film opens with a stylised image of a pulsating heart, violently red. It cuts to a collage of photographs, a mass of traces of incidental moments and individual lives. As the camera moves over the photographs we catch a brief image of the virtual possibilities that exist within the film. These multiple, infinite stories could have been told. The film bears only a metonymic relation to this series of destinies; from the outset it signals its own partial status, its dependence on the exclusion of the majority of its material. From this mosaic, the film settles on three individuals. These destinies are by no means exceptional or even exemplary. The protagonists are rather part of a mass of living human matter that can be observed and recorded. Resnais cuts from the collage of snapshot photographs to a series of still images of plants, creatures, objects (recalling the images of peacetime which return, seemingly randomly, in *La Jetée*, or the close-up shots of objects at the start of *Muriel*). At moments the film resembles a slide show or photograph album as existence is reduced to a series of fixed frames, their connections supplied by the viewer. Voices accompany the collage of images and we can just pick out those of the individuals we recognise later as the three protagonists of the film. But at this stage they are part of an indiscriminate mass, like the first voices in *L'Année dernière à Marienbad*.

The film moves nevertheless to highlight its three protagonists and we are offered a sketch of the destiny of each. Text is read by an announcer and the face of the protagonist in question is shown as a cameo within the frame while we see abbreviated scenes from the individual's life. There is a sense that these lives have been lived before the film is made, that each destiny has been forged and, as viewers, we will only see glimpses, disarranged, of a life in process. The brevity, yet specificity, of each biographical account draws attention to the absurdity of the details which make up each individual life. The first protagonist is Jean Le Gall (Roger Pierre), born 4 August 1929 in the Morbihan. After the Ecole Normale Supérieure, he taught history in a Paris lycée and then in 1975 was chosen as head of radio news. He lost his post in 1977 and went on to write about his experiences in radio. The second protagonist, Janine Garnier (Nicole Garcia), was born in the 20e arrondissement in Paris on 13 January 1948. Her father was a worker at the Renault factory and her family were Communist supporters. After training as a secretary she became involved in the theatre and after a career on the stage moved into management with a textile company. The third protagonist, René Ragueneau, was born on 27 December 1941 at Torfou in the department of Maine et Loire. His parents were farmers and after working on the family farm he went to work for a textile company. While these three figures, from different social milieux, will weave the drama of the film, its images part of the fabric of their lives, the film also presents its fourth figure, Henri Laborit, in the same manner. We learn that Henri Laborit was born on 21 November 1914 at Hanoi in Indochina; his education, career and academc awards are cited as if he were another of Resnais's characters (although his participation in the film is purely in the present with no animation of his past life).

Mon oncle d'Amérique seeks to set up mirroring patterns between art and science through its own internal reflections. The manner of presentation of Laborit mirrors that of the protagonists, despite his different status with relation to the film's drama. Fusing fiction and documentary, Resnais opens space in the film for Laborit to offer short discourses on human behaviour. We see him talking to camera, presenting his ideas as if he were in a documentary. The experimental basis of his work is reflected as Resnais illustrates Laborit's ideas with close-up scenarios showing laboratory rats. The relation of these scenarios, and of Laborit's discourses, to the action in the film as a whole is further suggested as in its late stages we see both Le Gall and Ragueneau in rat form, with rat faces, acting out their own dilemmas.

Reflections move back and forwards between protagonists and rats, between the lived reality of the protagonists, the laboratory reality of the rats, and the surreal world where the two – rat and human – are fused. Further mirrorings exist, too, between the lived reality of the protagonists captured in Resnais's images, and tableaux from other French movies which are spliced into the film. Not content to draw these in as cinematic allusions, Resnais includes in each protagonist's biography the name of a French actor to whom each is devoted. For Jean Le Gall, this is Danielle Darrieux, for Janine Garnier, Jean Marais, and for René Ragueneau, Jean Gabin. Miniature clips of these actors appear at moments mirroring the responses of Resnais's protagonists. The mimicry between scenes works formally to create *Mon oncle d'Amérique* as a hall of mirrors, one image heightening and doubling the effect of another (Benayoun suggests that Resnais and Gruault even considered making the film entirely out of clips (Benayoun 1980: 179)). The repetitions also bring in questions about identification as the protagonists may assume the role of the actor they admire, and about the unconscious as the intrusive image seems in each case to offer, in distilled form, the truth of the scene it doubles.

Moving between art and science, the film is a composite puzzle. In the biography of Janine we glimpse a set of Russian dolls in her childhood bedroom; we see these again later in the film in her dressing room. For Prédal, the film suggests here that the world is made up of a system of interlocking pieces like these Russian dolls (Prédal 1996: 15). In parallel with this composite view of the world, the film adopts a complex structure. While the protagonists' lives seem lived in advance from the start, we still witness the development of each protagonist, as the reflections and differences between their experiences are worked through. This forward flow of the narrative is also interrupted halfway through, the pieces re-arranged. As Penelope Houston observes: 'The second half opens with more from Dr Laborit, and a return to the images of childhood, the pieces of the mosaic now forming a clearer, subtler pattern at this intersection of past and future' (Houston 1980–81: 63). Commenting on the disparate strands of the film, Resnais observes: 'Que de la rencontre d'éléments *a priori* hétérogènes va naître quelque chose, qu'on ne peut pas toujours prévoir' (*L'Avant-scène* 1981: 6).[1] *Mon oncle d'Amérique*

1 'That from the encounter of previously heterogeneous elements something will emerge, that one cannot always foresee'.

resembles the narrative structure of Woolf's *The Waves* where infinitely sentient individual lives lie in parallel with a more abstract narrative of time passing and the day fading. Resnais is willing to let gaps remain, to leave the lives he represents unresolved. The film exists as a series of experiments whose result remains unknown. In observing these experiments, the viewer is drawn in particular to question the relation between collective experience and individual destiny.

Houston writes of *Mon oncle d'Amérique*: 'Not since *Muriel*, perhaps, has Resnais made a film structured for such precise, delicate, and sympathetic effects; and it may not be coincidental that this is also the first film he has made for many years, really since *Muriel*, which is wholly French and of the present' (Houston 1980–81: 63). A trend in discussion of the film has indeed emphasised its status as a record of France at a period of transition. Catherine Brunet suggests that despite his reputation as a filmmaker concerned with memory and forgetting, Resnais captures the present era in which he films with extraordinary acuity (Brunet 2003: 49). She continues to argue that, in representing France at the end of the 1970s, '[*Mon oncle d'Amérique*] témoigne d'une société en profonde mutation: il montre tout à la fois les éléments d'une France finissante et l'émergence de nouvelles structures économiques engendrant en particulier des comportements différents' (Brunet 2003: 50).[2] Le Gall represents a privileged social class in France, with his ENS (Ecole Normale Supérieure) education and his inherited family house, the Villa Beauséjour; his loss of his post at Radio France testifies to political changes under Giscard d'Estaing. Janine Garnier, with her Communist parents and home in Belleville, is representative of a politically engaged proletariat. We see her leave this background behind in her bid to find self-expression in acting and then in her more desultory move into industry. Brunet aligns the role of Communism in Janine's family with that of the Catholic Church in René Ragueneau's rural milieu. Ragueneau moves from the family holding into a job in industry, but then that job becomes increasingly pressurised and uncertain. He serves to draw attention to the insecurity in the workplace and the socio-economic changes in France in this period. Focusing importantly on the

2 '[*Mon oncle d'Amérique*] bears witness to a profoundly changing society: at the same time it shows elements of a France near extinction and the emergence of new economic structures in particular bringing about different behaviour'.

representation of society and change in the film, Keith Reader argues, indeed, that Resnais, like Perec, should be seen as heir to the nineteenth-century novelists (Reader 1996).

The historical specificity of the film also has a bearing on its representation of Laborit. Combs speaks of confusion over whether the film is 'illustrating' Laborit's theories on behaviour (Combs 1980: 239). Prédal argues that: 'Certes le didactisme de *Mon oncle d'Amérique* n'est qu'un jeu s'appuyant sur des explications séduisantes parce que simplistes et mécanistes' (Prédal 1996: 156).³ For Reader: 'Laborit foregrounds the animal and instinctual elements in human behaviour – flight from stress, the defence of territory – in a way that led unwary critics to view the film as little more than an endorsement of then-unfashionable Right-wing theories of biological determinism' (Reader 1996: 177). For Reader, further, Laborit's Right-wing establishment behaviourism is 'abundantly satirized by Resnais' (Reader 1996: 178). Resnais's treatment of Laborit in *Mon oncle d'Amérique* certainly can be seen as an elaborate game. He takes Laborit's theories and works out what it would mean to illustrate them in a film. As we watch the unfolding paths of the lives of the three protagonists, we see at moments how far they can be arranged according to the patterns in human behaviour Laborit has identified. This works not to prove the theories as such, but to show how lives can be deciphered though a particular grid, visualised in scenarios. While the film seems, on one level, to allow Laborit to hold an explanatory role with relation to the other protagonists, it is also, as remarked above, relevant that Resnais should present him self-consciously as a character in the film. In this sense we may read Laborit too, and his theories of behaviourism, as a product of a particular period and society. Resnais relativises Laborit, his life, his works, with relation to other individual destinies in late 1970s France.

Laborit is offered the first words of the film: 'La seule raison d'être d'un être, c'est d'être, c'est à dire de maintenir sa structure. C'est de se maintenir en vie. Sans ça, il n'y aurait pas d'être' (*L'Avant-scène* 1981: 11).⁴ He then expands on this further, repeating and elaborating his terms:

---

3 'Of course the didacticism of *Mon oncle d'Amérique* is only a game depending on explanations which are seductive because they are simplistic and mechanistic'.
4 'A being's only reason for being is to be, that is to maintain its structure. To keep itself alive. Without that, there would be no being'.

Ainsi une pulsion pousse les êtres vivants à maintenir leur équilibre biologique, leur structure vivante, à se maintenir en vie. Et cette pulsion va s'exprimer dans quatre comportements de base: un comportement de consommation, c'est le plus simple, le plus banal, il assouvit un besoin fondamental, boire, manger, copuler. Un comportement de fuite, un comportement de lutte et un comportement d'inhibition (*L'Avant-scène* 1981: 12).[5]

Disconcertingly, further into the film Laborit can be heard beginning again: 'On peut donc distinguer quatre types principaux de comportements' (*L'Avant-scène* 1981: 24).[6] His ideas return as a refrain in the film. Their calm, measured presentation by Laborit, his gentle didacticism, seems gradually belied by the growing mess around the characters. Laborit's voice and observations begin to dominate the second half of the film and with this increasing presence we find him precipitating ideas precisely about dominance: 'La recherche de la dominance, dans un espace qu'on peut appeler le territoire, est la base fondamentale de tous les comportements humains, et ceci en pleine inconscience des motivations' (*L'Avant-scène* 1981: 54).[7] The fatalism of the last words of the film seems particularly keen: 'Tant que l'on n'aura pas diffusé très largement à travers les hommes de cette planète la façon dont fonctionne leur cerveau, la façon dont ils l'utilisent, et tant qu'on aura pas dit que, jusqu'ici, ça a toujours été pour dominer l'autre, il y a peu de chances qu'il y ait quelque chose qui change' (*L'Avant-scène* 1981: 69–70).[8]

By letting Laborit's words begin to dominate, Resnais establishes, ironically, some critical distance from them. Domination and aggression, the violent submission of the other to the will of the self,

5 'Thus a drive urges living beings to maintain their biological equilibrium, their living structure, to keep themselves alive. And this drive will be expressed in four basic modes of behaviour: the mode of consumption, which is the simplest, the most banal, satisfying a fundamental need, drinking, eating, copulating. Modes of flight, fighting and inhibition'.
6 'One can make out four principal types of behaviour'.
7 'The search for domination, in a space that can be called the territory, is the fundamental basis of all human behaviour, and quite without conscious motivation'.
8 'For as long as people of this planet are not informed about the way their brain functions, the way they use it, and for as long as we don't admit that, up until now, it has always been used to dominate the other, there is little chance that anything will change'.

have been insistently his subject. Yet he looks precisely for a more compassionate or attentive mode of engagement between individuals. In *Mon oncle d'Amérique*, Resnais contests the dominant theory of Laborit by focusing on the affect, emotional and bodily pain of the protagonists as they engage in Laborit's scenarios. The protagonists are more than laboratory rodents, yet even in his presentation of the actual rats Resnais draws out pathos. Set against Laborit's voice-over we see a female laboratory technician stroking one of the rats. In the second half of the film rat images thread through the enactments of human behaviour. Laborit's experiments are seen in omniscient overhead shots as we see the rat undergoing various ordeals. After Laborit shows the conditioned rat unable to avoid an electric shock, Resnais offers an unusual close-up of the rat in a state of anxiety. Its face stares straight to camera, its fur on end, catching the light. The rat's experience is shot on a human scale and, as elsewhere in his films, Resnais indiscriminately responds to physical and mental suffering. Indeed, against Laborit, the rat images of *Mon oncle d'Amérique* represent an unconscious truth about the protagonists as they contend with conflict. Rather than illustrate their behaviour mechanistically, the rat images make visible, in miniature animal forms, the unspoken and uncomprehending pain and fear of his protagonists. Shots of the wild boar, glimpsed early in the film and seen later, dying and dead as Janine confronts Le Gall, function similarly. In these images, Resnais pays homage to Renoir's shooting scene in *La Règle du jeu*. Cutting between the shot boar and Janine herself, he allows the viewer to reconsider the sentience and the pathos conjured in shots of a dying creature.

Reader, contesting Laborit's presence in the film, sees the protagonists as desiring machines, in Deleuze and Guattari's terms (Reader 1996). Such a reading stresses the potential in the individual, the way in which his or her destiny is constantly becoming and in process. Such process knows conflict and pain but, as Reader writes: 'For Deleuze and Guattari, these fractures and malfunctionings carry the charge of a certain *jouissance* that is glumly absent from the world Resnais depicts' (Reader 1996: 179). Resnais's vision is manifestly melancholic; as Jan Dawson recognises, however, 'there is a beauty to the spectacle of human defeat which cannot be rationalized in terms of behavioral patterns' (Dawson 1980: 23). Benayoun, stressing too the ways in which the film outstrips Laborit, writes that the multitude of scientific, sentimental and symbolic information the film offers only makes the lives of its protagonists seem more intense and inexplicable (Benayoun 2002a: 265).

Referring to the title of the film, Richard Combs writes: 'Even the notion of the "American uncle" operates with some ambiguity in the film: the unrealistic hope of some salvation outside ourselves, or an imaginative challenge to which we fail to respond?' (Combs 1980: 240). Reference to the American uncle is made lightly in the film; it surfaces first in an argument between Ragueneau and his wife. Ragueneau says that any time people mentioned change to his father he would speak of his American uncle, who ended up on the streets in Chicago. Ragueneau counters, against his father, that his uncle's fate was never proved. For Oudart, 'L'Amérique est tout à fait absente du film de Resnais, absente lourdement' (Oudart 1980: 48).[9] The American uncle himself is structurally missing, an object outside the frame of the film nevertheless determining the narrative of failed aspirations and desires. Yet America itself is figured, in a collage of shots at the end of the film described in the screenplay:

> De l'image de Janine et de Jean se battant, on passe à des paysages de villes en ruine que nous explorons. Nous avançons le long d'une rue vide d'une cité antique en ruine (Utica, en Tunisie, par exemple), ou d'une ville moderne abandonnée par ses habitants (la partie sud du quartier du Bronx à New York, ou la ville de Cleveland dans l'Ohio, ou encore le cimetière de Wood Lawn à New York, avec ses mausolées géants) (Resnais 1980: 147).[10]

Using an impressionistic creative geography, Resnais cuts between locations as his tracking camera moves past row upon row of derelict buildings on unmarked streets. Prefiguring the desolate collage at the end of Lars von Trier's *Dogville* (2003), Resnais's dream of America in *Mon oncle d'Amérique* opens a space of anomie and despair at the end of the film which has only this empty, anonymous hinterland beyond its frame. Seeking some escape, the camera closes

9 'America is entirely absent from Resnais's film, massively absent'.
10 'From the image of Janine and Jean fighting, we move on to explore landscapes of towns in ruins. We move down an empty street of an ancient city in ruins (Utica, in Tunisia, for example), or of a modern city abandoned by its inhabitants (the South Bronx in New York, or the city of Cleveland in Ohio, or even the Wood Lawn cemetery in New York with its giant mausoleums)'.

in on an urban mural, 'The American Forest', which Resnais saw by chance on a street in New York. The mural offers an image of painted nature, something verdant, but, as Brunet notes: 'cette unique note de verdure paraît d'autant plus dérisoire que, plus la caméra se rapproche, plus les traces de peinture s'effacent au profit de la brique sale' (Brunet 2003: 60).[11] For Brunet, Resnais approaches abstraction as his camera moves so close to the brickwork that the shape of both building and painted design are lost in close-up detail. Resnais himself has wondered how to approach detail without losing a sense of the whole (*L'Avant-scène* 1981: 7). The painted brickwork seems an abstract double of the wall of photographs at the start, so many traces of information which risk losing all connotative or expressive power, viewed from too great or too little a distance. Further, the painted brickwork visually echoes foliage seen from within the rat's cage in one of Laborit's early experiments. The mesh of the cage recalls the patterns of the brickwork. The mural at the close bricks in the film in this way, whilst apparently opening an illusion of a verdant escape or retreat.

Mon oncle d'Amérique privileges pathos more than Laborit, making us aware of protagonists as sentient fearing subjects whose desire, however failed or hopeless, still impels them beyond the limits of their lives. The film reaches an impasse: Ragueneau has made a suicide attempt which fails, but he will surely lose his job; Janine and Le Gall are left wrestling with one another like Jacob and the Angel. Resnais counters Laborit by offering no solutions, by making a film which emerges not as lesson but as elegy, an album of images of a present era but also, within the broader frame of his filmmaking, a more universal engagement with failed and failing lives.

La Vie est un roman (1983)

Resnais continued to work with Gruault on his next two films. As a collage film, *La Vie est un roman* recalls *Mon oncle d'Amérique* but is too caricatural, and too dissonant, to achieve its coruscating engagement with individual destinies. When *La Vie est un roman* came out in

---

11 'this single touch of verdure seems all the more derisory because, the closer the camera gets, the more the traces of paint lay bare the dirty brick beneath'.

Paris, *Le Monde* declared it 'a catastrophe' (see Serceau 2003: 61). Combs notes that unease quickly hardened into dissatisfaction with the film (Combs 1984: 135). Adair, aptly, writes: 'As a film it is utterly without antecedents, a prime number' (Adair 1983: 200). He notes that it is weakest in 'its exclusively intellectual discourse' (Adair 1983: 201). The film was conceived, initially, as a more spectacular and hybrid work. In line with a concern which will dominate his filmmaking in one way or another for the next two decades, Resnais notes: 'Il y avait d'abord le très fort désir de faire un film où le parler et le chanter alterneraient' (Daney and Dubroux 1983: 28).[12] For Serceau, however, 'ce sont précisément les parties chantées qui créent un incontestable malaise' (Serceau 2003: 66).[13]

Despite its discordant reception, *La Vie est un roman* is in one way a key work in Resnais's corpus in marking the arrival of Sabine Azéma, the muse of his later years around whom Resnais would create a new circle. Resnais notes: 'Je tire un énorme plaisir, personnellement, en tant que spectateur, de la notion de troupe. Je suis ravi quand je vais voir un film de Bergman, et je dirais presque que j'irais voir n'importe lequel rien que pour cela. Parce qu'il me plaît de retrouver la troupe et de voir en garagiste l'acteur qui faisait le chevalier dans le film précédent' (Masson 2002a: 171).[14] In *La Vie est un roman*, Sabine Azéma joins Pierre Arditi (who had already appeared in a minor role in *Mon oncle d'Amérique*), Fanny Ardant and André Dussollier. The four play together again in *L'Amour à mort* and *Mélo*. Arditi and Azéma alone play in *Smoking* and *No Smoking* and, latterly, in *Pas sur la bouche*. Dussollier joins them, in between, in *On connaît la chanson*.

Azéma is indeed the real revelation of *La Vie est un roman*. Critics comment on her qualities as *ingénue* and on her youthful enthusiasm (Masson 2002a: 285). She is literally driven into the film at the start, the film focusing on her face, the very timbre of her voice lightening

---

12 'First of all there was the very strong desire to make a film where dialogue and song would alternate'.
13 'it is precisely the parts in song which create an unquestionable unease'.
14 'Personally, as a spectator, I draw an enormous pleasure from the notion of a company. I am delighted when I go to see a Bergman film, and I would almost say that I would go and see any film just for this. Because I like to recognise the company and to see the actor who was a knight in the previous film now playing the part of a garage mechanic'.

the scenes in which she plays. Azéma is radiant in the film, if occasionally edgy or high-pitched. In interview, Azéma speaks of the extraordinary gift Resnais gave her in using her for the film (Thomas 1989: 93) and of the inspiration Resnais offers to his actors (Thomas 1989: 92).

Azéma stars in the contemporary strands of the film, where it comes closest to the historical vision of *Mon oncle d'Amérique*. For Prédal, the film is a lucid biopsy of our era's utopias (Prédal 1996: 98). In the contemporary strands, in the words of Masson, Resnais ridicules pedagogues (Masson 2002a: 284). He shows a group of teachers and educational experts gathering for a conference on 'Education de l'imagination'. The acting style and scenarios presented are so overstretched that it is hard to see the film either as defence or critique of the methods of education it explores. As Masson notes, the shots are fairly loosely composed and dispersed (Masson 2002a: 288), offering a liberty or even a bagginess to the whole.

The visual style of the other two historical strands creates a more unified effect. Intercut with the modern narration are scenes from a generic, and fantastic, medieval era. (As Thevenet notes there is little logic in the interweaving of these periods (Thevenet 1983: 6).) The medieval scenes largely fail to engage the viewer; Serceau suggests this may be because no close shots are used, leaving us to view the scenes from afar (Serceau 2003: 65). Resnais collaborates here on the design of the film with cartoonist Enki Bilal. The sets and visual effects are created through a technique of painting on glass (first used in cinema by Méliès). The fantasmagoric, bejewelled constructions, the fantasy foliage of the medieval sequences, are two-dimensional illusions painted on glass, given substance by their relation to the material objects and human figures within the frame. Such a technique, explored and illustrated elaborately in Thevenet's book *Images pour un film: Les décors d'Enki Bilal pour* La Vie est un roman *d'Alain Resnais*, adds to the visual experimentation of the film, though the final images, and dark colours, are not visually appealing.

Bilal's world of the imagination, caught on glass, also illuminates the first and most effective strand of *La Vie est un roman*. The film opens with a close-up on the face of Fanny Ardant. She plays Livia, a young woman in evening dress who is being driven with her suitor (André Dussollier) to a mysterious gathering in the forest of the Ardennes. They alight from their carriage, stepping into one of the most memorable scenes of the film. We see a gathered ensemble in evening dress out in an icy landscape (shot from overhead). The images recall *L'Année dernière à Marienbad* or *Stavisky*. Here we see ornately dressed individuals, an ensemble with men in dark suits and top hats and women in shimmering velvet and jewel-encrusted dresses, against the wastes of the landscape. They have been summoned to the site of a future building project. Their host, Forbek (Ruggero Raimondi), unveils a model of a fantasy palace he will build on this site. We see a model in miniature designed by Bilal, anticipating the stylisation of his medieval sequences. It is as if the palace at Marienbad has been redesigned and extended by Gaudi or Hundertwasser. In interview Resnais alludes to the extravagant mansions in California or New England as his inspiration. Adair describes the fantasy palace as 'a Radiant City, Wellsian, Wellesian and Orwellian, in the depths of the Ardennes (or Arden) Forest' (Adair 1983: 201). As his references imply, the fantasy palace embodies a vision of the future. Forbek presents the palace as location of future harmony and happiness. This gathering takes place, however, in 1914, on the eve of the First World War. Mass trauma is figured most minimally as fires burn behind the model of the palace. Forbek gathers his friends once more five years later when the palace has been built, now out of joint with the post-war era. At his house party, Forbek serves an elixir of forgetting, an exquisite pale green philtre served in crystalline cocktail glasses. His guests, dressed in densely pleated pink robes, pass out as they recline, like sleeping figures in an Albert Moore painting.

La Vie est un roman is one of Resnais's bizarrest films, in particular as it incorporates the themes – memory, forgetting, historical knowledge – that he has treated more soberly elsewhere. Adair again sums the film up aptly as he says (alluding to one of the influences behind Forbek): '*La vie est un roman* is a folly, in the architectural sense of the word, the sense in which it is applied to Beckford's Fonthill' (Adair 1983: 200). For Lardeau, the film is more than the sum of its parts (Lardeau 1983: 41); for Adair, the film gathers coherence in retrospect. After this ensemble piece, Resnais expresses the need to work with a smaller cast, on a more restricted canvas.

L'Amour à mort (1984)

L'Amour à mort opens with red titles on a black background: Resnais asked his cinematographer, Sacha Vierny, to use a restricted palette of red, black and gold throughout (Prédal 1996: 68). For François Thomas (2002a: 298), the film depends on a broader series of strong contrasts, the most striking of which are those between life and death. Indeed *L'Amour à mort* plays on the hesitation between animate and inanimate which runs through Resnais's films. This is mapped on a metaphysical and erotic scale in *L'Amour à mort* where Resnais's protagonists offer religious meditations on ressurrection and the afterlife and debate the possibility of love unto death.

The drama of Gruault's plot centres around four protagonists: Simon (Pierre Arditi), an archeologist; Elisabeth (Sabine Azéma), a botanist and Simon's lover of a few months; and Judith (Fanny Ardant) and Jérôme (André Dussollier), friends of Simon and pastors in the local community. Close to the start of the film Simon is viewed in agony, then he is pronounced dead by an elderly doctor. As Elisabeth attempts to rally from this shock, she sees Simon coming down the spiral staircase of their apartment. He has returned to her from the dead. The majority of the film takes place in a doubtful interlude between living and dying. While Simon has returned and is palpably present, verifiably alive, some shadow of death has been cast over him. Like *Je t'aime je t'aime*, the film draws inevitably towards his second death and subsequent burial, closing the space and time of hesitation, of wish-fulfilment, it has provided. The last parts of the film concern Elisabeth's attempts to persuade her pastor friends that she must accompany Simon in death by suicide.

The film is most interesting in its exploration of the return from the dead by Simon. This is rendered not a puzzle that has to be solved in the film but merely part of its dream logic, and its attempt to reveal some truth of the experience of responding to the death of the other. The very impossibility of sense-making, of comprehension, that death generates, is conveyed in the film's interruption of logic, in the time between Simon's first and second death. Associated with this interruption in both temporal and medical logic are a series of interludes which in turn disrupt the progress of the film as narrative, allowing it to exist on a more formal or abstract plane. Resnais claims that the origin of the film was in music and that he wanted to use music differently from in his other films (Masson and Thomas 2002: 306). He uses here the music of Hans Werner Henze and he allows it to stand alone in the interludes between the film's action scenes. Resnais contemplated offering interludes of complete blankness where the viewer merely listened to Henze's music. In the completed film he uses a varied series of shots of illuminated particles falling against darkness. Prédal notes that these interludes have been interpreted as speaking of death's ascendancy, but might equally offer an image of love's devotion (Prédal 1996: 136). For Le Roux, more prosaically, the shots are reminiscent of shaken snow globes (Le Roux 1984: 47). For Resnais there was no symbolism in these interludes: 'Ce que j'ai cherché avec les particules, c'est à obtenir une image non figurative qui permette au spectateur de mieux suivre la musique' (Masson and Thomas 2002: 309).[15] However they are interpreted, these interludes work in the film to speak of something beyond or beside the narrative; they set it in a different perspective, allowing it to be suddenly obscured and removed from vision. The film remains fissured by moments which suspend sense-making, leaving the spectator interrupted.

The screenplay's treatment of death and resurrection are nevertheless also visceral and embodied (Le Roux 1984: 46). In some respects *L'Amour à mort* echoes the treatment of the dying and dead body in *Hiroshima mon amour*. Where the French woman in the earlier film finds her dead lover, embodied, resurrected, in the figure of the Japanese lover, in *L'Amour à mort* Resnais echoes this erotic death encounter in shots of a resurrected Simon and Elisabeth making love. Hands clasping and contorting are again a visual motif. Parallels are drawn aurally between Elisabeth's pleasure with Simon and her later grief. Like the woman in Hiroshima, in the film's strange hiatus Elisabeth encounters Simon as dying and yet also as already dead. The film is haunted by her attempts to verify that he is still alive; she literally tracks him through the countryside, through the house, as the camera itself, oddly animate, tracks through trees (echoing *Providence*) in the opening of the film.

As Thierry Jousse points out, we are always with Elisabeth in the film – we do not know anything that she does not know (Jousse and Never 1993: 29). Simon's death encounter may be the subject of the

---

15 'What I wanted to do with the particles, was to achieve a non-figurative image which would allow the spectator to focus better on the music'.

film, but it is Elisabeth's response to this, and the exacerbation of her hopeless love for him, which seems to fascinate Resnais. He chose to film *L'Amour à mort*, like *Le Chant du styrène* and *L'Année dernière à Marienbad*, in CinemaScope. He recounts that an advantage of CinemaScope is that it allows close-ups of faces without the concommittant loss of a relation of those figures to the space around them. For Resnais, 'Très rapidement, il y avait l'idée que c'était un film de visages' (Masson and Thomas 2002: 316);[16] in this respect the film bears comparison in particular with the films of Bergman. In *L'Amour à mort*, the face we see abundantly is the loving, mourning visage of Sabine Azéma. She may not conjure the pathos of Bergman's actresses, or the mad sobriety of Charlotte Rampling in a comparable role in François Ozon's *Sous le sable* (2000), but Azéma carries the film with fervent enthusiasm. She tells François Thomas: 'j'ai joué les scènes de *L'Amour à mort* avec ces cordes qui résonnaient dans ma tête comme des hurlements de bête blessée' (Thomas 1989: 103).[17] In preparing for the film Resnais required her to read Henry James's tale, 'The Altar of the Dead'; he asked her to look at the paintings of Munch. Through art, literature and music he conjured the sepulchral, heistant world of *L'Amour à mort*, a world whose reach stretches into their next film, *Mélo*.

In *L'Amour à mort*, Elisabeth states: 'ma seule religion, c'est Simon'.[18] Masson questions: 'c'est un autosacrifice humain, appelé par des voix infernales. La décision d'Elisabeth exprime l'absolu de l'amour?' (Masson 2002b: 294).[19] Elisabeth seems obdurate, fanatical, in her bid to follow Simon to death. While Judith and Jérôme reason with her and offer theological arguments against suicide, the film seems to cherish Elisabeth's passion for Simon. Azéma sacrifices herself impulsively as Elisabeth, as she will again commit suicide in *Mélo*. Resnais pursues his fascination with love-lorn women, and Azéma meets his every demand in her acting. The relatively cool reception of *L'Amour à mort* may suggest that viewers are less willing to follow this lead.

16 'Almost immediately I had the idea that this was a film of faces'.
17 'I played the scenes from *L'Amour à mort* with these string notes echoing in my head like the cries of a wounded creature'.
18 'Simon is my only religion'.
19 'it is a suicidal human sacrifice, summoned by infernal voices. Does Elisabeth's decision express the absolute of love?'.

Mélo (1986)

Resnais's company returns to play in *Mélo*. In the mid-1980s Resnais was working on a project with the novelist Milan Kundera. This failed, leaving Resnais in search of a script at short notice. He selected Henry Bernstein's play *Mélo*, written in 1929 and filmed at least four times through the 1930s. As Johnson writes: 'Henry Bernstein's *Mélo* is a 1929 French counterpart of a "well-made" Broadway play (and indeed it was soon translated to Broadway) – a psychological drama involving a sexual triangle between bourgeois characters' (Johnson 1988: 24). The drama centres around a handful of characters (for Robert Benayoun it is a classic *ménage à trois* (Benayoun 2002c: 330)). Pierre (Pierre Arditi) and Marcel (André Dussollier) have trained as violinists; Marcel now has an international solo career. Pierre, living in a suburban house in Montrouge, has married Romaine, also called by the diminutive Maniche (Sabine Azéma), the younger sister of his dead first wife. Over dinner Romaine desires Marcel and a relationship develops between them, though this is strained as Marcel goes on tour. Romaine begins to poison Pierre, but, caught between love and guilt, she drowns herself instead. The end of the play takes place three years later after Pierre has married his companion Christiane (Fanny Ardant). He confronts Marcel about his possible affair with Romaine. Marcel denies this to the end and the play finishes with the two friends playing a sonata by Brahms which has been key to desire and inter-relation throughout the film.

Resnais comments that he was not allowed to see the play in his childhood, but that his parents brought him back the programme (Sotinel 2003: 30). He admits that he was keen to create an adaptation of the play he would have wished to see (Thomas 2002b: 336). *Mélo* was made on a low budget – 7 million francs – and in a 23-day shoot, with 12 days of rehearsals in the Boulogne studios in advance. Combs suggests that Resnais has turned the period between the wars into 'a kind of personal *rétro* cinema: a time of false promises and illusory hopes which the films are designed to trap – a contradictory task – in a precisely constructed, concrete, almost materialist frame' (Combs 1987: 131). The film looks back to *Stavisky* and looks forward to *Pas sur la bouche*, yet it also provides its own hermetic world. *Mélo* takes us into the intimacy of a *ménage* and rarefies its every emotion. Resnais brings polish and control to the adaptation. It is a glittering and asphyxiating work, vivified in particular by the performances from Dussollier and Azéma.

Mélo opens with images of a finely manicured hand turning the pages of a theatre programme. Recalling Resnais as a child, this immediately emphasises the theatricality of the production; yet it works also to focus on the tactile and on the privilege of cinema in bringing us up close to the drama of the play. The opening is seductive in its presentation of the cast – we see glamorous photographs of Azéma and Ardant – and also in inserting us into the expectant moments, the material reality of theatre-going, before the action begins. Resnais shows a red stage curtain which returns between each act. Theatricality is emphasised in the filming of large proportions of the drama on enclosed sets. While the first scene is an evening meal in a garden, the sky above the garden is a stylised midnight blue. The characters inhabit a sparkling, painted world. The interiors – a bachelor apartment, a glamorous nightclub – are exquisite art deco set pieces. The apartment is in muted and luxurious beige and camel with decorative frosted glass windows. The night club, with its mirrored walls, is constructed as a space of disorientaton as we catch reflected glimpses of the characters dancing the tango. This motif of broken reflections is repeated in the film where we see Romaine through window frames and layers of glass as she reaches the decision to commit suicide, and Marcel in a wall of mirrors as he is confronted by Pierre at the end. For Prédal: '*Mélo* assume le cinéma en tant que spectacle et non miroir du réel' (Prédal 1996: 26).[20] Far from capturing the real world, the mirrors of *Mélo* construct an ever-reflecting, self-enclosed, transient reality.

For Johnson, 'the whole of *Mélo* can be compared to a chamber piece in three movements' (Johnson 1988: 26). His use of the term 'chamber piece' recalls the enclosure and interiority of the film, yet it also likens Resnais's film to the music he treats as subject. This is a film about an intrigue, and romantic rivalry, between musicians. There is a realist dimension in its use of music. A particular piece, the Brahms G Major Violin Sonata, plays through *Mélo*. For Johnson, Resnais's film takes on the very qualities of such a chamber piece in its intensity, control and intimacy. Echoing Proust's use of the Vinteuil sonata to calibrate the love between Swann and Odette in *Un Amour*

---

20 '*Mélo* adopts cinema as spectacle and not mirror of the real'.

de Swann, the music played in the film acts as a metonym for desire, for feelings of longing, and memory and mourning, which remain outside language. Prédal writes: 'jouer la sonate = faire l'amour' (Prédal 1996: 58).[21] Romaine goes to Marcel's apartment and they play the sonata together (she questions whether she could have played this in front of Pierre). The music implies the merger of the two figures as Romaine accompanies Marcel's violin as she has previously accompanied Pierre. Yet the music is also part of the relation between Marcel and Pierre. Pierre says of the sonata, 'elle évoque toute notre jeunesse à Marcel et à moi' (*L'Avant-scène* 1987: 13).[22] The film ends as the two men play the Brahms sonata together. The friendship and rivalry between the two men never supplants the intense romance at the centre, yet *Mélo* is most concerned with that romance viewed through the frame of the friendship betrayed.

Loss is central to the aesthetic of *Mélo*. On one level the film is a nostalgic recreation of a past era of filmmaking. Azéma notes of Resnais: 'Il a toute une collection de photographies d'actrices de l'époque, des tas de livres, et donc on faisait des choix pour les costumes, la coiffure, le maquillage' (Thomas 1989: 97).[23] Romaine is an incarnation of a lost icon, a collaged figure who is both 'femme-enfant' (Benayoun 2002c: 330) and silent movie star (Toubiana 1986: 14). She is fragile, diaphanous, poised between madness and her imminent death by drowning. For Toubiana this fleeting quality stretches to the whole of the film; he writes, in words which foreshadow *Pas sur la bouche*: '*Mélo* ... est un film spectral, où les personnages, les figures visibles, venues du théâtre, ne sont au fond que des apparences' (Toubiana 1986: 13).[24]

Where the use of music is Proustian, Resnais also lingers, like Swann, on imagery of flowers. Where Stavisky has showered Arlette with white flowers, Marcel brings Romaine deep red roses. The roses become a symbol in their love affair, beyond her death. Toubiana mentions the scene where 'Marcel Blanc, en cachette de son rival, pose délicatement ses lèvres sur le pétale rouge, donnant ainsi un

---

21 'playing the sonata = making love'.
22 'for Marcel and me, it evokes our whole youth'.
23 'He has a whole collection of photographs of actresses of the period, piles of books, and so we made choices for the costumes, hair and make-up'.
24 '*Mélo* ... is a spectral film, where the characters, visible figures from the theatre, are really only semblances'.

dernier baiser à une morte, collant sa bouche sur les traces disparues de celle de Romaine' (Toubiana 1986: 15).[25] The rose petal pressed in her diary, a commemorative fragment, a fragile relic, survives the love affair. Resnais's attention to the relic indicates the pathos with which he invests material objects in his filming of memory. *Mélo* is a loving return to Bernstein's original, yet a re-adaptation which reflects on questions of loss and melancholy, on the past as enclosed world which the director can only approach imperfectly, mournfully, in his film-making.

I Want to Go Home (1989), *Gershwin* (1992)

I Want to Go Home is Resnais's second English-language film. It seems a comic reflection of *Providence*, with its mansion and house-party in the French countryside. The film opens with shots of an aircraft flying from New York to Paris. The shots have the artifical colour and texture of Resnais's later fake images of the Paris sky-line in *On connaît la chanson*. In *I Want to Go Home* a young woman flies to Paris to study Flaubert with the French intellectual Christian Gauthier (Gérard Depardieu). For Alain Masson, *I Want to Go Home* is a film about the American vision of French culture (Masson 2002c: 376). The film recalls the dislocations of *Providence*; it also looks forward to the hybrid cinematic space, neither England nor France, of *Smoking* and *No Smoking*.

In developing the project, Resnais approached American cartoonist Jules Feiffer, who was known for comic strips on love, politics, age and depression. Feiffer provided the script and Resnais took it into production alone in France, beginning filming in autumn 1988. The film was received with a standing ovation at the Venice Film Festival in 1989 and Feiffer received the award for best script. But the film was not widely distributed and, in Feiffer's words, remained, 'unseen and unseeable', in the United States (McGilligan 1990: 146). Resnais acknowledges his lack of success with *I Want to Go Home* (Jousse and Nevers 1993: 26). On the one hand it is a nostalgic film about Americans in Paris (as his star cartoonist, Joey Wellman, Resnais

25 'While his rival is not looking, Marcel Blanc delicately puts his lips on the red petal, thus giving a last kiss to a dead woman, pressing his mouth against the vanished traces of Romaine's'.

casts Adolph Green, screenwriter of *Singin' in the Rain* (1952)). On the other, it seeks, more rawly, to investigate family material.

Despite interest in *bandes dessinées*, Resnais insists that *I Want to Go Home* does not bear the influence of cartoon in its form (Prédal 1996: 73). The film follows forms of American comedy, interrupted by the appearance of an animated cat, Hepp Cat, Wellman's cartoon character and 'le surmoi félin et animé de Joey Wellman et de sa fille' ('the animated, feline superego of Joey Wellman and his daughter') (Gras 1989: 45). Hepp Cat breaks the surface of the film allowing it some hybridity and also giving expression to the antagonism and desires of its characters. The device signals Resnais's interest in intrusions and borrowings from other genres; it also foregrounds an unwitting psychic symbiosis between his two protagonists, Wellman and his daughter.

The film stages a protracted *dialogue de sourds* between the two. Elsie, having left Cleveland for Paris, does not write to her father for two years. Her resentment stems from the separation of her parents and her enmity towards Wellman's new partner. In Paris their hostilities continue in failed phone calls and encounters until they are reconciled at a costume party in the family house of Christian Gauthier. Elsie here returns to fragments of her childhood and memories of her father drawing for her as a child. These memories allow the father and daughter to refind one another; she returns to the United States at the end while he stays in France. Gras comments on 'l'indéfinissable distanciation/affection qui caractérise le rapport du spectateur aux personnages des films de Resnais' (Gras 1989: 47).[26] Wellman and Elsie often appear caricatural, occasionally surprising us with their sentience and depth of feeling.

In a late scene, Wellman looks for someone to speak English to him in the local village. The villagers gradually gather around him in an amused crowd. When Elsie comes to find him, he is ensconced in cross-cultural dialogue, drawing cartoons. Elsie apologises to him and they hug and reconcile. As he holds her hand, a child approaches the table and smiles at Wellman. He looks from Elsie to the child as he says: 'I don't know if I'm ready to go home yet'. The child seems to stand as an image of the Elsie he has left before, but she is smiling at

26 'the undefinable distancing/affection which characterises the spectator's relation to the characters in Resnais's films'.

him now. The film calls for filial piety in the figure of the smiling child; it forgives the father who again seeks leave of absence. The child glimpsed here is played by Ludivine Sagnier, offering a moment of recognition for viewers who will see her later in the films of François Ozon.

I Want to Go Home anticipates the playfulness of Resnais's works of the following decade but does not equal their formal invention, reach or poise. He would follow the film with an unexpected return to documentary. He was commissioned to direct a project about Gershwin for the series *L'Encyclopédie audiovisuelle* (other films in the series included an entry on Darwin by Peter Greenaway). *Gershwin* received negative press when it was shown on TV in the UK; François Thomas, writing in *Positif*, shows more sympathy (2002c). In *Gershwin*, Resnais disrupts chronology; his account of the composer's life begins with forgetting, with Gershwin experiencing a traumatic moment of amnesia while playing in a concert in June 1937. This amnesia led to headaches, anxiety attacks and the subsequent diagnosis of a brain tumour and early death. His body was buried in the Westchester Hills cemetery in New York State. Early in the film, and at its close, Resnais shows beautifully framed shots of the imposing mausoleum. In a documentary which is largely a chamber piece, shot in the studio or in interiors, these vivid cemetery shots connect with the broader field of Resnais's filmmaking (Thomas makes a link to the shots of the Parc Monceau in *Stavisky* (2002c: 388)). Resnais creates a traumatised account of Gershwin's life, taking his decline and death as its frame. He stresses the sobriety and melancholy of Gershwin's music, in contrast to the unbridled optimism of his brother Ira's lyrics.

Resnais offers a cinematic and theatrical appreciation of Gershwin, with comments from Martin Scorsese and Bertrand Tavernier amongst others. Arditi and Azéma read the commentary; we also recognise Adolph Green from *I Want to Go Home*, here with his partner Betty Comden. Resnais stresses the cultural and ethnic hybridity of Gershwin's musical background on Tin Pan Alley, but any direct purchase on the social reality of Gershwin's past and career is slowly dissipated as the film favours a roving gaze over static images of the past, captured from an original fresco painted by Guy Peellaert. The last parts of the film indulge in an extraordinary rolling programme of Gershwin's productions where we hear snatches of a decade of works. *Gershwin* confirms Resnais's extreme interest in the rhythm and affect of documentary where meaning is created not so much in individual shots or sequences as in the move between them. While commentators note a return to the forms with which Resnais started his film career in *Gershwin*, this film too seems to anticipate his next decade of filmmaking, with its variations on a theme and increasingly musical compositions.

References

Adair, Gilbert (1983) 'Un Deux Trois: Films by Resnais, Rohmer and the Straubs', *Sight and Sound*, 52:3 (summer), pp. 200–2.

L'Avant-scène du cinéma: Mon oncle d'Amérique, 263 (March 1981).

L'Avant-scène du cinéma: Mélo, 359 (April 1987).

Benayoun, Robert (1980) *Alain Resnais: arpenteur de l'imaginaire* (Paris: Stock/Cinéma).

Benayoun, Robert (2002a) 'Le retour au pays natal', in Stéphane Goudet (ed.), Positif, *revue de cinéma: Alain Resnais* (Paris: Gallimard [Folio]), pp. 260–74.

Benayoun, Robert (2002b) '"Proust, jamais!": entretien avec Alain Resnais', in Stéphane Goudet (ed.), Positif, *revue de cinéma: Alain Resnais* (Paris: Gallimard [Folio]), pp. 275–81.

Benayoun, Robert (2002c) 'Palimpseste de vérité', in Stéphane Goudet (ed.), Positif, *revue de cinéma: Alain Resnais* (Paris: Gallimard [Folio]), pp. 326–31.

Brunet, Catherine (2003) '"La nouvelle France" de *Mon oncle d'Amérique*', *Contre Bande* 'Alain Resnais', 9, pp. 49–60.

Combs, Richard (1980) '*Mon oncle d'Amérique (My American Uncle)*', *Monthly Film Bulletin*, 47:563 (December), pp. 239–40.

Combs, Richard (1984) '*La Vie est un roman (Life Is a Bed of Roses)*', *Monthly Film Bulletin*, 51:604 (May), pp. 135–6.

Combs, Richard (1987) '*Mélo*', *Monthly Film Bulletin*, 54:640 (May), pp. 131–5.

Daney, Serge and Danièle Dubroux (1983) 'Entretien avec Alain Resnais', *Cahiers du cinéma*, 347 (May), pp. 26–36.

Dawson, Jan (1980) 'French Uncles', *Film Comment*, 16:5 (September–October), pp. 18, 20–3.

Gras, Pierre (1989) 'Alain Resnais: L'illusion librement acceptée', *La Revue du cinéma*, 453 (October), pp. 43–52.

Houston, Penelope (1980–81) 'The Animal Condition: *Mon oncle d'Amérique*', *Sight and Sound*, 50:1 (winter), pp. 62–3.

Johnson, William (1988) '*Mélo*', *Film Quarterly*, 41:4 (summer), pp. 24–7.

Jousse, Thierry and Camille Nevers (1993) 'Entretien avec Alain Resnais', *Cahiers du cinéma*, 474 (December), pp. 22–9.

Lardeau, Yann (1983) 'Les trois âges du bonheur', *Cahiers du cinéma*, 347 (May), pp. 38–41.

Le Roux, Hervé (1984) 'Le Ressuscité d'Uzès', *Cahiers du cinéma*, 364 (October), pp. 45–9.
Masson, Alain (2002a) 'Pour jouer, pour savoir', in Stéphane Goudet (ed.), Positif, *revue de cinéma: Alain Resnais* (Paris: Gallimard [Folio]), pp. 284–90.
Masson, Alain (2002b) 'La religion ou la foi', in Stéphane Goudet (ed.), Positif, *revue de cinéma: Alain Resnais* (Paris: Gallimard [Folio]), pp. 292–7.
Masson, Alain (2002c) 'Riant avec leurs amis', in Stéphane Goudet (ed.), Positif, *revue de cinéma: Alain Resnais* (Paris: Gallimard [Folio]), pp. 374–9.
Masson, Alain and François Thomas (2002) '"Le langage de la passion"; entretien avec Alain Resnais', in Stéphane Goudet (ed.), Positif, *revue de cinéma: Alain Resnais* (Paris: Gallimard [Folio]), pp. 305–23.
McGilligan, Pat (1990) 'Feiffer: Resnais and an "elderly has-been cartoonist"', *Sight and Sound*, 59:3 (summer), p. 146.
Oudart, Jean-Pierre (1980) '*Mon oncle d'Amérique*', *Cahiers du cinéma*, 314 (July–August), pp. 48–51.
Prédal, René (1968) *Alain Resnais* (Paris: Lettres Modernes [Etudes Cinématographiques]).
Reader, Keith (1996) 'Giscardian desiring machines: Alain Resnais's *Mon oncle d'Amérique*', *Journal of European Studies*, 26, pp. 175–84.
Resnais, Alain (1980) *Mon oncle d'Amérique* (Réalisation d'Alain Resnais. Scénario de Jean Gruault) (Paris: Editions Albatros).
Serceau, Daniel (2003) 'La vie est un roman, pour celui qui l'écrit', *Contre Bande* 'Alain Resnais', 9, pp. 61–72.
Sotinel, Thomas (2003) 'Alain Resnais, réalisateur: "Il y avait une folie à la Raymond Queneau dans ce livret"', *Le Monde* (3 December), p. 30.
Thevenet, Jean-Marc (1983) *Images pour un film: Les décors d'Enki Bilal pour La Vie est un roman d'Alain Resnais* (Paris: Dargaud).
Thomas, François (1989) *L'Atelier d'Alain Resnais* (Paris: Flammarion).
Thomas, François (2002a) 'Concert en chambre obscure', in Stéphane Goudet (ed.), Positif, *revue de cinéma: Alain Resnais* (Paris: Gallimard [Folio]), pp. 298–304.
Thomas, François (2002b) '"Mademoiselle Zambeaux, s'il vous plaît!": entretien avec Alain Resnais', in Stéphane Goudet (ed.), Positif, *revue de cinéma: Alain Resnais* (Paris: Gallimard [Folio]), pp. 332–51.
Thomas, François (2002c) 'Fontaine de jouvence', in Stéphane Goudet (ed.), Positif, *revue de cinéma: Alain Resnais* (Paris: Gallimard [Folio]), pp. 382–9.
Toubiana, Serge (1986) 'Rosebud: *Mélo* d'Alain Resnais', *Cahiers du cinéma*, 387 (September), pp. 12–15.

8

Smoking/No Smoking (1993), *On connaît la chanson* (1997), *Pas sur la bouche* (2003)

The films which Resnais has made since the early 1990s, *Smoking* and *No Smoking* (adaptations by Agnès Jaoui and Jean-Pierre Bacri of Alan Ayckbourn's plays *Intimate Exchanges*), *On connaît la chanson* (an original script by Jaoui and Bacri, distinguished in particular in its use of popular songs) and finally *Pas sur la bouche* (an adaptation of a 1925 operetta by André Barde and Maurice Yvain) could not seem more different from the documentaries, and traumatic subjects, with which Resnais is first associated. While each film continues to show the director choosing a new and divergent path, the late films are nevertheless haunted by certain echoes. Each in its own way explores a sense of déjà vu and of uncanny familiarity.

This late period shows Resnais knowing unexpected success. *Smoking* and *No Smoking* won the Prix Louis Delluc in 1993, the Silver Bear at Berlin and 5 Césars in 1994. *On connaît la chanson* won 7 Césars in 1997 and has been Resnais's most popular film to date. He says in interview in *Sight and Sound*: 'The success of *On connaît la chanson* is a complete mystery to me – my fourteenth film and finally everybody likes it!' (Duynslaegher 1998: 18). In 2003, *Pas sur la bouche* was awaited with ceremony and excitement in the Paris cinephile and cinema-going community, with early set reports in *Première* and television coverage.

Smoking and No Smoking

Discussing *Smoking* and *No Smoking*, Resnais says:

> J'étais aussi attiré par cette espèce de nostalgie qu'on retrouve dans une page de Kundera au début de *L'Insoutenable Légèreté de l'être*, quand le héros regarde le mur d'en face et se dit que quelle que soit la décision qu'il prendra, il ne pourra jamais savoir ce qu'aurait donné l'autre; une vie ressemble toujours à une esquisse, à l'ébauche d'un tableau qui ne sera jamais achevé: 'Ne pouvoir vivre qu'une vie, c'est comme ne pas vivre du tout' (Thomas 2002a: 407–8).[1]

In *Je t'aime je t'aime* Resnais shows a man re-viewing scenes from his past life, at random (at the will of a malfunctioning machine). Ridder's life is open to interpretation, yet its events are singular and irrevocable, leading inexorably, in whatever order, to his death by suicide. In *Smoking* and *No Smoking* Resnais pursues his interest in the narrative of a life one can conceive or imagine. The films allow the spectator to visualise divergent destinies for Resnais's protagonists, supposedly letting us imagine the virtual possibilities which inhere in any choice or chance decision (and this experimentation leads critics to see the films as part of a new trend of ludic films). Resnais gives us multiple sketches of his characters' lives yet, as I will go on to discuss below, the effect of this proliferation of destinies is peculiarly disheartening.

Resnais saw Alan Ayckbourn's play *Absurd Person Singular* in London in 1972 and since then continues to see his plays. Ayckbourn met Resnais at his theatre in Scarborough during the production of *The Revengers' Comedies*. Resnais later contacted Ayckbourn to enquire about adapting *Intimate Exchanges*; these plays were a singular project, composed of eight separate parts, each to be staged on a different night, with two actors, a man and a woman, playing all the parts. Philip Strick explains the structure of the plays: 'Sixteen divergent conclusions sprout from eight main events derived in turn from four sessions of enlightenment, two introductory encounters and one

---

[1] 'I was also attracted by the type of longing you find in a page near the start of Kundera's *The Unbearable Lightness of Being*, when the hero looks at the wall opposite and says to himself that whatever decision he takes, he can never know the outcome of any other; a life is always like a sketch, an outline of a painting that will never be finished: "Only being able to live one life is like not living at all"'.

moment of decision' (Strick 1994b: 47). The plays have been seldom performed. Resnais admits: 'c'est peut-être grâce à sa disparition rapide de la scène londonienne, que, ne l'ayant pas vue, j'ai pu songer à la mettre en scène...' (Jousse and Nevers 1993: 23).[2]

Resnais approached actors and screenwriters Agnès Jaoui and Jean-Pierre Bacri asking them to adapt the plays in a French version. (Jaoui and Bacri had previously written the screenplay for Philippe Muyl's film *Cuisine et dépendances* (1992) and they would go on to write and star in Cédric Klapisch's *Un Air de famille* (1996); Jaoui directed *Le Goût des autres* in 2000.) Approaching *Intimate Exchanges* Resnais decided to make two films, each of which explores an extending series of possibilities. He leaves out two of Ayckbourn's strands, suggesting they are too typically English (one shows a cricket match, the other a medieval pageant). In *Smoking* and *No Smoking*, following *Intimate Exchanges*, there is one initial scene, in which the protagonist Celia Teasedale comes out into her garden in the midst of spring cleaning. In *Smoking*, she smokes a cigarette and is visited by a man named Lionel Hepplewick. After this scene, the film jumps forward to a scene 'Cinq jours plus tard', then to a following scene 'Cinq semaines plus tard' and then to the culmination of the first strand 'Cinq années plus tard'. After these first four scenes, the narrative rewinds and we enter the first avowedly virtual strand as we see the intertitle 'Ou bien'.[3] *Smoking* then shows an alternative scene of culmination, 'Cinq années plus tard'. Then with a further 'Ou bien' we jump back again to see an alternative scenario 'Cinq semaines plus tard' followed by two further possible scenarios 'Cinq années plus tard'. The narrative rewinds once more so that we find ourselves now, again, at the end of the first episode and see an alternative 'Cinq jours plus tard', followed sequentially by a scene 'Cinq semaines plus tard' and a further 'Cinq années plus tard' and then one further, alternative, 'Cinq années plus tard', offering twelve separate scenarios in all. *No Smoking* follows an equivalent pattern beginning where Celia comes out into the garden and, this time, chooses not to smoke. From this tiny decision a series of variant destinies unfold, leading to another film of twelve evolving but conflicting scenarios.

2 'it is perhaps because of their quick disappearance from the London stage that, not having seen them, I could think of filming them...'.
3 'Five days later'; 'Five weeks later'; 'Five years later'; 'Or rather'.

There is an identical preface at the start of each film where actor Peter Hudson introduces us to the setting, a fictional village, Hutton Buscel 'dans le Yorkshire'. Resnais's image of Yorkshire is deliberately stylised. This effect is enhanced where each scene is demarcated by a brightly coloured drawing by the artist Floc'h. French is spoken in Resnais's Yorkshire; indeed, as Philip Strick comments, 'its inhabitants all appear to be strikingly overdressed French immigrants engaged in a subtly Anglophobic charade' (Strick 1994b: 47). The films are disconcerting in their relation to realism. On the level of detail they are strikingly precise. Resnais chooses British brands of cigarettes and alcohol. Sabine Azéma, the main actress, chose clothes for her characters on a trip to England. Even the soundtrack is apt; as Resnais says, his sounds – seagulls, bells, children on a playing field, church hymns – are properly English (Thomas 2002a: 416). The film's music is composed by John Pattison, who has worked frequently for Ayckbourn. Yet in the language they use, their acting style, gestures and range of references, the actors Sabine Azéma and Pierre Arditi, who play all the parts, appear singularly French.

This discrepancy adds to the levels of unreality in *Smoking* and *No Smoking*. Just as Resnais creatively merges France and England, so he moves freely between theatrical and cinematic conventions. Jonathan Romney describes the films as 'theatrical cinema in the fullest sense of the term' (Romney 1994: 10); in this respect the films recall *Mélo* and indeed look forward to *Pas sur la bouche*. For Romney, 'it's as if the phantom presence of the proscenium arch were hovering invisibly over the action' (Romney 1994: 10).Theatricality is enhanced by the fact that the films were made entirely within the Arpajon studios. Resnais's set designer, Jacques Saulnier, spent eight days taking photographs in Yorskhire and then concocted a Yorkshire house and garden, hotel terrace, golf club and church fête. Resnais has expressed a preference for working in the studio, and for the continuity of filming these conditions allow (he wonders too if this preference derives from the influence of 1930s cinema). Studio conditions offer control over the setting, its presentation and lighting. Renato Berta, the cinematographer, speaks for example of the care with which (using computer technology) he lit the second scene of *No Smoking*, a dinner on the terrace where the sun sets and night falls (Berthomé and Thomas 2002: 450). (Similar effects are created in a sunset scene in *On connaît la chanson*.) Jean-Louis Leutrat has commented:

'Resnais aime les univers artificiels déjà constitués, à partir desquels il peut prendre son élan et organiser ses propres variations' (Leutrat 2002: 396).[4] While Ayckbourn's plays provide these artificial worlds, with their variations, the very conditions of production of *Smoking* and *No Smoking* in the artificially lit studio add a further level of control and construction.

The sense of theatricality is further enhanced in the acting style of the two players. There are nine parts in the films, five female and four male, and just two actors, Azéma and Arditi (a trailer for *Pas sur la bouche* comments on their inseparability). With reference to *Smoking* and *No Smoking*, Strick writes: 'Sabine Azéma and Pierre Arditi respond magnificently to a unique invitation to show off, and do so without apparent exhaustion' (Strick 1994b: 48). (Arditi says of Resnais: 'Personne n'a porté sur moi un regard aussi intense que le sien, à part ma mère: il me regarde comme un objet précieux, et du coup je deviens précieux' (Kohn 2002: 425).)[5] The use of single actors to play multiple roles recalls the theatre as does Resnais's refusal to let two characters played by the same actor appear in the same frame. This would have been possible in cinema; its avoidance adds to the questions about verisimilitude in the pair of films. The timing of the actors' exits and entrances in different roles is such as to give the effect that they have very rapidly, but plausibly, changed costume. In this sense the conventions of the stage are upheld again, with gentle parody.

While the use of two actors offers a theatrical constraint, it also opens up reflection on the relations and differences between the characters. In *Smoking* the major couple presented are Toby and Celia Teasedale, a headmaster and his wife. They interact with an alternative couple, Lionel Hepplewick, the school caretaker, and Sylvie Bell who is Celia's cleaner. In *No Smoking*, while Celia is still central at the start, Miles Combs, Toby's best friend, and his wife Rowena gradually take centre stage, while Lionel and Sylvie also enter the narrative at various points. Through costume changes and stereotyping, the characters are easily delineated. They seem at times almost a set of puppets or figures escaped from an Ionesco play. Yet Resnais does not let us fix them like this, adding uncertainty to the way we perceive them.

4 'Resnais likes already constructed, artificial worlds, which he can use as a point of departure for his own variations'.

5 'No one but my mother has looked at me as intensely as he does: he looks at me like a precious object, and immediately I become precious'.

Azéma stresses that the characters themselves are always in transition in the individual scenes (Strauss and Taboulay 1993: 30). Each character's identity is shifting, as both actors in turn shift between characters. This sense of characters changing through their interactions links the films with Resnais's earlier works. The class and gender demarcations in *Smoking* and *No Smoking* are, however, somewhat cruder. A further constraint coming from the use of only two actors is that each scene depends on a male–female exchange. (*On connaît la chanson* is richer in embracing the complexity of the relationship between sisters Odile and Camille, and the friendship between Nicolas and Simon.) If the roles are more stereotyped in *Smoking* and *No Smoking* there is also something disquieting in the repetitions between the scenes and in the reappearance of certain needs, desires and betrayals between the characters. For Strick, 'Ayckbourn's pageant becomes self-evidently the story of just two people, exploring a multiplicity of possible lives. They could even be just Celia' (Strick 1994b: 48). For Sizaret, 'Alain Resnais s'intéresse ... aux constantes des personnages, aux lois internes qui les animent' (Sizaret 2003: 93).[6] We are left uncertain whether these characters are shadows, personae of a single person, or whether they are differentiated individuals whose needs and impulses move in parallel, bearing witness to their broader social and psychological conditioning (echoing in this respect Resnais's work in *Mon oncle d'Amérique*).

Smoking and *No Smoking* are supposedly an answer to Kundera's grief that we can only know one life and not all a life's virtual possibilities. Yet Resnais's approach to these virtual lives seems stark and melancholy. In his volume on Kieślowski, *The Fright of Real Tears*, Žižek argues: 'a new "life experience" is in the air, a perception of life that explodes the form of the linear, centred narrative and renders life as a multiform flow' (Žižek 2001: 78). He refers to such films as Kieślowski's *Blind Chance* (1987) and Tom Tykwer's *Run Lola Run* (1998) (acknowledging that a fuller representation of virtual destinies may be found in hypertext). Yet Resnais already in narrative cinema goes some way to eschewing linearity and singularity of narrative; further he may anticipate in *Smoking* and *No Smoking* some of the conclusions Žižek draws about the filming of virtual lives.

6 'Alain Resnais is interested ... in the constants in the characters, in the internal laws which animate them'.

In *Blind Chance*, three alternative destinies are shown for one individual, their divergence depending on a dream-like moment where he does, or does not, catch a train. Each episode is imagined fully with its passions and commitments, its moments of fear, intensity and futility. While Witek has differing levels of success in each, for me there is no sense of prioritisation of these virtual destinies; more properly there is interest in the possibility in each narrative strand. Žižek argues differently that it is only the third strand that is 'real', that we see two alternative life histories as Witek faces the moment of death. Whichever reading one accepts, the film itself, at the level of style and diegesis, marks no distinction between the three virtual strands or two virtual and one 'real'. Indeed the very realism of Kieślowski's film perversely heightens the effect and disorientation of his filming of virtual destinies.

In *Smoking* and *No Smoking*, what I see as the open meditation of *Blind Chance* is replaced by steadily more claustrophobic narratives (and here my reading follows that of Nicole Sizaret). On one level, Resnais's characters may be heard to voice the existential queries which concern Kundera or Kieślowski: near the end of the first section, 'Cinq années plus tard', of *Smoking*, Celia and Lionel wonder what might have happened if they had continued a catering business together. Celia says, however, that no one knows what would have happened. This statement of apparent fact is beautifully contradicted by the intrusion of the first 'Ou bien' sequence, working precisely to imagine how things might have been otherwise. Curious about their destiny though they may be, on another level Resnais's characters still lead one-dimensional lives. While the viewer of the films, with omniscient privileges, is curious about the possibilities that open up, through the diegesis and manner of representation we quickly lose any sense that one life will be preferable to another; each has its limits, its ennui. The confirmation of this in, effectively, twenty-four different scenes, all with a false sense of chirpy composure and suburban calm, is strongly unsettling. Further, the sense of reality only half-realised which is conveyed by the falsity and theatricality of the settings serves the purpose of Resnais's film about the unbearable similarity, and disappointment, of alternative destinies very well.

In *Smoking* and *No Smoking* Resnais works, in Žižek's terms, to illustrate the possibility that 'other possible outcomes are not simply cancelled out but continue to haunt our "true" reality as a spectre of what might have happened' (Žižek 2001: 79). Resnais's characters are themselves not aware of these spectres; it is left to the viewer to perceive this (traumatic) ghosting of reality. Žižek sees such spectres 'conferring on our reality the status of extreme fragility and contingency' (Žižek 2001: 79). Indeed he argues that, the '(false) ordinary perception that we live in one "true" reality ... relieves us from the unbearable awareness of the multitude of alternative universes which envelop us' (Žižek 2001: 79). Resnais shows a fraction of this multitude; this alone is disquieting where even a limited range of plural destinies unsettle a perception of reality as singular or fixed. Showing further, as Resnais does, that the choice between these realities depends on inconsequential chance and that each separate destiny is itself, in turn, at once routine and fateful lends a devastating effect to the films. Žižek writes: 'Kieślowski's universe is one created by a perverse, confused and idiotic God who screwed up the work of Creation, producing an imperfect world, and then tried to save whatever could be saved by repeated new attempts' (Žižek 2001: 94). This seems apt for Resnais too, who in his insistent repetitions and in the painted artifice of *Smoking* and *No Smoking* shows still more literally a view of reality as a series of botched attempts, imperfect, unfinished, yet finite destinies.

While they offer the viewer little pleasure in the prospect of alternative destinies, the films may hold our attention through their formal innovation. Strick comments that 'a shape can be found in the bewildering checks and renewals of [the characters'] behaviour' (Strick 1994b: 47); Neyrat speaks of the films in terms of mosaic (Neyrat 1998: 73). For Romney, with material reference to their setting, the films form 'a crazy-paving garden of narrative' (Romney 1994: 10). Philippon admits that despite the structure and instructions that accompany the films, a moment comes when we are hopelessly (for him also 'deliciously') lost (Philippon 1993: 21). The films play between form and formlessness. The initial structure is carefully delineated; events and settings, in different permutations, return. Yet the episodes are themselves of strikingly different lengths, as if Resnais allows each to respond to the dramatic needs of the plot and emotions. While each film follows some sense of sequence, Resnais claims that the two films themselves are complementary and not sequential. There is a tendency to see *Smoking*, the film of increased activity and humour, with more focus on Celia herself, as the point of departure, and *No Smoking* as its more melancholy shadow. Yet Resnais himself wishes our choice between the films to be entirely aleatory (Philippon 1993: 20). Whichever way round the films are viewed, there is a sense that the viewing of the first will impact on the viewing of the second. While, for the characters, the slate seems to be wiped clean after each virtual history of their lives, for the spectator, seeing a second variation does not entirely efface the memory of a first (Philippon 1993: 21). The films together build a dizzying sense of déjà vu as we see their protagonists embarking on different, yet similar, emotional and existential journeys in the proliferating narrative strands.

This sense of déjà vu is further enhanced, and complicated, as we recognise returning concerns from Resnais's other films. Vincent Amiel writes, referring to any Resnais film: 'Et l'on a beau puiser dans la raison, dans la conscience claire, dans les articulations fournies par le film, il demeure des taches sombres, des terres inconnues où n'aborder qu'avec difficulté' (Amiel 2002: 19).[7] In *Smoking* and *No Smoking*, this sense of the 'tache sombre' or 'terre inconnue' is rendered literal on the studio stage. As Leutrat comments: 'Il existe ... une réserve spatiale, remise ou refuge, d'où sortent et dans laquelle pénètrent les personnages à tour de rôle' (Leutrat 2002: 397–8).[8] The function of this 'réserve spatiale' – in most scenes a shed of some sorts – is firstly theatrical: it is a space into which characters can disappear and from which others may emerge; it is a space from which sounds may emanate while the actor is invisible. It also has a practical function within the narrative in each case (as the shed gardener Lionel Heppelwick clears out in *Smoking*; as the refuge of Miles Combs and Sylvie Bell on their fated, foggy walk in *No Smoking*). Yet more than this, the 'réserve' forms a space that we cannot see or enter, a blindspot or blot. It is like the rooms not entered in *Marienbad*, the solipsistic sphere in *Je t'aime, je t'aime*, the lodge at the end of *Stavisky*. Resnais disrupts our viewing and knowledge in even the late films (where his films have perpetually been concerned with what cannot be seen and known of trauma, of desire and of the

7 'And one searches in vain through the rationale, the self-awareness, the articulations provided by the film, dark blots remain, unknown stretches that can only be approached with difficulty'.

8 'There is a spatial reserve, a shed or refuge, in and out of which the characters come in turn'.

other). It seems significant that the 'réserve' is associated with the male characters in the two late films; in one closing sequence of *No Smoking*, when a lean-to in the cemetery has been dedicated to the memory of Miles Combs, who has perished in the fog falling over the cliff into the unknown, Rowena, Sylvie and Celia in turn visit the commemorative spot, paying homage in different ways to their love for Miles as absent other. (Love in *Smoking* and *No Smoking* is, though less poetic, in many ways as mystifying and non-reciprocal as in *L'Année dernière à Marienbad*.)

If the male characters, played by Arditi, are associated with this unseen enclosed spot, and literally with reserve, Azéma plays the female characters with more openess and febrile energy. Celia in one strand of *Smoking* and Rowena in another of *No Smoking* are seen to succumb to madness or hysteria. In *Smoking*, Celia, who has become uncontrollable, is literally wrapped in a tablecloth, a white winding sheet, at the garden fête. She emerges at the end and we see her face out of the sheet, distressed, disoriented, broken and child-like. In the following scene, a lengthy five years later, we see her sitting numbed on a bench, recalling Riva in *Hiroshima mon amour*. Despite the broad brushstrokes and the exuberance of her acting style, Azéma manages to bring pathos to her portrayal of the women in the films, and Celia in particular. Where, as Rowena, Azéma often wears her own clothes (in red and black) as Celia she wears rose colours, dresses with white collars, clothes that are at once girlish and subdued. Yet in the frenzy of Celia's madness, and the expressivity of her face and features, Azéma conveys the depth of feeling of her character so we glimpse her life, its proliferating destinies, as tragedy, not satire. Strick writes: 'it is feasible to regard Resnais as the constant and hopeful companion of "lost" women' (Strick 1994a: 15). It is in his exploration of a woman grieving her own fate or fates, that we witness the delicacy and attention of Resnais's filmmaking.

In *No Smoking*, Rowena asks Miles: 'tu te souviens de tout ce qu'on voulait faire?'.[9] She expresses the nostalgia that underlies Resnais's project, its exploration of failed aspirations, of narrative lines and lives which might or might not be followed. *Smoking* and *No Smoking* are, despite their length, restless plays which depend largely on the characters' exits and entrances to trigger action and move the narra-

9 'Do you remember everything we wanted to do?'.

tives forward. The films reflect the tedium and vanity of individual lives, love, domesticity, yet show too how the lives it represents are still alive to pain and the ever present wish for alternative paths.

On connaît la chanson

On connaît la chanson opens with a stylised titles sequence, drawn by Floc'h. Clean line drawings are embellished with cut and pasted photographs. There is a drawing of a Greek column (such an image appears in all Resnais's films); this is followed by a dedication to British playwright Denis Potter, whose work, most famously *The Singing Detective*, inspired Resnais, Jaoui and Bacri. We see images of the screenwriters and director – their photographed faces superimposed over cartoon bodies – and then members of the cast. The blend of fantasy and reality, incarnated in the film in the move from realist action to lip-synched song sequences, is indicated graphically from the opening. While there is melancholy in *On connaît la chanson* it is, arguably, Resnais's most endearing film and clearly the funniest.

Resnais asked Jaoui and Bacri to write an original script for him; their collective project resulted in *On connaît la chanson*. They worked by taping sections of dialogue and sending these to Resnais. The choice of songs was also integral to the writing of the script. Director and screenwriters variously suggested and chose songs which would function directly in relation to the script and its on-going narrative (as illustration and not diversion). Resnais is famous for distancing the screenwriter from the actual shoot; this would prove impossible in *On connaît la chanson* where Jaoui and Bacri were also to star in the film.

Critical responses to *On connaît la chanson* have been mixed. Philip Kemp describes the film as 'a light, beguiling romantic comedy' (Kemp 1998: 55). French critics have found more in the film, and have focused on its blending of humour and melancholy. Yann Tobin explains: 'Mais l'enjouement de cette oeuvre brillante cache, comme derrière le plaisir ophulsien, une poignante mélancolie' (Tobin 2002: 456).[10] René Prédal continues: 'Il est donc question de faire rire, mais avec des stressés, des mélancoliques, des angoissés, des hypocondriaques,

---

10 'But the playfulness of this brilliant work, like the pleasure in Ophuls's films, hides a poignant melancholy'.

des spasmophiles, névrosés ou schizophrènes, avec des couples qui se trompent ou se séparent' (Prédal 2003: 111).[11] For Prédal, Resnais's film creates 'un univers d'incompréhensions' ('a world of misunderstandings') (Prédal 2003: 112). For Resnais the film is about appearance and misunderstanding (Thomas 2002b: 469). He says in interview, in terms which recall earlier reflections on *L'Année dernière à Marienbad*: 'On renonce à certaines décisions parce qu'on pense à l'interprétation qui en sera faite, on tient toujours à ce que l'image, généralement positive, qu'on projette soit comprise par l'autre, sans se rendre compte qu'elle sera reçue par celui-ci d'une manière souvent très différente' (Thomas 2002b: 469).[12] *On connaît la chanson* exposes characters in interaction, misapprehending each other, their interconnections and their unspoken desires. Resnais treats these themes lightly in the film, unsettling viewers. This film is a layered, veiled representation, a shimmering set of scenes which induce the vertigo and malaise from which the characters themselves suffer.

Ostensibly this is a film about two sisters, Odile (Sabine Azéma) and Camille Lalande (Agnès Jaoui). Odile is married to Claude (Pierre Arditi) who, as she does not realise, is having an affair. Camille has recently finished a doctoral thesis and is working as a tour-guide in Paris; she meets Marc (Lambert Wilson), an estate agent, with whom she becomes romantically involved. She is courted more gently by Simon (André Dussolier), who is older, who writes radio plays and who also works for Marc. Simon spends much time showing flats to Nicolas (Jean-Pierre Bacri), who is a sometime suitor to Odile, and who has returned to Paris despite his marriage to an English wife (Jane Birkin). The plot arises out of the coincidental encounters between these characters. Its points of decision and conflict depend on Camille's intellectual and emotional life (her 'soutenance de thèse' (PhD viva voce), her choice between Marc and Simon) and on Odile's wish to move to a more spacious apartment, with a beautiful view over Paris. Its point of culmination is a party held by Odile. Despite its

---

11 'So it's a question of creating humour, but with the stressed, melancholy and anxious, hypochondriacs, spasmophiliacs, neurotics or schizophrenics, with couples cheating on each other or breaking up'.
12 'One doesn't take certain decisions because one thinks about how they will be interpreted, one always wants the generally positive image one projects to be understood by the other, without realising that it will often be received by him or her in a very different way'.

differences from much of Resnais's work, this is a film where he pursues his interest in questions of emotion (heightened or banal) and in the mapping of relations and relationships across space, both material location and an imagined city of Paris.

The opening of the film has disturbed critics. We hear the directorial voice of Agnès Jaoui, Camille as tour-guide, over the opening credits (she begins 'on y va', 'tout le monde est là?').[13] But the first image we see, emerging out of the darkness of the frame, is the Nazi flag. There follows an over-acted image of von Choltitz, the German commander in Paris, receiving a call from Hitler to destroy the city. After he has taken the call, we see his face in close-up; as he speaks, or rather perfectly lip-synchs, we hear instead Josephine Baker singing 'J'ai deux amours' (the song continues, 'mon pays et Paris').[14] René Prédal writes: 'Début étonnant: l'épisode de la destruction évitée de la capitale en 1944 réduit au ridicule d'un dilemme de music-hall dans une sorte de prologue extérieur à l'intrigue proprement dite, insert en forme de flash-back illustrant le commentaire du guide' (Prédal 2003: 99).[15] However irreverant, the scene serves to indicate that Resnais's film will, as ever, allow mental and material reality to collide and in this film in a hyperbolic fashion. The scene ends with three accelerated pans downwards into darkness, accompanied by the sound of Paris traffic. The traffic noise acts as a bridge to the opening of the film proper where we see Camille's gloved hand pointing out the window of the building, on the rue de Rivoli, where the decision to spare Paris was taken. The shots themselves seem to vanish, spiralling away. The film derides this fantasised history – the material of guided tours and tourist routes (recall the atomic tour bus glimpsed in *Hiroshima mon amour*). The shots which seem at first, as Prédal suggests, exterior to the film as a whole, can also be grouped with two other hyperbolic scenarios. In the first Camille and Simon, on another tour, emerge from the métro to see members of the Garde républicaine pass by on horseback. Camille is enraptured with the sight; Simon is then seen himself on horseback, lip-synching to Alain Bashung's 'Vertige de

13 'off we go'; 'is everyone with me?'.
14 'I have two loves'; 'my country and Paris'.
15 'An astonishing start: the episode of the avoidance of the destruction of the capital in 1944 reduced to a music-hall dilemma in a sort of prologue exterior to the plot proper, an insert in the form of a flashback illustrating the guide's commentary'.

l'amour'. In the second scene, Camille goes down steps in a restaurant to visit the bathroom to find herself descending into a dark, surreal scenario of medieval peasants, on the banks of a lake (the scene is a material embodiment of the subject of her thesis). Other mental images are seen in the film, for example where Claude imagines how he will leave Odile, but such other images are shot within the realist register of the rest of the film. In this way, Resnais creates layers of different competing realities in the film; he takes us to extremes of the ludicrous as well as offering more familiar subjective images.

The use of songs throughout *On connaît la chanson* further relates to this layering of reality. Stéphane Bouquet takes a strict view of Resnais's tactics, writing that the grafting of music-hall techniques onto realist cinema creates a profound distancing effect (Bouquet 1997: 47). Other critics have placed Resnais in the company of Terence Davies or Woody Allen. Resnais himself clearly opposes the sense that his film is distanced from realism in its use of songs. He says in interview in *Sight and Sound*: 'I'd even defend the film as a realist document because in daily life, when our minds wander off, we often hear fragments of popular songs in our heads' (Duynslaegher 1998: 14). Bacri, too, comments on the way songs can sometimes reveal what we are thinking (Rouyer and Tobin 2002: 490). Both suggest that the songs work as indicators of, or interference from, the characters' mental lives. In this way the use of songs in *On connaît la chanson* directly pursues Resnais's interest in procedures of representing the imaginary and emotional life of both individuals and collective groups. Critics have aligned *On connaît la chanson* with *Mon oncle d'Amérique* with its use of intercalated extracts from films, or with *I Want to Go Home* with its speaking cartoon characters. On a psychological level this works to uphold a notion of collective or social memory, as the songs (or films) become a bank of sounds (or images) which resonate for characters and audience, which offer a form and means of expression for emotions, sensations and memories.

Resnais has always been interested in music and its mnemonic capacities; he has chosen the composers with whom he has worked on his films very carefully. Where language is often seen in Resnais's cinema as an indirect or inadequate means of expression, music at times takes the place of words. This is witnessed, for example, in *Hiroshima mon amour* in the form of the waltz, written especially for Resnais by Georges Delerue, which the heroine hears on a juke-box.

Here the sounds in Hiroshima seem in tune with and to be summoned from her psyche; as Henri Colpi suggests, the waltz reminds the heroine of her youth (Colpi 1960: 4). In *On connaît la chanson* Resnais, Jaoui and Bacri use a range of twentieth-century songs, from performers such as Arletty, Piaf, Charles Aznavour, Dalida, Johnny Hallyday and Jane Birkin. Critics have seen these choices as evidence of Resnais's interest in aligning popular culture with high art. Resnais is dismissive of such hierarchical divisions, however, commenting on the emotions conjured by popular songs (de Baecque and Lalanne 1997: 51); and specifying elsewhere: 'Chez Piaf ou Trenet, les sentiments sont parfois décrits avec une plus grande précision que dans un roman subtil et de bon goût' (Thomas 2002b: 468).[16] His response to songs, and the way they are used in *On connaît la chanson*, seems to recall T.S. Eliot's thoughts of a 'worn-out common song ... recalling things that other people have desired'. For Prédal, Resnais shows the role of such music in human sentiment and the imagination (Prédal 2003: 105), yet also uses the songs as a form of interior monologue for the characters.

Resnais also uses the songs specifically as a means of creating connections between the characters, signalling interconnectivity. Stéphane Bouquet (referring also to Thierry Jousse) speaks of the songs creating an effect of 'surconversation' (Bouquet 1998: 49), as opposed to the notion of 'sous-conversation' found in Sarraute. 'Sous-conversation' is a stream of inner thoughts, impulses and motives, represented by Sarraute and other experimental novelists not merely as a stream of consciousness but as part of a web of unspoken connections and points of conflict in social inter-relations. 'Surconversation' exists in addition to spoken language but, in *On connaît la chanson*, it can be heard directly and is made up of cited, repeated fragments of song. It still holds a revelatory power with relation to the language of spoken relations, shadowing and enhancing that language, showing its emotion and forces in hyperbolic forms. Part of the humour of *On connaît la chanson* derives from feelings unspoken. Through song, the reserved character Simon can voice the strength of his attraction to Camille as he impersonates the more macho male singers Alain Bashung, Eddy Mitchell and Johnny Hallyday. When Simon sees

---

16 'In Piaf or Trenet, feelings are sometimes described with greater precision than in a subtle and high-brow novel'.

Camille in the library, he lip-synchs to Gilbert Bécaud's 'Nathalie'; later when he is showing an apartment to Nicolas, and is thinking of Camille, the song is heard like mental interference. In another example, Simon and Nicolas sing Jane Birkin's 'Quoi' in the bathroom of an apartment they are viewing. They are shown both in the frame, in a single take, singing the song as a duet. Later in the film, Birkin herself sings the song at the Eurostar terminal at the Gare du Nord. The songs circulate in the characters' spaces, sometimes heard on the radio. This live, aural material is there in the atmosphere around the characters and it attaches at moments to their emotions and becomes briefly their means of expression.

Resnais also uses the songs to create manoeuvres in editing and mnemonic triggers for the spectator. Particularly striking is the rendition of Sylvie Vartan's 'Ce soir je serai la plus belle pour aller danser' ('tonight I will be the most beautiful going dancing') as the characters prepare for Odile's house-warming. The scene starts and ends with Marc in front of his bathroom mirror singing. Through the song the film cuts to each character in turn viewed in a mirror, singing along. We move through the major characters – Odile, Simon, Camille, Nicolas – and back to Marc, then through the characters again, this time with Odile and Camille's father inserted, busy shaving. Marc closes the sequence. The *mise-en-scène* of each intercut shot is similar – each character is viewed from behind with their mirrored reflection in focus. Each is mirrored, they mirror each other, and their expectations are mirrored in the words of the song. The characters, and actors, are seen as a collective group, yet the pathos with which they are viewed and the precision of the details of each shot (Odile's gestures as she combs her hair, the objects and garments in each room) allow each individual to stand out.

As often in his films, Resnais plays here between the collective and the individual. This is witnessed too in scenes showing the house-warming party itself in the goldfish bowl of Odile's flat with its panoramic view of Paris. Emphasising flow and interconnectivity superimposed over the images of the guests we view at certain moments spectral images of jellyfish (*méduses* in French). Internet reviews of the film contain a number of bemused comments. Bouquet offers a fuller explanation, suggesting that Resnais represents distress, anxiety and unease through the images of these illusory sea creatures (Bouquet 1998: 49). Prédal, too, associates the jellyfish with anxiety (as felt in the queasy sound accompanying each shot) but refuses to ascribe them a single signification. Resnais says in interview: 'Je tenais à ce que ces plans restent une énigme, qu'ils ajoutent du mystère et ne constituent surtout pas un symbole' (de Baecque and Lalanne 1997: 52),[17] although he acknowledges that the characters are indecisive, they float, like jellyfish; he also specifies more practically: 'Plastiquement, elles me servent en effet de liaison entre les plans: elles unifient et fluidifient la soirée' (Thomas 2002b: 477).[18] The association of this aquatic world with anxiety is emphasised in the strongest image where Odile's horror, on discovering that her view will be lost as a result of a proximate building project, is given moving visual form in a flash shot of a mammoth octopus. Yet, as she is later comforted by Claude, the seaworld around the characters becomes more harmonious. As Claude François sings 'Chanson populaire' the jellyfish pulse on the screen more peaceably, their formation now a visual pattern superimposed over a shot of Claude clasping Odile, her pale face a further fissure in the image, reflecting the irridescent substance of the fish. These jellyfish with their crystalline, moving, reflective bodies are not so much symbols as mediators, as reflectors, absorbing and transferring the emotion and sensation of the pool in which they circulate. They signal in their moves the interconnections between this group; sea creatures here for Resnais, like the waves for Virginia Woolf, serve to say something of the common unconscious, of the ripples which move between individuals in a circle or community.

In interview, Resnais also draws attention to another sea creature, not spotted literally in *On connaît la chanson*. He talks about the hermit crab, that small creature without its own shell which moves between the dead shells of other crustaceans, seeking a new habitat as its body grows and changes. In these terms Resnais speaks of the desire to move house, which is one of the themes of *On connaît la chanson*. In exploring space and the city, as in other respects, Resnais plays between the natural and the artificial. From the start, this has been signalled as a film about Paris and the chance survival of the city – Paris destroyed, as viewed for example in Chris Marker's dystopian

17 'I wanted these shots to remain an enigma, for them to add mystery and above all not to be symbolic'.

18 'From the point of view of form, they work for me as a link between shots: they make the gathering unified and fluid'.

La Jetée, is a possibility which shadows the film (and indeed the fragility and mutability of structures, urban and domestic, are integral to the film). Since Paris is saved, Camille can chart its tourist routes for her international public. Resnais films, unusually this late in his career, on location, showing us the rue de Rivoli with its colonnades and the Place de la Concorde, the Buttes-Chaumont park with its Pont des Suicidés and mock temple, and the Paris cemetery Père Lachaise. He revisits the macabre and marmoreal Paris of Stavisky's memories of the Parc Monceau, of the cemetery in *La Guerre est finie*. Apparently Resnais wished also to film in the catacombs at Denfert-Rochereau, but this did not prove possible. He films on location, but shows shots of a city which can be formally identified with the imaginary spaces and subjective vision of his films. In addition, he films a confected Paris created in the studio, notably in the party scenes in Odile's flat where a realistic painted image stands in for the panoramic view over the city. Resnais creates no hierarchical relation between painted and stone Paris; he shows each as images, as different representations which will be overlaid in different ways in his film.

Further, the city is mapped as a location of encounters and interconnections, in keeping with one of the main thematic strands of the film (and indeed with the Surrealist aesthetic that Benayoun and others have seen persisting in Resnais's work). For Prédal, Paris is here 'une ville-puzzle' (Prédal 2003: 110); the statue, 'Les Polypores' by Jean-Yves Lechevallier (in the place Jean Cocteau in the 15e arrondissement), is the rendez-vous point for Odile and Marc when she visits her future flat; it is the point where Marc and Camille meet, on several occasions, once accidentally viewed from above by Simon and Nicolas as they are viewing another apartment. The characters are continually catching glimpses of each other in this city which becomes a mirror to their hopes and fears of romantic encounter and betrayal. The spaces of the city are always in part subjective and reflective of the characters' inner states. This is witnessed, for example, in a scene where Nicolas has come to dine with Odile and Claude, and Claude is seen alone in the kitchen (adorned with a teatowel from Scarborough as miniature reminder of *Smoking* and *No Smoking*) singing Charles Aznavour's 'Et moi dans mon coin'. He sees Odile and Nicolas alone in the sitting room, a lit vignette, and returns to his solitude in the kitchen. Seamlessly following the lyrics of the song, the film cuts to a later scene with Odile and Claude alone.

Their old apartment, with its faded green walls and small spaces, seems to enclose them and to speak of the slight atrophy in their relations. Elsewhere in the film, the majority of the interior spaces are empty apartments viewed by Simon and Nicolas, so many virtual spaces, and lives, which Nicolas could inhabit but chooses not to. The characters are rarely at home in this film; their homes are unsettling or cluttered spaces. The spatial paragon of the film is Odile's new apartment, the space where Marc and Camille will view a romantic sunset, the lavish space, decorated with modern art, of the final house-warming. Yet this too is seen as locus of horror as the building project opposite is revealed.

On connaît la chanson ends, as it began, in a different register, humorously, here with Odile's father alone in the apartment looking at an Al Jolson album and wondering, 'il y a quelqu'un qui connaît cette chanson?'.[19] The film has been reassuring in reconciling Odile and Claude and in signalling that Camille, seeking comfort in Simon's arms, may make this better romantic choice. Resnais leaves us with stability and affection, antidotes to the vertigo of the apartment or Paris itself as aquarium or flotation tank. The film is resolved as romantic comedy, anticipating in this respect his work in *Pas sur la bouche*. Yet the brilliance of *On connaît la chanson* lies in its ability, despite its levity and humour, to enter spaces and plumb depths often untouched in such material. *On connaît la chanson* is a slippery film, its pleasures come and go, like the refrains of the songs it echoes, like its reflections on its characters' needs and desires.

Pas sur la bouche

Pas sur la bouche, Resnais's latest film, was released in Paris on 3 December 2003. In its first week it was beaten at the box office by *Finding Nemo* and *Kill Bill Volume 1* in their second week, *S.W.A.T.* and *Love Actually* in their first week on release. Despite fairly unanimous French critical acclaim, *Pas sur la bouche* did not equal the box-office success of *On connaît la chanson* (though, as Vincendeau notes, 'it delighted French audiences' (Vincendeau 2004: 66)).

Resnais returns in his newest film to the territory of *Mélo*,

19 'is there anyone who knows this song?'.

adaptating a *comédie musicale* written by André Barde with music by Maurice Yvain, first produced on 17 February 1925 at the Théâtre des Nouveautés. Resnais needed a script at short notice since his project for a film *Or...*, with an original script by Michel Debris, had to be postponed. The world of the *comédie musicale* or light operetta was familiar to him from childhood trips to Paris to see such productions with his parents. He describes his immense pleasure hearing the music of Maurice Yvain and his consequent decision to film *Pas sur la bouche*. The film was made entirely in the Arpajon studios, allowing Resnais again the luxury of filming in chronological sequence. The film groups together members of Resnais's company, Sabine Azéma and Pierre Arditi. Lambert Wilson returns from *On connaît la chanson*; veteran comic actor Darry Cowl cross-dresses as a concierge; Audrey Tautou and Isabelle Nanty, who worked together previously in *Amélie* (2001), play the other female leads.

The plot of *Pas sur la bouche* is slight and fairly dated (Vincendeau nevertheless makes a strong case for the sophistication regarding gender that is found in the genre Resnais adapts here). The plot circles around Gilberte Valandray (Sabine Azéma), whose husband Georges (Pierre Arditi) believes he married a virginal bride. This illusion is threatened as he meets Eric Thomson (Lambert Wilson), an American businessman, who has been Gilberte's lover. Like Valandray, Thomson too is threatened by female sexuality and it is his phobia about kissing which gives the work its title. After much play with various suitors and younger lovers, the work resolves in an unexpected romance, and full kiss, between Thomson and Gilberte's sister Arlette (Isabelle Nanty), and restored marital harmony between Gilberte and Georges. The plot itself is of little consequence; it is instead the vehicle for a proliferating series of comic scenarios, of variations on thwarted or consummated desire. Resnais circulated Lubitsch's 1925 adaptation of *Lady Windermere's Fan* amongst his cast to intimate the tone of the film. Critics responding to the experimental and bizarre in the film have aligned it rather with Vian and Queneau (Sotinel 2003: 30). The film's success, and pathos, lie also in several features which bind it into Resnais's oeuvre as a whole.

In the first place, in this film even more than in *On connaît la chanson*, Resnais realises his early dream of making a musical. Bruno Fontaine, with whom he had collaborated on the previous film, worked painstakingly with the actors (see Thomas 2003) to achieve a musical film with actors singing, not singers acting (only Lambert Wilson had sung professionally before). Resnais has spoken of his love of American musicals, of Fred Astaire and Ginger Rogers (Benayoun 1980: 23), but also mentions in interview a possibly unconscious French influence: 'J'aime les films de Jacques Demy et aimais beaucoup l'homme. Pourtant, étrangement, à aucun moment je n'ai pensé à lui pendant le tournage. Peut-être m'a-t-il quand même influencé? J'aime bien cette idée d'être influencé consciemment ou non' (Resnais 2003: 38).[20]

Like Demy, Resnais in *Pas sur la bouche* constructs a stylised world. Key here are the elaborate décors designed by Jacques Saulnier, who worked with Resnais from *L'Année dernière à Marienbad* onwards. The set is constructed as an extraordinarily ornate carapace. It provides a range of patterns and textures for the viewer's visual and tactile delectation. In one of the opening shots, a circular tea-table with miniature éclairs and macaroons is seen from above as an elaborate mosaic. The sets favour rich colours: reds, burgundy, deep wood shades. This effect of luxury, protection, texture, is enhanced in the 'garçonnière de style bordel chinois' (Douin 2003: 30) where the red damask chairs have raised, silky, floral patterns, the cushions are encrusted in gold, and the maze of woodwork catches the eye in interlocking patterns.[21] The set is finely worked, carefully wrought, to express the material reality of the film's era, yet also to enhance its visual stylisation and physical appeal. Every detail, every drape is lovingly arranged in a re-creation which speaks of its own excess, its own hyberbole.

This tactile fashioning of a past reality extends beyond the décor to the costumes (designed by Jackie Budin) and the actors themselves. At the centre of the film is Sabine Azéma and she is entirely radiant and pliable. With her beautifully cut hair red and shining, dressed in crushed velvet and at moments literally dripping in jewels she seems to have emanated from the set. Her masquerade of femininity and the hyberbole of the film are pushed to extremes as she dresses up in a magnificent Spanish dancer's costume with embroidered waistcoat and full, swirling black net skirt. Her dancing and energy here, her

20 'I like Jacques Demy's films and liked the man a lot. However, strangely, I never thought of him during the shoot. Perhaps he influenced me even so? I like this idea of being influenced, consciously or not'.

21 'bachelor flat in the style of a Chinese bordello'.

moves to entertain and enrapture the filmmaker, cast and audience (captured too in the images of the published *carnet de tournage* (diary of the shoot)) speak of her indispensability to the film, of her position as tightly wound spring released at its centre. Against the repression of the two male protagonists, Resnais sets in contrast the passion and delirious energy of Azéma.

Pas sur la bouche may not be Resnais's swansong; there is the promise of another film, and this latest is itself is so alive and effervescent. Yet several times in interviews a more melancholy dimension to *Pas sur la bouche* can be glimpsed. Two pieces which appeared in *Cahiers du cinéma* remark on the dizzying technical virtuosity of the film and in particular on its visual effects: its opening with *ombres chinoises* (shadow theatre) offering silhouettes of the characters, and its visual device whereby characters vanish, literally disappearing from view without leaving the frame (see Frodon 2003, and Burdeau and Frodon 2003). Resnais says in the interview which accompanies his *carnet de tournage*: 'J'imagine parfois que tous ces personnages sont des fantômes. Initialement, j'avais prévu un petit prélude. La caméra se promenait sur l'île de la Grande-Jatte, on y racontait la vie d'autrefois. Puis on s'arrêtait devant la façade d'un hôtel particulier hanté chaque nuit par ses anciens occupants' (Resnais 2003: 91).[22] The protagonists of the *comédie musicale* are so lightly characterised, so diaphanous, though dressed up like marionettes or dolls, it is easy to see them like the figures in *Marienbad* as phantoms, ghosts of a past world. Seeming to allude silently to this earlier film, Resnais admits: 'J'ai tourné *Pas sur la bouche* avec cette impression d'ectoplasmes, de cimetières, de feux follets, de personnages qui accomplissent toutes les nuits les mêmes rites sans bien savoir ce que signifient ces conventions' (Thomas 2003: 86).[23]

Pas sur la bouche is an animation of a forgotten operetta, frothy, evanescent, inconsequential. Yet it echoes Resnais's concern more broadly to trace past sensations and moments of being, to watch them

22 'I sometimes imagine that all these characters are phantoms. Initially I had planned a short prelude. The camera would move over the île de la Grande-Jatte, while a tale of the past there was told. Then you would stop before the façade of a private mansion haunted each night by its former inhabitants'.

23 'I filmed *Pas sur la bouche* with this impression of ectoplasm, of cemeteries, of phantom lights, of figures who carry out the same rituals every night without knowing the meaning of their actions'.

take form on film, in memory and fantasy, then allow them to dissipate, to disappear. His filmmaking testifies to such hesitations between memory and forgetting, between the quick and the dead. The materials, the matter, the physical sensations of his films never deny the move into oblivion and forgetting his work anticipates; his loving animation of the past, as erotic ideal, as sensory refuge, exists in symbiotic relation with his bid to move onward into an uncertain future, beyond the closure of his sets, out into the darkness and madness of the gardens of *Marienbad*.

References

Amiel, Vincent (2002) 'Resnais, la construction du désordre', in Stéphane Goudet (ed.), Positif, *revue de cinéma: Alain Resnais* (Paris: Gallimard [Folio]), pp. 13–20.

Baecque, Antoine de and Jean-Marc Lalanne (1997) 'Le goût de la chansonnette: Entretien avec Alain Resnais', *Cahiers du cinéma*, 518 (November), pp. 50–3.

Benayoun, Robert (1980) *Alain Resnais: arpenteur de l'imaginaire* (Paris: Stock/ Cinéma).

Berthomé, Jean-Pierre and François Thomas (2002) 'Soleils en studio: Entretien avec Renato Berta', in Stéphane Goudet (ed.), Positif, *revue de cinéma: Alain Resnais* (Paris: Gallimard [Folio]), pp. 445–53.

Bouquet, Stéphane (1997) 'La vie n'est pas un roman: *On connaît la chanson* d'Alain Resnais', *Cahiers du cinéma*, 518 (November), pp. 46–9.

Burdeau, Emmanuel and Jean-Michel Frodon (2003) 'Alain Resnais: "Voulez-vous jouer avec nous?"', *Cahiers du cinéma*, 585 (December), pp. 22–6.

Colpi, Henri (1960) 'Musique d'Hiroshima', *Cahiers du cinéma*, 18:103 (January), pp. 1–14.

Douin, Jean-Luc (2003) '*Pas sur la bouche* d'Alain Resnais', *Le Monde* (3 December), p. 30.

Duynslaegher, Patrick (1998) 'The Accidental Tourist (including interview with Alain Resnais)', *Sight and Sound*, 8:12 (December), pp. 14–18.

Frodon, Jean-Michel (2003) 'Le Jeu de la règle: *Pas sur la bouche* d'Alain Resnais', *Cahiers du cinéma*, 585 (December), pp. 20–2.

Jousse, Thierry and Camille Nevers (1993) 'Entretien avec Alain Resnais', *Cahiers du cinéma*, 474 (December), pp. 22–9.

Kemp, Philip (1998) '*On connaît la chanson*', *Sight and Sound*, 8:12 (December), pp. 54–5.

Kohn, Olivier (2002) 'Toby or not Toby: Entretien avec Pierre Arditi', in Stéphane Goudet (ed.), Positif, *revue de cinéma: Alain Resnais* (Paris: Gallimard [Folio]), pp. 419–26.

Leutrat, Jean-Louis (2002) 'Hutton Buscel, ou bien... ou bien...', in Stéphane

Goudet (ed.), Positif, *revue de cinéma: Alain Resnais* (Paris: Gallimard [Folio]), pp. 396–404.

Neyrat, Cyril (1998) 'Stable/Instable: Formes et figures de l'instabilité dans le cinéma d'Alain Resnais', DEA d'études cinématographiques, sous la direction de M. Jean-Louis Leutrat, Université de la Sorbonne Nouvelle – Paris III.

Philippon, Alain (1993) 'Vertiges du double', *Cahiers du cinéma*, 474 (December), pp. 20–1.

Prédal, René (2003) 'Un jeu de l'oie à cases musicales... *On connaît la chanson*', *Contre Bande: Alain Resnais*, 9, pp. 99–114.

Resnais, Alain (2003) *Pas sur la bouche: carnet de tournage* (Arles: Actes Sud).

Romney, Jonathan (1994) 'Rules of the Game', *Sight and Sound*, 4:9 (September), pp. 10–13.

Rouyer, Philippe and Yann Tobin (2002) 'Ecrire pour jouer, jouer pour écrire: Entretien avec Agnès Jaoui et Jean-Pierre Bacri', in Stéphane Goudet (ed.), Positif, *revue de cinéma: Alain Resnais* (Paris: Gallimard [Folio]), pp. 482–90.

Sizaret, Nicole (2003) '*Smoking-No Smoking*: Les douzes faims (moins une) du spectateur', *Contre Bande: Alain Resnais*, 9, pp. 85–97.

Sotinel, Thomas (2003) 'Alain Resnais, réalisateur: "Il y avait une folie à la Raymond Queneau dans ce livret"', *Le Monde* (3 December), p. 30.

Strauss, Frédéric and Camille Taboulay (1993) 'Nectar d'acteurs: Entretien avec Sabine Azéma et Pierre Arditi', *Cahiers du cinéma*, 474 (December), pp. 30–3.

Strick, Philip (1994a) 'Waiting for the end', *Sight and Sound*, 4:9 (September), pp. 14–15.

Strick, Philip (1994b) '*Smoking / No Smoking*', *Sight and Sound*, 4:9 (September), pp. 46–8.

Thomas, François (2002a) 'Le point de vue de la mouette: Entretien avec Alain Resnais', in Stéphane Goudet (ed.), Positif, *revue de cinéma: Alain Resnais* (Paris: Gallimard [Folio]), pp. 405–18.

Thomas, François (2002b) 'D'un coquillage à l'autre: Entretien avec Alain Resnais', in Stéphane Goudet (ed.), Positif, *revue de cinéma: Alain Resnais* (Paris: Gallimard [Folio]), pp. 467–81.

Thomas, François (2003) 'Bruno Fontaine: Faire de la musique avec des acteurs', *Positif,* 514 (December), pp. 88–94.

Tobin, Yann (2002) 'Singing, no singing', in Stéphane Goudet (ed.), Positif, *revue de cinéma: Alain Resnais* (Paris: Gallimard [Folio]), pp. 456–60.

Vincendeau, Ginette (2004) '*Pas sur la bouche*', *Sight and Sound*, 14:5 (May), p. 66.

Žižek, Slavoj (2001) *The Fright of Real Tears: Krzysztof Kieslowski between Theory and Post-Theory* (London: British Film Institute).

Conclusion

Little mention has been made here of Resnais's relation to his contemporaries; I have explored his work in some isolation, despite my interest in the critical commentaries on his work. Positioning Resnais, retrospectively, in French cinema is a complex task. *Hiroshima mon amour* was acclaimed in *Cahiers du cinéma* on its release, and Resnais's early work received with massive enthusiasm by directors and critics in France in the late 1950s and early 1960s; his moving camerawork and energetic filming of urban and exterior spaces align him in principle with a new aesthetic in French cinema, yet he was never directly involved in the Nouvelle Vague. His politics, his scepticism, his solipsism, his specific visual sense and the very grammar of his editing leave him apart (or link him more properly with his predecessors, with Vigo or Cocteau perhaps, or with Bresson). Certainly his documentary impulse and purchase on history align him latterly with the work of Godard, in particular as Godard contends with cinema, war and trauma in such works as *Histoire(s) du cinéma* and *Notre musique*. Resnais's films of the 1980s bear comparison with late Truffaut – specifically, for example, in their mutual use of scripts by Jean Gruault. Yet the directors whose work and whose cinematic trajectory since the 1950s bear closest comparison to Resnais are his early collaborators Chris Marker and Agnès Varda, whose relation to the Nouvelle Vague was, like Resnais's, tangential, and whose very different works over subsequent decades are yet equally marked by attention to memory, virtuality and mourning on the one hand, and to the textures, shapes and surfaces of the material world on the other.

Setting Resnais apart in this volume, I have sought to respect the singularity of his filmmaking career. More than many directors,

Resnais would seem to defy an auteurist approach, not in any overt dismissal of auteur theory or in his avowed lack of interest in writing the scripts of his films, but in the extraordinary departures and reinventions of his long career, in the displacement of his attention to new narratives and genres, to new forms of innovation. Respecting this in analysis of a career, I find myself moved in part to treat each film in isolation, envisaging each project as a tabula rasa, as a new opportunity for critical intervention and sensory engagement. This approach, with its attendant risks, is one way towards understanding the rhythm of Resnais's filmmaking career, his refusal of overt repetition, the challenge he meets at every juncture in his move to reinvent his cinematic vision. For me his films demand this kind of selective attention; such attention is perhaps necessary in particular to allow the later films to be viewed on their own terms and not to be overshadowed by such unequalled and inimitable works as *Hiroshima mon amour* or *L'Année dernière à Marienbad*, films which obtrude magnificently in Resnais's filmmaking, and more broadly in modern cinema.

Yet inevitably – despite my syncopated, even amnesiac, approach to Resnais's filmmaking – my project also seeks to identify certain recurring motifs, cycles of repetition, recollections of one film within another. On one level, there are of course material similarities in Resnais's working methods on even highly diverse films. He has been distinctive in assembling a crew and troupe which collaborate with him extensively; in the latter part of his career he specifically favours work in the studio with this discreet group of actors and artists. In addition, specific collaboration with authors (novelists and playwrights rather than screenwriters specifically) is pursued through much of his career; over and again he returns to the same strategy whereby he allows an author creative freedom in the construction of a text and allows himself equal liberty in its visual interpretation. Each text is a challenge or catalyst for the filmmaker; in his engagement with such extraneous textual material Resnais (constantly) allows his films to differ internally, to respond visually and technically to a new irritant or inspiration. Such disjunctive collaboration has allowed his films to be inflected by and imbricated with the work of some of the key literary figures of (post)modernity; in this respect, as well, Resnais stands largely apart in modern French cinema.

Beyond these fairly constant conditions of creation and production,

I recognise here that Resnais's works also tend to brood over certain issues. While other critics are sensitive to different points of return in Resnais, my readings have worked in particular around issues of identity, its fragility and transience, around the uncertainty and lack of knowledge which infest and fissure human interaction and desire. These issues are integrally bound up with the approaches – the questioning of memory and trauma on the one hand, of the senses and material world on the other – which I have adopted in treating Resnais: theories of traumatic memory stress an uncertain, intermittent relation to past events, showing the subject possessed by, rather than possessing, a knowledge of the past, of the other; writers on the senses in cinema have emphasised the suspicion of the visual which motivates a move towards more embodied modes of representation in a bid to glean an imprint, sensory evidence, of a lost history or hidden other. Examining fantasy as it facilitates and complicates human interaction, Resnais shows figures remaining veiled and screened from one another; contending with loss and mourning, he animates lost objects of desire, half-living, half-dead, cinematic hallucinations, haunting the stage of his sets. Disruptions in relations between self and other are the matter of his filmmaking (this quality inspiring the summoning of his name in discussion of later realist directors such as Agnès Jaoui). In his sensitivity to our failure to know the other and our failure to relinquish the other (once lost or dead), Resnais sets new standards in the French film.

Despite such brooding, his films continually move on: his work is itinerant and mobile, restless in its search for departure. The bid to move, and move on, is witnessed in his visual tracking of ambulation, through the streets of Hiroshima, through the corridors and alleys of Marienbad: the urban film, discussed as such here, gives way to the more figurative, labyrinthine films of virtual, mirroring, crystalline spaces. This trajectory, this move from film to film, reveals the correlation in Resnais's filming between real and imaginary spaces, between the built environment and the reality of the mind; in his film style he allows no distinction between the two, he dissolves any difference between external and internal in his emphasis on the uncanny similarities, indeed the total resemblance between lived, remembered and imagined spaces. The same shapes, viewpoints and vistas return as his later films enter new conceptual spaces, where dramas of parallel and alternative histories begin to dominate. The compulsive repetitions of traumatic remembering, the itinerant footsteps through an estranged urban environment, return in more abstract forms in the circling, dizzying structural repetitions used to represent virtual or hypothetical lives; here characters mourn not only the other they have lost or have not known, but the other they might themselves have been.

Vincent Amiel, reflecting on Resnais's works from the new perspective offered by *Pas sur la bouche*, writes: 'Mais ils [ses films] s'appellent aussi mutuellement, et leur autonomie lacunaire ne cesse de dire que chacun est un fragment d'une même démarche' (Amiel 2003: 95).[1] Acknowledging the lacunary nature of each single work, Amiel yet seems to anticipate here some completion in the oeuvre as a whole. I suggest, in contrast, that Resnais's work, despite its precision, its maniacal attention to detail, will always leave something missing. Films of rupture, fracture, illusion and departure – traumatised works despite their visual pleasures – Resnais's works across his career haunt each other, displace and dispel one another, with no move to plenitude or completion. Rather he calls us to respond to their passing pleasures, distractions, as we also acknowledge the deep melancholy, the stringency, the control and candour of his vision.

References

Amiel, Vincent (2003) 'Des histoires qui s'échappent: Trajectoire d'une oeuvre', *Positif*, 514 (December), pp. 95–7.

---

1 'But they [his films] also call out to one another, and the way they lack wholeness individually continually reveals the way each is a fragment of a single enterprise'.

Filmography

***Van Gogh**, 1948, 20 mins, b/w*

Production: Panthéon Production
Conception: Robert Hessens, Gaston Diehl
Text: Gaston Diehl, read by Claude Dauphin
Editing: Alain Resnais
Photography: Henri Ferrand
Music: Jacques Besse
Sound: Studios Saint-Maurice

***Paul Gauguin**, 1950, 12 mins, b/w*

Production: Panthéon Production
Conception: Gaston Diehl
Text: extracts by Gauguin, read by Jean Servais
Editing: Alain Resnais
Photography: Henri Ferrand
Music: Darius Milhaud
Sound: Pierre-Louis Calvet

***Guernica**, 1950, 12 mins, b/w*

Co-director: Robert Hessens
Production: Panthéon Production
Text: Paul Eluard, read by Maria Casarès and Jacques Pruvost
Editing: Alain Resnais
Photography: Henri Ferrand
Music: Guy Bernard, directed by Mac Vaubourgoin
Sound: Pierre-Louis Calvet

Les Statues meurent aussi (Statues also Die) 1950–53, 30 mins, b/w

Production: Présence Africaine, Tadié-Cinéma
Conception and text: Chris Marker, read by Jean Negroni
Editing: Alain Resnais
Photography: Ghislain Cloquet
Music: Guy Bernard
Sound: Studio Marignan

Nuit et brouillard (Night and Fog), 1955, 31 mins, b/w and col.

Production: Argos Films, Como Films, Cocinor
Text: Jean Cayrol, read by Michel Bouquet
Editing: Henri Colpi, Jasmine Chasney
Photography: Ghislain Cloquet
Music: Hanns Eisler
Sound: Studios Marignan

Toute la mémoire du monde (All the Memory of the World), 1956, 22 mins, b/w

Production: Films de la Pléiade (Pierre Braunberger)
Text: Remi Forlano, read by Jacques Dumesnil
Editing: Alain Resnais, Anne Sarraute, Claudine Merlin
Photography: Ghislain Cloquet, assisted by Pierre Goupil
Music: Maurice Jarre, directed by Georges Delerue
Sound: Studios Marignan

Le Chant du Styrène (The Song of Styrene), 1958, 19 mins, col.

Production: Films de la Pléiade (Pierre Braunberger)
Text: Raymond Queneau, read by Pierre Dux
Editing: Alain Resnais, Claudine Merlin
Photography: Sacha Vierny
Music: Pierre Barbaud, directed by Georges Delerue
Sound: Studios Marignan

Hiroshima mon amour, 1959, 91 mins, b/w

Production: Argos Films, Como Films, Daïeï, Pathe Overseas
Screenplay: Marguerite Duras
Editing: Henri Colpi, Jasmine Chasney
Photography: Takahashi Michio (Japan), Sacha Vierny (France)
Sets: Esaka, Mayo, Petri

Music: Giovanni Fusco
Sound: Yamamoto, Pierre Calvet
Cast: Emmanuelle Riva (Elle), Eiji Okada (Lui), Bernard Fresson (German soldier), Stella Dassas (mother), Pierre Barbaud (father).

L'Année dernière à Marienbad (*Last Year in Marienbad*), 1961, 93 mins, b/w

Production: Terra Film, Société nouvelle des films Cormoran, Argos films, Tamara, Cinetel, Pre-Ci-Tel, Silver Films, Como Films, Cineriz (Rome)
Screenplay: Alain Robbe-Grillet
Editing: Henri Colpi
Photography: Sacha Vierny
Sets: Jacques Saulnier
Music: Francis Seyrig
Sound: Guy Villette
Cast: Delphine Seyrig (A), Giorgio Albertazzi (X), Sacha Pitoeff (M)

Muriel ou le temps d'un retour (*Muriel, or The Time of Return*), 1963, 116 mins, col.

Production: Argos Films, Alpha Productions, Éclair, Films de la Pléiade, Dear Films (Rome)
Screenplay: Jean Cayrol
Editing: Kenout Peltier
Photography: Sacha Vierny
Sets: Jacques Saulnier
Music: Hans Werner Henze
Sound: Antoine Bonfanti
Cast: Delphine Seyrig (Hélène Aughain), Jean-Pierre Kérien (Alphonse Noyard), Jean-Baptiste Thierrée (Bernard Aughain), Nita Klein (Françoise)

La Guerre est finie (*The War is Over*), 1966, 121 mins, b/w

Production: Sofracima, Europa Film (Stockholm)
Screenplay: Jorge Semprun
Editing: Eric Pluet
Photography: Sacha Vierny
Sets: Jacques Saulnier
Music: Giovanni Fusco

Sound: Antoine Bonfanti
Cast: Yves Montand (Diego Mora), Ingrid Thulin (Marianne), Geneviève Bujold (Nadine Sallanches), Jean Dasté (le chef du réseau), Paul Crauchet (Roberto)

Loin du Viêt-Nam (Far from Vietnam), 1967 ('Claude Ridder'), 15 mins, col.

Production: S.L.O.N. (Chris Marker)
Screenplay: Jacques Sternberg
Editing: Colette Leloup
Photography: Denys Clerval
Sound: Antoine Bonfanti
Cast: Bernard Fresson (Claude Ridder), Karen Blanguernon (la jeune femme)

Je t'aime je t'aime, 1968, 91 mins, col.

Production: Parc Film, Fox Europa
Screenplay: Jacques Sternberg
Editing: Colette Leloup, Albert Jurgenson
Photography: Jean Boffety
Sets: Jacques Dugied, Auguste Pace (the sphere)
Music: Krzysztof Penderecki
Sound: Antoine Bonfanti
Cast: Claude Rich (Claude Ridder), Olga Georges-Picot (Catrine), Anouk Ferjac (Wiana), Van Doude (le chef du centre), Alain Mac Moy (technicien du Crespel)

Stavisky, 1974, 115 mins, col.

Production: Cérito Films, Ariane Films, Euro International (Rome)
Screenplay: Jorge Semprun
Editing: Albert Jurgenson
Photography: Sacha Vierny
Sets: Jacques Saulnier
Music: Stephen Sondheim
Sound: Jean-Pierre Ruh, Bernard Bats
Cast: Jean-Paul Belmondo (Serge Alexandre/Stavisky), Charles Boyer (baron Raoul), François Perrier (Albert Borelli), Annie Duperey (Arlette), Michael Lonsdale (docteur Mézy), Van Doude (inspecteur principal Gardet)

Providence, 1977, 110 mins, col.

Production: Action Film, S.F.P., F.R.3, Citel Film (Geneva)
Screenplay: David Mercer
Editing: Albert Jurgenson
Photography: Ricardo Aronovich
Sets: Jacques Saulnier
Music: Miklós Rózsa
Sound: René Magnol
Cast: John Gielgud (Clive Langham), Dirk Bogarde (Claud Langham), Ellen Burstyn (Sonia Langham), David Warner (Kevin Woodford), Elaine Stritch (Molly Langham and Helen Wiener)

Mon oncle d'Amérique (My American Uncle), 1980, 125 mins, col.

Production: Philippe Dussart, Andrea Films, T.F.1
Screenplay: Jean Gruault, drawing on the work of Henri Laborit
Editing: Albert Jurgenson
Photography: Sacha Vierny
Sets: Jacques Saulnier
Music: Arié Dzierlatka
Sound: Jean-Pierre Ruh
Cast: Roger Pierre (Jean Le Gall), Nicole Garcia (Janine Garnier), Gérard Depardieu (René Ragueneau), Henri Laborit (himself), Pierre Arditi (Zambeaux), Nelly Borgeaud (Arlette Le Gall), Marie Dubois (Thérèse Ragueneau)

La Vie est un roman (Life is a Bed of Roses), 1983, 111 mins, col.

Production: Philippe Dussart, Soprofilms, Films A.2, Fideline Films, Films Ariane, Filmedis
Screenplay: Jean Gruault
Editing: Albert Jurgenson
Photography: Bruno Nuytten
Sets: Jacques Saulnier and Enki Bilal
Music: M. Philippe-Gérard
Sound: Pierre Lenoir
Cast: Ruggero Raimondi (le comte Forbek), Sabine Azéma (Elisabeth Rousseau), Vittorio Gassman (Walter Guarini), Géraldine Chaplin (Nora Winkle), Robert Manuel (Georges Leroux), Pierre Arditi (Robert Dufresne), Martine Kelly (Claudine Obertin), Véronique Silver (Nathalie Holberg), Fanny Ardant (Livia), André Dussollier (Raoul)

L'Amour à mort (Love Unto Death), 1984, 112 mins, col.

Production: Philippe Dussart, Les Films Ariane, Films A2
Screenplay: Jean Gruault
Editing: Albert Jurgenson
Photography: Sacha Vierny
Sets: Jacques Saulnier
Music: Hans Werner Henze
Sound: Pierre Gamet
Cast: Sabine Azéma (Elisabeth Sutter), Pierre Arditi (Simon), André Dussollier (Jérôme), Fanny Ardant (Judith), Jean Dasté (docteur Rozier)

Mélo, 1986, 112 mins, col.

Production: MK2 et Films A2
Screenplay: from the play by Henry Bernstein
Editing: Albert Jurgenson
Photography: Charlie Van Damme
Sets: Jacques Saulnier
Music: M. Philippe-Gérard
Sound: Henri Morelle
Cast: Sabine Azéma (Romaine), Pierre Arditi (Pierre), André Dussollier (Marcel), Fanny Ardant (Christiane)

I Want to Go Home, 1989, 105 mins, col.

Production: MK2 Productions, Films A2, La SEPT, Investimage, Sofinergie, Sofima, Centre National de la Cinématographie
Screenplay: Jules Feiffer
Editing: Albert Jurgenson
Photography: Charlie Van Damme
Sets: Jacques Saulnier
Music: John Kander
Sound: Jean-Claude Laureux
Cast: Adolphe Green, Laura Benson, Linda Lavin, Gérard Depardieu, Micheline Presle, John Ashton, François-Eric Gendron, Géraldine Chaplin

Gershwin, 1992, 52 mins, col.

Production: A2, Telemax, les Editions audiovisuelles, Centre National de la Cinématographie, ministère de la culture et de la communication

(DMD), Procirep, conseil de l'Europe (fonds Eurimages), Sofica Cofimage 3, RAI 2, Channel 4
Text: Edward Jablonski, read by Pierre Arditi, Sabine Azéma, Lambert Wilson
Editing: Albert Jurgenson
Photography: Ned Burgess
Musical Advisor: Philippe Baudoin
Sound: Bernard Bats
Cast: Philippe Baudouin (pianist and composer), Betty Comden (librettist), Adolph Green (librettist), John Guare (writer), Edward Jablonski (author of three books on Gershwin), John Kander (pianist and composer), Martin Scorsese (filmmaker), Bertrand Tavernier (filmmaker), Alicia Zizzo (pianist and composer)

Smoking and **No Smoking**, 1993, 146 mins and 147 mins respectively, col.

Production: Arena Films, Caméra One, France 2 Cinéma, Canal +, Centre Nationale de la Cinématographie, ProcirepAlia Film, Vega Film
Screenplay: adapted from Alan Ayckbourn's *Intimate Exchanges* by Agnès Jaoui and Jean-Pierre Bacri
Editing: Albert Jurgenson
Photography: Renato Berta
Sets: Jacques Saulnier
Music: John Pattison
Sound: Gérard Lamps, Bernard Bats
Cast: Sabine Azéma (Celia Teasdale, Rowena Coombes, Sylvie Bell, Irene Pridworthy, Josephine Hamilton), Pierre Arditi (Toby Teasdale, Miles Coombes, Lionel Hepplewick, Joe Hepplewick) and the voice of Peter Hudson

On connaît la chanson (*Same Old Song*), 1997, 122 mins, col.

Production: Arena Films, Caméra One, France 2 Cinéma, Vega Film, Greenpoint, Canal+, Cofimage 9, Sofineurope, Alia Film (Rome), Télévision Suisse Romande, The European Co-production fund (London)
Screenplay: Agnès Jaoui and Jean-Pierre Bacri
Editing: Hervé de Luze
Photography: Renato Berta
Sets: Jacques Saulnier
Music: Bruno Fontaine

Sound: Pierre Lenoir
Cast: Agnès Jaoui (Camille Lalande), Sabine Azéma (Odile Lalande), Jean-Pierre Bacri (Nicolas), André Dussollier (Simon), Lambert Wilson (Marc Duveyrier), Pierre Arditi (Claude), Jane Birkin (Jane), Jean-Paul Roussillon (father)

Pas sur la bouche (Not on the Lips), 2003, 115 mins, col.
Production: Arena Films, France 2 Cinéma, France 3 Cinéma, Arcade, Vega Film, Canal +, Cinecinema, La Télévision Suisse Romande
Screenplay: from the operetta by André Barde and Maurice Yvain
Editing: Hervé de Luze
Photography: Renato Berta
Sets: Jacques Saulnier
Music: Bruno Fontaine
Sound: Jean-Marie Blondel
Cast: Sabine Azéma (Gilberte Valandray), Isabelle Nanty (Arlette Poumaillac), Audrey Tautou (Huguette Verberie), Pierre Arditi (Georges Valandray), Darry Cowl (Madame Foin), Jalil Lespert (Charley), Daniel Prévost (Faradel), Lambert Wilson (Eric Thomson)

Select bibliography

Armes, Roy, *The Cinema of Alain Resnais* (London: Zwemmer, 1968). A clear early study.

Bailblé, Claude, Michel Marie, Marie-Claire Ropars, *Muriel* (Paris: Editions Galilée, 1974). A case study which offers extensive, rich analysis of *Muriel*.

Benayoun, Robert, *Alain Resnais: arpenteur de l'imaginaire de Hiroshima à Mélo* (Paris: Ramsay [Ramsay Poche Cinéma], 1986). Lively discussion and a number of interviews with Resnais.

Bersani, Leo and Ulysse Dutoit, *Arts of Impoverishment: Beckett, Rothko, Resnais* (Cambridge MA: Harvard University Press, 1993). A highly original and theoretical section on Resnais's films.

Bounoure, Gaston, *Alain Resnais* (Cinéma d'aujourd'hui 5) (Paris: Seghers, 1974). An authoritative and personal account.

Callev, Haim, *The Stream of Consciousness in the Films of Alain Resnais* (New York: McGruer Publishing, 1997). Clear and well-directed discussion, with detailed readings of key scenes.

Caruth, Cathy, *Unclaimed Experience: Trauma, Narrative, and History* (Baltimore MD and London: The Johns Hopkins University Press, 1996). Extended discussion of trauma with a key chapter on *Hiroshima mon amour*.

Contre Bande 'Alain Resnais', no. 9 (2003). Special issue of a journal drawing together some of the finest recent French critical discussion of Resnais.

Cowie, Peter, *Antonioni, Bergman, Resnais* (London: The Tantivy Press, 1963). Fine early discussion of Resnais as *auteur*.

Daney, Serge, *Ciné Journal. Volume II 1983-1986* (Paris: Petite bibliothèque des Cahiers du Cinéma, 1998). Brief, but key critical account of Resnais, history and modernity.

Deleuze, Gilles, *Cinéma 2: L'Image-temps* (Paris: Minuit, 1985). A theoretical and philosophical discussion of post-war cinema which offers some scintillating readings of Resnais's films.

Fleischer, Alain, *L'Art d'Alain Resnais* (Paris: Editions du Centre Georges Pompidou, 1998). A brief study offering discussion of the early documentaries.

Goudet, Stéphane (ed.), Positif, *revue de cinéma: Alain Resnais* (Paris: Gallimard [Collection Folio], 2002). An essential collection which draws together all the articles on Resnais which have appeared in *Positif* and numerous interviews.

Greene, Naomi, *Landscapes of Loss: The National Past in Postwar French Cinema* (Princeton NJ: Princeton University Press, 1999). An excellent chapter on Resnais with reference to trauma, history and censorship.

Ishaghpour, Youssef, *D'une image à l'autre: La représentation dans le cinéma d'aujourd'hui* (Paris: Editions Denoël/Gonthier, 1982). This contains a groundbreaking essay on Resnais.

Kreidl, John Francis, *Alain Resnais* (Boston MA: Twayne Publishers, 1977). A useful early study.

Leperchey, Sarah, *Alain Resnais: Une lecture topologique* (Paris: L'Harmattan, 2000). An original and engaging synthetic discussion, drawing on Deleuze and questions of space.

Leutrat, Jean-Louis, *Hiroshima mon amour* (Paris: Nathan, 1994).

Leutrat, Jean-Louis, *L'Année dernière à Marienbad* (London: BFI Film Classics, 2000). Studies of individual films, these two volumes by Leutrat offer fine, detailed analysis by Resnais's current major French critic.

Monaco, James, *Alain Resnais* (New York: Oxford University Press, 1979). A lively and approachable account.

Nowell Smith, Geoffrey, 'L'Année dernière à Marienbad', *New Left Review*, 13–14 (January–April 1962), pp. 146–150. A gritty early article.

Oms, Marcel, *Alain Resnais* (Paris: Rivages "Rivages Cinéma", 1988). A good, authoritative account.

Prédal, René, *Alain Resnais* (Paris: Lettres Modernes [Etudes Cinématographiques], 1968). An excellent integrated discussion of Resnais's first two decades of filmmaking.

Prédal, René, *L'Itinéraire d'Alain Resnais* (Paris: Lettres Modernes

[Etudes Cinématographiques], 1996). The most striking thematic and formal discussion of Resnais's work, which offers new attention to the later films.

Ropars-Wuilleumier, Marie-Claire, 'How History begets meaning: Alain Resnais's *Hiroshima mon amour*', in Susan Hayward and Ginette Vincendeau (eds), *French Film: Texts and Contexts* (London and New York: Routledge, 1990), pp. 173-85. A subtle and incisive reading of *Hiroshima mon amour* by one of Resnais's finest critics.

Sweet, Freddy, *The Film Narratives of Alain Resnais* (Ann Arbor MI: University of Michigan Press, 1981). Good, clear discussion.

Thomas, François, *L'Atelier d'Alain Resnais* (Paris: Flammarion, 1989). Focus on Resnais's many long-time collaborators, including detailed interviews.

Ward, John, *Alain Resnais or the Theme of Time* (London: Secker & Warburg/British Film Institute, 1968). An account of Resnais's early films, drawing on the work of Henri Bergson.

Index

Adair, Gilbert 108, 143–4, 157, 159
Agamben, Giorgio 31
Air de famille, Un 173
Altman, Robert 135
Améry, Jean 31
Amiel, Vincent 179, 198
L'Amour à mort 147, 148, 157, 160–2
L'Année dernière à Marienbad 6, 11, 40–1, 67–85, 87, 89, 94, 96–7, 103–4, 114, 115, 116, 119, 120, 127, 129, 134, 138, 147, 148, 159, 162, 179, 180, 182, 192, 193, 196
Antonioni, Michelangelo 51, 67
Ardant, Fanny 157, 158–9, 160, 163, 164
Arditi, Pierre 157, 160, 163, 168, 174, 175, 180, 182, 190
Arletty (Léonie Bathiat) 185
Armes, Roy 79
Astaire, Fred 191
L'Avant-scène du cinéma 131
Aventures de Harry Dickson 108
Ayckbourn, Alan 171, 172, 173, 175, 176
Azéma, Sabine 115, 157–8, 160, 162, 163, 164, 165, 168, 174, 175, 176, 180, 182, 190, 191–2
Aznavour, Charles 185, 188

Bacon, Francis 137, 139
Bacri, Jean-Pierre 171, 173, 181, 182, 184, 185
Baker, Josephine 183
Barde, André 171, 190

Bardot, Brigitte 73
Baroncelli, Jean de 111
Bashung, Alain 183–4, 185
Bazin, André 27
Bécaud, Gilbert 186
Beckford, William 159
Belle et la bête, La 67
Belmondo, Jean-Paul 123, 125
Benayoun, Robert 28–9, 81–2, 91, 100, 111–12, 142, 154–5, 163, 188
Bergman, Ingmar 67, 110, 157, 162
Bernini, Gian Lorenzo 83
Bernstein, Henry 163, 166
Bersani, Leo 5–6, 27, 49, 85, 97, 98, 139
Berta, Renato 174
Beylie, Claude 129, 131
Bilal, Enki 158, 159
Birds, The 88
Birkin, Jane 182, 185, 186
Blind Chance 176–7
Böcklin, Arnold 1
Bodard, Mag 122
Bogarde, Dirk 131, 132, 133, 143
Boltanski, Christian 60
Boomeester, Christine 17
Boudjedra, Rachid 89
Bounoure, Gaston 2–3, 16, 25, 122, 126
Bouquet, Michel 24
Bouquet, Stéphane 184, 185, 186
Brahms, Johannes 163, 164, 165
Brancusi, Constantin 119
Bresson, Robert 20, 195
Breton, André 131

Britton, Celia 99
Brooks, Louise 73
Brunet, Catherine 151, 156
Brunius, Jacques 76
Bruno, Giuliana 10–11, 58
Budin, Jackie 191
Bujold, Geneviève 115, 116
Burstyn, Ellen 133

Cahiers du cinéma 26, 88, 192, 195
Callev, Haim 76, 113, 115, 119, 136, 137, 142
Caruth, Cathy 4–5, 52, 56, 57–8, 59
Casarès, Maria 20
Cayrol, Jean 20, 24–7, 30, 31–2, 87, 89, 90–1, 94, 98–9, 102, 108
Certeau, Michel de 60–1
Chagrin et la pitié, Le 25
Chambre verte, La 148
Chant du styrène, Le 36–7, 162
Chekhov, Anton 3, 67
Chirico, Giorgio de 131
Ciné-Club 18
Citizen Kane 131
Cocteau, Jean 20, 81, 195
Colpi, Henri 50, 63–4, 185
Combs, Richard 152, 155, 157, 163
Comden, Betty 168
Conformist, The 123
Courau, Pierre 68
Cowie, Peter 36, 81
Cowl, Darry 190
Cuisine et dépendances 173

Dalida (Yolanda Gigliotti) 185
Daney, Serge 5, 14
Darrieux, Danielle 150
Dauman, Anatole 25
Dawson, Jan 128, 154
Debris, Michel 190
Delerue, Georges 184
Deleuze, Gilles 6, 12, 14, 52, 53, 54, 63, 72–3, 92, 100, 105, 118, 120, 121, 126, 154
Delvaux, Paul 82, 131
Demeure, Jacques 113
Demy, Jacques 3, 191
Depardieu, Gérard 166
Dietrich, Marlene 129
Dimendberg, Edward 36

Dogville 155
Doniol-Valcroze, Jacques 32, 33
Double Vie de Véronique, La 144
Draughtsman's Contract, The 67
Duperey, Anny 129
Duras, Marguerite 46, 47, 48, 49, 51, 57, 65, 67, 68, 108, 117, 129
Dürer, Albrecht 36
Dussollier, André 157, 158, 160, 163, 164, 182
Dutoit, Ulysse 5–6, 27, 49, 85, 97, 98, 139

L'Eclisse 51
Eisenstein, Sergei/Eisensteinian 9–10, 88
Eisler, Hanns 24, 50
Eliot, T.S. 185
Eluard, Paul 20
L'Encyclopédie audiovisuelle 168
L'Enfant sauvage 148
Erickson, Kai 74
Ernst, Max 3, 82
Esprit 111

Fantômas 3
Farnsworth, Rodney 133, 140, 141
Feiffer, Jules 166
Fellini, Federico 67
Fieschi, Jean-André 88
Films in Review 47
Flaubert, Gustave 99, 166
Fleischer, Alain 19
Floc'h, Jean-Claude 174, 181
Fontaine, Bruno 190–1
Forty, Adrian 60
Foucault, Michel 36
Francesca, Piero della 17
François, Claude 187
Fresson, Bernard 117
Freud, Sigmund 136
Froment, Raymond 68
Fusco, Giovanni 50

Gabin, Jean 150
Garbo, Greta 74, 129
Garcia, Nicole 149
Gauguin, Paul 19
Gershwin 123, 168–9
Gershwin, George 168

Gielgud, John 132, 136–7
Godard, Jean-Luc 6, 9, 31, 98, 195
Goetz, Henri 17
Gogh, Vincent van 17–19, 36
Goût des autres, Le 173
Goya, Francisco de 36
Gras, Pierre 167
Great Gatsby, The 123
Green, Adolph 167, 168
Greenaway, Peter 67, 168
Greene, Graham 132
Greene, Naomi 5, 24, 35, 74, 90, 91, 94, 123–4, 133
Gruault, Jean 148, 156, 160, 195
Guattari, Felix 154
Guernica 19–21, 36, 60, 110
Guerre est finie, La 85, 106, 108, 109–16, 121, 188

Hallyday, Johnny 185
Hartung, Hans 17
Hellwig, Klaus 131
Henze, Hans Werner 161
Higgins, Lynn 47, 59
Hiroshima mon amour 2, 5, 8, 16, 19, 20, 29, 39, 46–65, 68, 72–3, 74, 77, 81, 84, 87, 89, 92, 96, 100, 101, 114, 115, 117, 125, 161, 180, 183, 184, 195, 196
Histoire(s) du cinéma 195
Hitchcock, Alfred 67, 88, 114
Houston, Penelope 77, 98, 103, 110, 114, 150, 151
Hudson, Peter 174
Huyssen, Andreas 59

Ibsen, Henrik 73, 74
India Song 67, 129
Insdorf, Annette 29
Ionesco, Eugène 175
Ishaghpour, Youssef 1–2, 8, 9, 10
I Want to Go Home 147, 166–8, 184

James, Henry 143, 162
Jaoui, Agnès 171, 173, 181, 182, 183, 185, 197
Jebb, Julian 119
Je t'aime je t'aime 13, 108, 117–23, 160, 172, 179
Jetée, La 30, 67, 122, 148, 188

Johnson, Barbara 82–3
Johnson, William 163, 164
Jolson, Al 189
Jousse, Thierry 161, 185
Joyce, James 118
Jules et Jim 148

Kael, Pauline 50
Kafka, Franz 36
Kemp, Philip 181
Kieślowski, Krzysztof 13, 144, 176, 177, 178
Kinder, Marsha 135, 143
Klapisch, Cédric 173
Klarsfeld, Serge 26
Klein, Nita 115
Kline, T. Jefferson 68, 74
Krantz, Charles 26, 27, 32
Kreidl, John Francis 89, 114, 117, 128
Kristeva, Julia 55, 57
Krutnick, Frank 63
Kundera, Milan 163, 172, 176, 177

Laborit, Henri 147–8, 152, 154, 156
Lacan, Jacques/Lacanian 68, 71, 83, 139
LaCapra, Dominick 33
Lanzmann, Claude 7–8, 26–7, 28, 31
Lardeau, Yann 159
Leperchey, Sarah 12, 56, 75, 87, 95, 101
Le Roux, Hervé 161
Lettres françaises, Les 20, 33
Leutrat, Jean-Louis 47, 48, 63, 69, 81, 84, 87, 174, 179
Levi, Primo 31
Liandrat-Guigues, Suzanne 117–18
Lifton, Robert Jay 47, 48–9
Loin du Viêt-nam 108, 117
Losey, Joseph 131, 143
Lost Highway 138
Lovecraft, H.P. 108
Lubitsch, Ernst 190
Lynch, David 138

Magritte, René 3, 82, 131
Maillot, Pierre 139, 140, 143
Mallarmé, Stéphane 126
Man Ray 73
Mansfield, Katherine 2
Marais, Jean 150

Marie, Michel 89
Marker, Chris 7, 22–3, 25, 30, 67, 108, 117, 122, 187–8, 195
Marks, Laura 7–8, 9, 11
Masson, Alain 158, 162, 166
Méliès, Georges 158
Mélo 44, 123, 147, 157, 162, 163–6, 174, 189–90
Mercer, David 131–2, 133, 134, 136, 137, 139
Mettey, Marcel 9, 88, 112, 114
Michael, Robert 26
Michel, Henri 25
Michio, Takashi 49
Miller, Lee 73
Milne, Tom 88, 90, 108, 113, 128
Minotaure 3
Monaco, James 22, 33, 49, 81, 101, 108, 117, 128, 132, 137
Monde, Le 111, 157
Monk, Thelonius 122
Mon oncle d'Amérique 1, 43–4, 144, 147–56, 157, 158, 176, 184
Monster Maker, The 108
Montand, Yves 111
Monthly Film Bulletin 88, 115
Mulholland Drive 138
Munch, Edvard 162
Muriel ou le temps d'un retour 5, 37, 42, 85, 87–106, 114, 115, 141, 148, 151
Muyl, Philippe 173

Nanty, Isabelle 190
Neyrat, Cyril 11, 178
Nora, Pierre 34–5, 59, 64
No Smoking 13, 157, 166, 171–81
Notre Musique 31, 195
Nuit et brouillard 2, 5, 19, 20, 22, 24–33, 34, 36, 39, 46, 48, 50, 58, 69, 81, 93–4, 133, 134, 140
Nysenholc, Adolphe 27

O'Brien, Alyssa 90, 91, 94, 98
Ollier, Claude 88
On connaît la chanson 45, 120, 157, 166, 171, 176, 181–9
Ophuls, Marcel 25
Or... 190
Orphée 67, 81

Oudart, Jean-Pierre 155
Ozon, François 162, 168

Pandora's Box 73
Paris 1900 3
Parkes, Graham 73–4
Pas sur la bouche 45, 123, 157, 163, 165, 171, 174, 189–93, 198
Pattison, John 174
Paul Gauguin 19
Peellaert, Guy 168
Perec, Georges 98, 152
Philippon, Alain 178–9
Piaf, Edith 185
Picasso, Pablo 19, 21
Pierce, Constance 132, 137, 143
Pierre, Roger 149
Pinel, Vincent 28, 29
Pingaud, Bernard 63, 64
Piranesi, Giovanni 34
Pointe courte, La 3
Positif 113, 168
Potter, Denis 181
Prédal, René 9–10, 112, 117, 122, 125, 126, 127, 134, 139, 150, 152, 158, 161, 164, 165, 181–2, 183, 185, 186, 188
Première 171
Proust, Marcel/Proustian 2, 23, 64, 164–5
Providence 13, 122, 131–45, 161, 166

Queneau, Raymond 36, 190

Raimondi, Ruggero 159
Rampling, Charlotte 162
Rascaroli, Laura 138, 143
Raskin, Richard 26, 27, 28, 33
Rayns, Tony 126, 128
Reader, Keith 152, 154
Redon, Odilon 36
Règle du jeu, La 67, 128, 154
Rembrandt 140
Renoir, Jean 154
Repérages 141, 144
Rich, Claude 117
Richardson, Christine 34, 35
Riley, Michael M 143
Robbe-Grillet, Alain 68, 70, 74, 75, 77, 79, 82, 83, 84, 94, 108

Romney, Jonathan 174, 178
Ropars-Wuilleumier, Marie-Claire 49, 54, 58, 64, 88–9, 95–6, 99, 100, 111
Rosenbaum, Jonathan 124
Run Lola Run 176

Sade, Marquis de 108, 131
Sadoul, Georges 20
Sagan, Françoise 48
Sagnier, Ludivine 168
Sarraute, Nathalie 185
Sartre, Jean-Paul 89
Saulnier, Jacques 174, 191
Scarry, Elaine 55, 99–100
Scorsese, Martin 168
Scudéry, Madeleine de 10
Semprun, Jorge 109–10, 111, 123, 128, 141, 144
Serceau, Daniel 157, 158
Seyrig, Delphine 73–4, 79, 82, 87–8, 103–4, 115
Shakespeare, William/Shakespearean 126, 137
Shoah 27, 32
Shoos, Diane 135, 136, 140–1, 143
Sight and Sound 88, 108, 171, 184
Silence, The 67
Singin' in the Rain 167
Sizaret, Nicole 176, 177
Smoking 13, 157, 166, 171–81
Sontag, Susan 11, 98
Sous le sable 162
Spadone, Pierre-Louis 61
Statues meurent aussi, Les 19, 22–4, 46
Stavisky 13, 85, 108 109, 122, 123–9, 159, 163, 168, 179
Stavisky, Serge Alexandre 124, 125
Stendhal/Stendhalian 115
Sternberg, Jacques 117, 118, 119
Strick, Philip 121, 122, 174, 175, 176, 178, 180
Stritch, Elaine 133, 135, 140

Tautou, Audrey 190
Tavernier, Bertrand 168
Thevenet, Jean-Marc 158

Thirard, Paul Louis 120
Thomas, François 17, 160, 162, 168
Three Women 135
Thulin, Ingrid 110, 116
Tobin, Yann 181
To Catch a Thief 67
Tomlinson, Emily 33, 89, 105
Toubiana, Serge 165
Toute la mémoire du monde 33–6, 69
Trenet, Charles 185
Trier, Lars von 155
Triumph of the Will 30
Trotsky, Leon 124
Truffaut, François 18, 26, 148, 195
Tykwer, Tom 176

Van Gogh 17–19
Varda, Agnès 3, 195
Vartan, Sylvie 186
Védrès, Nicole 3
Velázquez, Diego 136
Vertigo 67
Vian, Boris 190
Vie est un roman, La 115, 147, 148, 156–9
Vierny, Sacha 49, 74, 160
Vigo, Jean 195
Vincendeau, Ginette 189, 190
Visconti, Luchino 131, 143
Visiteurs du soir, Les 67
Vitoux, Frédéric 123, 124, 128

Walker, Alexander 88
Ward, John 113
Warner, David 133
Wert, William F. van 131
Weyergans, François 83
Williams, Alan 88
Williams, Linda 57
Wilson, Lambert 182, 190, 191
Woolf, Virginia 99, 118, 120, 151, 187
Wormser, Olga 25, 27
Worton, Michael 82

Yvain, Maurice 171, 190

Zizek, Slavoj 32, 71, 138, 144, 176, 177–8

EU authorised representative for GPSR:
Easy Access System Europe, Mustamäe tee 50,
10621 Tallinn, Estonia
gpsr.requests@easproject.com

www.ingramcontent.com/pod-product-compliance
Ingram Content Group UK Ltd.
Pitfield, Milton Keynes, MK11 3LW, UK
UKHW021829140426
5217IPUK00021B/1347

EU GSPR Authorised Reprsentative
Logos Europe, 9 rue Nicolas Poussin
1700, La Rochelle, France
Phone: +33 (0) 6 67 93 73 78
E-mail: contact@logoseurope.eu

www.ingramcontent.com/pod-product-compliance
Ingram Content Group UK Ltd.
Pitfield, Milton Keynes, MK11 3LW, UK
UKHW021829140426
5217IPUK00021B/1344